Doing Capitalism in the Innovation Economy

The Innovation Economy begins with discovery and culminates in speculation. Over some 250 years, economic growth has been driven by successive processes of trial and error: upstream exercises in research and invention, and downstream experiments in exploiting the new economic space opened by innovation. Drawing on his professional experiences, William H. Janeway provides an accessible pathway for readers to appreciate the dynamics of the Innovation Economy. He combines personal reflections from a career spanning forty years in venture capital with the development of an original theory of the role of asset bubbles in financing technological innovation and of the role of the state in playing an enabling role in the innovation process. Today, with the state frozen as an economic actor and access to the public equity markets only open to a minority, the Innovation Economy is stalled; learning the lessons from this book will contribute to its renewal.

WILLIAM H. JANEWAY has been an active venture capital investor for forty years. In particular, he built and led the Warburg Pincus Technology Investment team that provided the financial backing to a series of companies which made critical contributions to building the internet economy. He received his Ph.D. in Economics from Cambridge, where he founded the Cambridge Endowment for Research in Finance, and is a Teaching Visitor in the Princeton Economics Department. He is a member of the Board of the Social Science Research Council and of the Institute for New Economic Thinking.

Doing Capitalism in the Innovation Economy

Markets, Speculation and the State

WILLIAM H. JANEWAY

CAMBRIDGE
UNIVERSITY PRESS

CAMBRIDGE UNIVERSITY PRESS
Cambridge, New York, Melbourne, Madrid, Cape Town,
Singapore, São Paulo, Delhi, Mexico City

Cambridge University Press
The Edinburgh Building, Cambridge CB2 8RU, UK

Published in the United States of America by Cambridge University Press, New York

www.cambridge.org
Information on this title: www.cambridge.org/9781107031258

First published 2012

Printed and Bound in Great Britain by the MPG Books Group

A catalogue record for this publication is available from the British Library

Library of Congress Cataloguing in Publication data
Janeway, William H.
    Doing capitalism in the innovation economy : markets, speculation and the
    state / William H. Janeway.
        pages   cm
    Includes bibliographical references and index.
    ISBN 978-1-107-03125-8
    1. Venture capital.   2. Capitalism.   I. Title.
    HG4751.J37   2012
    332′.04154–dc23   2012019852

ISBN 978-1-107-03125-8 Hardback

"Bill Janeway, a key creator of modern venture capital, tells the amazing story of the intersection of economics and innovation. This book is essential to anyone who wants to understand technology and how its creation will be financed for decades to come."

Marc Andreessen, co-creator of the Internet browser, co-founder
of Netscape and Andreessen Horowitz

"Many people understand the political economic forces of our world. Add an understanding also of the financial forces at work in the modern economy and the list of wise people diminishes dramatically. Bill Janeway understands all three and writes about their interaction with great insight built on theoretical depth and practical experience. Read this book and your eyes will open to our current crisis and our prospect for the future."

Bill Bradley, former US Senator

"Written with flair and telling first-hand experience, William Janeway's *Doing Capitalism* is a terrific introduction to the world of venture capital. Along the way it is an insightful critique of economic models based on 'representative rational agents' and unlimited liquidity, a clarification of why continuous market models don't grasp the discontinuous world of finance, an explanation of the work irrationality and 'bubbles' do in technological innovation, and a call to recognize the necessary intersection of politics and economics. Both a 'must-read' and a fun read."

Craig Calhoun, Director of the London School of Economics

"When the despair of troubled economic conditions compels us to yearn for a better time, our fantasies gravitate to a savior called innovation. To discern whether such yearning attracts us to a mirage or to a sound basis for hope requires a discriminating and experienced mind. I know of no better mind in this realm than Bill Janeway, whom Hyman Minsky called a theorist–practitioner of financial economics. He has spent 40 years at the forefront of venture capital and financial economics. He takes us beyond mechanical details and reveals the deeper processes and interactions between state, market and finance that can foster and/or inhibit technological progress. *Doing Capitalism* leaves the neoclassical economic framework in tatters. It is a historically grounded and sophisticated look at how our society must rise to the challenges of collective action under radical uncertainty and integrate institutions on many levels to bring about the betterment of our human condition. This fine work will deepen your understanding of what innovation entails and impart a vision that will both surprise you, and inspire you, to move beyond your prejudices, whatever your political persuasion."

Rob Johnson, Executive Director of the Institute for
New Economic Thinking

"This is, quite simply, the only book I have read that does justice to the necessary interplay between the market of real goods and services, speculative financial markets, and the state. It is wise, insightful, and rich with both economic history and the personal stories of a brilliant investor. If you want to understand the innovation economy, go no farther: read this book."

Tim O'Reilly, Founder and CEO O'Reilly Media

"A powerful reinterpretation of capitalism, seen from above and lived from inside, by someone who is as much at home in the practical world of innovation and finance as in the abstract world of economic theory. Janeway's book is a fascinating double dip from theory to reality and back. Indispensable for anyone in finance or academia, in policy or politics, wanting to act intelligently in the post-bubble world and beyond."

Carlota Perez, Professor of Technology and Socio-Economic
Development, Tallinn University of Technology, Estonia, and LSE,
Cambridge and Sussex Universities in England

"This is a masterful historical and conceptual analysis of the Three Player Game between the state, private entrepreneurial innovation and financial capitalism. The state has a key role in funding scientific research that leads to innovation. Amply funded by financial capitalism, innovation is a source of long-term growth. But speculative funding of innovation is also associated with asset and credit bubbles that end up in financial crashes. Then, following Keynes, the state has to intervene again to limit the economic and financial fallout from such crashes. A Minsky-inspired synthesis of the financial excesses of Schumpeterian creative destruction, this book should be required reading for all."

Nouriel Roubini, Professor of Economics at New York University
and Chairman of Roubini Global Economics

"A revelatory exploration of the complex dynamics underlying the innovation economy and the inherent roles of speculation and waste as experienced by one of the great venture capitalists and political/economic thinkers of our age. This book provides a powerful framework for dealing with the economic challenges we are facing today. It couldn't have come at a better time!"

John Seely Brown, Former Chief Scientist of Xerox Corp
and Director of its Palo Alto Research Center (PARC)

"I have never held orthodox financial theory in high regard. I do not find it useful. It presumes a stability and certainty of knowing about the future that is both wrong and dangerously misleading. Bill Janeway can see that. He is both a practitioner and a financial theorist and his book, *Doing Capitalism*, is serious new economic thinking on the process of innovation. This is a realm where standard economic treatments do not get to the heart of the matter – dealing with radical uncertainty. Janeway applies keen insights from his experience as a venture capitalist and creates a vision of the interaction between governments, financiers, and firms that shows what institutions society must develop to foster innovation. I believe that *Doing Capitalism* will help all of us, whether academics, private sector leaders, or government officials, to see beyond shallow political dogma and move to a deeper understanding of challenges of technological advance."

George Soros, Chairman of Soros Fund Management

In memoriam, Ferdinand Eberstadt and Hyman Minsky

Contents

Figures and table

Figures

Table

Acknowledgements

This book would not have been conceived, let alone written, were it not for the goading and guidance of Richard Sennett. In the spring of 2009, Richard suggested that I assemble all my various writings over the near-forty years since the submission of my doctoral thesis into a "dossier" (his term). He agreed to read it through and offer his opinion as to whether a book might be developed from the assortment of published articles, private notes and more or less public lectures. Given his own extraordinary ability to render abstractions of experience into compelling literary form, as demonstrated in his many works that mediate between acute observation of how people live and work and sensitive interpretation of how they represent their living and working, this was not a proposal that I could refuse.

Richard's oversight of my first drafts brought both encouragement and discipline to the project. As a book did, indeed, begin to emerge, I began to seek comments from a range of scholars. First and repeatedly relevant in their responses were Barry Eichengreen and Carlota Perez. From early days, they understood my purpose and endeavored to help me keep control of a manuscript that threatened to veer in its later chapters from strategic analysis towards commentary on current events. And Carlota Perez has generously granted permission for reproduction of the graphics that appear as Figure 9.1 and Table 9.1.

As the book began to assume its final shape, constructive criticism was offered by Christopher Beauman, Mark Blyth, Craig Calhoun, Roman Frydman, Ira Katznelson, Henry Kressel, Paul Ricci, Jose Scheinkman, Til Schuermann and Catharine Stimpson. From their diverse domains of knowledge and analytical approaches, I have been privileged to receive questions, corrections and alerts, all of which have served to focus my efforts and the book's arguments. I must thank D'Maris Coffman of the Centre for Financial History at Newnham College for her contribution to my understanding of financial history generally and, specifically, for her aid in constructing Figure 7.1.

In parallel with the process of writing and rewriting the manuscript, I refined ways of communicating its narrative and analysis through two different styles of rhetoric. In particular, the discussion of the evolving role of venture capital in Chapter 4 reflects lectures contributed to the courses in Entrepreneurial Finance taught by Professor Antoinette Schoar at MIT Sloan School of Management and by Professor Alexander Ljungqvist at NYU Stern School of Business and Cambridge Judge Business School. The broader themes developed in the second half of the book variously arose in their nascent form as semi-formal presentations at each of two distinctive gatherings of people engaged in pushing the state of the art in information technology and deeply interested in the consequences thereof. I am very much indebted to Tim O'Reilly for my many opportunities to participate in the "FooCamp" and "SciFoo" gatherings that he originated and inspires, and to Mark Anderson for our repeated public conversations at his annual Future in Review conferences.

Closer to home, I and this book have been the beneficiary of discussions with my wife Weslie, my son Charles, and my brother Mike – discussions which in all three cases preceded by years my commitment to the writing and carried through to its completion. My thanks to them for their never unquestioning support is boundless.

Finally, when I circulated a mature manuscript, Chris Harrison of Cambridge University Press signally determined that this hybrid work of a "theorist-practitioner" of entrepreneurial finance could be worthy of publication. His support and sponsorship have been constant. A last word of thanks must go to my more-than-copy editor, Meg Cox, whose representation of the lay reader has contributed to the translation of much that was arcane into common speech.

After all aid solicited, offered and received, I do affirm my own sole responsibility for all errors of commission and omission and interpretation that reside herein.

Introduction: the Innovation Economy

The Innovation Economy begins with discovery and culminates in speculation. Over some 250 years, economic growth has been driven by successive processes of trial and error and error and error: upstream exercises in research and invention, and downstream experiments in exploiting the new economic space opened by innovation. Each of these activities necessarily generates much waste along the way: dead-end research programs, useless inventions and failed commercial ventures. In between, the innovations that have repeatedly transformed the architecture of the market economy, from canals to the internet, have required massive investments to construct networks whose value in use could not be imagined at the outset of deployment. And so at each stage the Innovation Economy depends on sources of funding that are decoupled from concern for economic return.

Upstream, when mechanical tinkering yielded to scientific discovery as the basis for economically meaningful innovation, funding initially was supplied by the great corporations that had been spawned by the second industrial revolution toward the end of the nineteenth century. These corporations, variously supported or at least tolerated by the state, channeled a portion of their profits into central research laboratories. By the time over the past generation that their seemingly unassailable market positions were lost to competition or deregulation, a cadre of American political entrepreneurs had successfully invented national security and human health as legitimizing rationales for direct state investment in science.[1]

The transformational networks of infrastructure that implement the Innovation Economy can be planned, built and funded by the state: the US interstate highway system is an outstanding exemplar. They can also be planned, built and funded by the willing collaboration of

[1] See D. M. Hart, *Forged Consensus: Science, Technology and Economic Policy in the United States, 1921–1953* (Princeton University Press, 1998), pp. 145–234.

1

promoters and speculators: the original British railway system is the exemplar. In each case, the calculus of expected economic return was a secondary consideration. Hence the endless miles of superhighway crossing the empty wastes and wilderness of the American West and the multiplication of competing routes and the destructive competition that followed hard on the British railway mania of the 1840s.

Downstream, the Innovation Economy is driven by financial speculation. Throughout the history of capitalism, financial bubbles have emerged and exploded wherever liquid markets in assets exist. The objects of speculation have ranged across a spectrum that challenges the imagination: from tulip bulbs, to gold and silver mines, to the debt of newly established countries of unknowable wealth and – again and again – by way of real estate and of the shares that represent ownership of corporations. The central dynamic is that the price of the financial asset is separated from any concern with the underlying cash flows – past, present or possible future – generated by the economic assets it represents. Speculators in the financial asset can and often do profit, even when the project they have financed fails. Inevitably, the speculation collapses: the more it has been fueled by credit and has infected the banking system, the more disastrous the economic consequences and the broader and more urgent the pleas for public relief.

Occasionally, decisively, the object of speculation is the financial representation of one of those fundamental technological innovations – canals, railroads, electrification, automobiles, airplanes, computers, the internet – the deployment of which at scale transforms the market economy, indeed creates a "new economy" from the wreckage of the financial bubble that attended its birth. Both upstream and downstream, absence of market discipline is the essence of the process. For, contrary to the central dogma of neoclassical economics, efficiency is not the virtue of a market economy whose growth is a function of the creative destruction identified by Joseph Schumpeter as the engine of economic development.[2] The prime virtue is the ability to tolerate unavoidable waste in the evolution of the Innovation Economy.[3] So the

---

[2] J. A. Schumpeter, *Business Cycles: A Theoretical, Historical and Statistical Analysis of the Capitalist Process* (London: McGraw-Hill, 1939), chaps. 1–3 and Schumpeter, *Capitalism, Socialism and Democracy*, 4th edn. (London: Allen & Unwin, 2010 [1943]), part II: "Can Capitalism Survive?"

[3] For a comprehensive analytical review of the literature on technological innovation as an evolutionary process, see G. Dosi and R. R. Nelson, "Technical

state has become central to the Innovation Economy's dynamics, both to fund the upstream research that generates discovery and invention, and to preserve continuity in the market economy when the speculative bubble that has funded its transformation bursts.

I have come to read this history as driven by three sets of continuous, reciprocal, interdependent games played between the state, the market economy and financial capitalism.[4] Through the centuries, the state and the market economy have variously collaborated and competed in the allocation of resources and the distribution of income and wealth. And financial capitalism has emerged to exploit discontinuities in the evolution of market and political processes, while it depends on those same processes for its prosperity and even at times for its survival.

The state, the market economy and financial capitalism are big, abstract concepts. Let me try to give each some substance.

By the state, I mean the political entity that has sufficient coercive authority to establish the rules for the other players. By definition it is able to exploit the other players, but it is also subject to their efforts to capture its authority or at least to bend it to their advantage. The state is the source of monopoly profits and privileges, but it also must have access to economic and financial resources to maintain itself and to pursue its objectives, whether they be wars of conquest or defense, or programs of economic development or social insurance. In principle, a state's authority may derive from the mandate of heaven or from popular sovereignty or from any of a variety of sources in between. Whatever the source of its power, the state is always subject to capture by economic or financial interests; rarely, if ever, is it useful to think of the state as monolithic.

By the market economy, I mean the institutions that enable the production and exchange of goods and services. It resides in marketplaces and trade fairs, entrepôts and caravan routes – anywhere the value of commodities is found in exchange, not merely in use. The market economy's virtues are regularity and predictability: ideally, atomistic competitors experience constant or diminishing returns in

---

Change and Industrial Dynamics as Evolutionary Processes," in B. H. Hall and N. Rosenberg (eds.), *Handbook of the Economics of Innovation*, 2 vols. (Amsterdam: North-Holland, 2010), vol. 1, pp. 51–127.

[4] For a set of relevant case studies that stops short of offering a comprehensive framework, see. R. Sylla, R. Tilly and G. Torella, *The State, the Financial System and Economic Modernization* (Cambridge University Press, 1999).

their own production functions and face well-behaved elasticities of demand from their trading partners, including utility-maximizing end consumers. In this utopian form, the market economy is the world of general-equilibrium theorizing and neoclassical economics. In its messy historical reality, it is the world of the "fair price" and of guild regulations, as it is of state-imposed tariffs and state-sanctioned monopolies. As Adam Smith understood, all who are subject to the rigors of competition seek to escape it. Those who can will innovate their way to market dominance and the enjoyment of economic rents, the profits a company can earn by escaping from competition. The many who fail can be expected to pursue countervailing relief, whether by conspiring to rig the market or by mobilizing intervention from outside the market's conventional confines.

Whereas the market economy is a world of continuity even when it fails to find and hold a state of equilibrium, the world of financial capitalism is one of discontinuous opportunism. The two are intimately related, for the market economy is not only a world of exchange; it is also, always and everywhere, a world of credit. Exchange and the production of goods for exchange must be financed from day to day, from month to month, and across years. Those who first provide credit have the potential to become capitalists as they dispose of liquid financial resources in order to exploit discontinuities in the market economy, and their impact on the market economy is disruptive. Whether invested in the opening of new trading relationships, development of innovative products or deployment of novel transportation and communication networks, financial capital earns its return by subjecting settled markets to new and powerful competition. As Fernand Braudel summarized the orthogonal relationship between capitalism and the market economy: "Capitalism does not invent ... the market or production or consumption, it merely uses them."[5]

From this dynamic and unstable configuration of political, economic and financial forces – this "three-player game" – has emerged a world in which state investment in fundamental research induces financial speculation to fund construction of transformational technological infrastructure, whose exploitation, in turn, raises living standards for everyone dependent on the productivity of the market economy. But

---

[5] F. Braudel, *Afterthoughts on Material Civilization and Capitalism* (Baltimore, MD: Johns Hopkins University Press, 1977), p. 75.

the three-player game is also responsible for a world in which bubbles and crashes in the financial system spill over and liquidate both the employed and their employers, generating appeals to the political process for redress and relief. In yet another version, we find ourselves in a world where "malefactors of great wealth" – to invoke Theodore Roosevelt's epithet – are able to exploit the political process in order to preserve and protect their exploitation of the market economy.

Over the past 250 years, the Innovation Economy has emerged from this intersection of political interests, economic incentives and financial speculation. Here, where the future is supposed to differ from the remembered past and the experienced present, one basic aspect of human existence is paramount: all who are engaged, singly and collectively, in the three-player game are subject to inescapable, irreducible uncertainty with respect to the full consequences of their actions, "the future," as Thomas Hobbes wrote, "being but a fiction of the mind."[6]

We rely to our own future peril on the patterns we imperfectly discern from the past. When, in 1937, John Maynard Keynes sought to convey to his fellow economists the kernel of his new general theory of employment, the theme he emphasized was the uncertainty that is native to the universe in which we exist, not an artifact of our inadequate ability to reason about that universe. This ontological uncertainty infuses economic and financial decision-making all the way down. Keynes wrote:

By "uncertain" knowledge ... I do not mean merely to distinguish what is known from what is merely probable ... The sense in which I am using the term is that in which the prospect of a European war is uncertain, or the price of copper and the rate of interest twenty years hence, or the obsolescence of a new invention, or the position of private wealth owners in the social system in 1970. About these matters there is no scientific basis on which to form any calculable probability whatever. We simply do not know.[7]

---

[6] T. Hobbes, *Leviathan*, ed. R. Tuck (Cambridge University Press, 1993 [1664]), p. 14.

[7] J. M. Keynes, "The General Theory of Employment," *Quarterly Journal of Economics* (February 1937), in E. Johnson and D. Moggridge (eds.), *The Collected Writings of John Maynard Keynes*, vol. 14 (Cambridge University Press and Macmillan for the Royal Economic Society, 1973 [1937]), pp. 112–113. Following Keynes's insight, the Cambridge economist Tony Lawson has explored in depth the difference between the ontological properties of the world and the theoretical properties of the models we construct in the hope of

The historian John Lewis Gaddis embraces and extends Keynes's assertion when he speaks of our world as compounded of continuities and contingencies:

The trouble with the future is that it is so much less knowable than the past. Because it lies on the other side of the singularity that is the present, all we can count on is that certain continuities from the past will extend into it, and that they will encounter uncertain contingencies. Some continuities will be sufficiently robust that contingencies will not deflect them: time will continue to pass; gravity will continue to keep us from flying off into space; people will still be born, grow old, and die. When it comes to the actions people themselves choose to take, though – when consciousness itself becomes a contingency – forecasting becomes a far more problematic exercise.[8]

I have lived in the Innovation Economy for forty years. I have learned that the ability of any player in the game to hedge against what cannot be anticipated – to hedge against crisis – is a joint function of assured access to cash and sufficient control of circumstances. Cash buys time to find out what is going on; control permits the player to use that time to shift the parameters of the problem. I learned about Cash and Control painfully through my apprenticeship in entrepreneurial finance. There, a new business's ability to generate positive cash flow from operations by selling goods and services to paying customers confers autonomy from the vagaries of the financial markets and the freedom to invest in future growth. There, too, evidence of effective control of the venture is demonstrated by the ability to fire the chief executive officer or to force a sale if the venture is floundering – or to recapitalize it and redirect it toward alternative opportunities.

As a student of financial crises, I have observed how large and systemically significant players have pursued equivalent strategies – from Jamie Dimon's construction of J. P. Morgan's "fortress balance sheet" in anticipation of the Crisis of 2008 to China's accumulation of $3 trillion of foreign exchange reserves – with consequences that feed back into the unstable dynamics of the global financial economy. In extremis,

---

understanding how the world works. See, for example, T. Lawson, *Reorienting Economics* (New York: Routledge, 2003) and T. Lawson, "The (Confused) State of Equilibrium Analysis in Modern Economics: An Explanation," *Journal of Post Keynesian Economics*, 27(3) (2005), 423–444.

[8] J. L. Gaddis, *The Landscape of History: How Historians Map the Past* (New York: Oxford University Press, 2004), p. 56.

when those who retain freedom of action find themselves on their own, then the panic-driven scramble for Cash and Control by each threatens the liquidation of all. But in normal times Cash and Control delivers liberation from the narrow constraints imposed by competitive markets and the perceived requirements of economic efficiency.

From the time Britain established the first industrial economy, mercantilism – export-led growth directly sponsored by state policies of protection and subsidy – has repeatedly succeeded in driving economic development.[9] As the prophet of "national economics," Friedrich List wrote in 1841:

Had the English left everything to itself – laissé faire and laissé aller – the merchants of the Steelyard would be still carrying on their trade in London, the Belgians would be still manufacturing cloth for the English, England would still have been the sheepyard for the Hansards.[10]

With remarkable foresight, List also recognized that strategic competitive advantage already turned on factors that transcend the relative costs of production:

The present state of the nations is the result of the accumulation of all discoveries, inventions, improvements, perfections, and exertions of all generations which have lived before us; they form the mental capital of the present human race, and every separate nation is productive only in the proportion in which it has known how to appropriate these attainments of former generations and to increase them by its own acquirements.[11]

Thus, List's book, titled *The National System of Political Economy*, "might just as well have been called *The National System of Innovation*."[12]

---

[9] For a succinct summary of the success of mercantilist policies, from the Meiji Restoration in Japan through contemporary China, see D. Rodrik, *The Globalization Paradox: Why Global Markets, States, and Democracy Can't Coexist* (New York: Norton, 2011), pp. 143–156.

[10] F. List, *The National System of Political Economy*, trans. Sampson S. Lloyd (New York: Augustus M. Kelly, 1966 [1841]), p. 25. The Hansards, also known as the "merchants of the Steelyard," were representatives of the trading cities of the Hanseatic League, which dominated English commerce prior to the seventeenth century.

[11] *Ibid.*, 140.

[12] L. Soete, B. Verspagen and B. ter Weel, "Systems of Innovation," in Hall and Rosenberg, *Handbook*, vol. 2, p. 1161.

Programs of measured mercantilism do more than enable relatively poor nations to foster industries able to compete in the global market and relatively rich nations to renew their favored position through investment in and sponsorship of discovery and invention. Surplus cash generated from economic activities, at the level of the individual firm as of the nation-state, buys insurance against what cannot be forecast and reduces dependence on the willingness of others to finance the continuity of economic life.

So, upstream and downstream, in normal times and in times of crisis, the dynamics of the Innovation Economy challenge inherited principles of mainstream economic theory and the theory of finance. Economists have long recognized, in theory, that market failure legitimizes state intervention.[13] And the market's failure to allocate sufficient resources to scientific discovery and technological invention is often cited as a prime example.[14] Yet as an effective rationale for state intervention, market failure has proved inadequate. Instead, causes that transcend economic calculation – national development, national security, conquest of disease – have been required. At a deeper level, neoclassical economics is irrelevant to understanding how the Innovation Economy evolves through historical time, for its core purpose is to identify the conditions under which a competitive market economy will reach an efficient, timeless equilibrium in the allocation of resources.[15] But excessive devotion to the principles of neoclassical economics has consequences.

Those who hold the state to rigorous criteria of efficiency in the allocation of resources not only inhibit toleration of the "Schumpeterian waste" inherent in the operation of the Innovation Economy. They also encourage toleration of the deadweight loss that is represented by unemployed resources of human labor and physical capital – what,

[13] W. J. Baumol, *Welfare Economics and the Theory of the State*, 2nd edn. (Cambridge, MA: Harvard University Press, 1969) and A. C. Pigou, *The Economics of Welfare*, 2 vols. (New York: Cosimo Classics, 2010 [1920]).

[14] The foundation texts are R. R. Nelson, "The Simple Economics of Basic Scientific Research," *Journal of Political Economy*, 67 (1959), pp. 297–306 and K. J. Arrow, "Economic Welfare and the Allocation of Resources for R&D," in K. J. Arrow (ed.), *Essays in the Theory of Risk-Bearing* (New York: American Elsevier, 1971 [1962]), pp. 144–163.

[15] For a relevant alternative approach that takes both time and uncertainty seriously, as discussed in Chapter 12, see R. R. Nelson and S. G. Winter, *An Evolutionary Theory of Economic Change* (Cambridge, MA: Belknap, 1982).

in recognition of Keynes's valiant assault on the phenomenon, I call "Keynesian waste." During the 1930s, Keynes sought to establish a new macroeconomic rationale for responsive state intervention independent of the specific projects it financed. He began with the recognition that the marginal productivity of unused resources is negative as skills atrophy and machines rust: any vehicle that sponsors incremental consumption by providing employment of whatever sort would be a less bad alternative. Keynes failed in this project. Tellingly, when full employment did return, it was the result of the most economically wasteful of all imaginable state investments, mobilization for total war.

In the postwar era, the Three-Player Game transformed small-state capitalism, whose final crisis was the Great Depression, into big-state capitalism, whose first global crisis seized the world beginning in 2007. Whereas Keynes was the most insightful analyst of the inherent instabilities that destroyed small-state capitalism, his post-Keynesian successor Hyman Minsky was the most prescient analyst of how those instabilities would be conditioned by the rise of big-state capitalism.

Writing twenty-five years ago, Minsky correctly anticipated that an activist central bank would validate the excesses that characterize financial crises in order to protect the market economy from their consequences, even while the big state maintained the cash flows critical to the market economy's continuity and provided the low-risk assets that investors demanded.[16] What he could not anticipate was this: as soon as the big state had saved financial capitalists from their own excesses in the course of limiting the impact of the crash on the market economy, those whom it saved would question the solvency of the very institution that had saved them.

Now, although Keynesian waste is at a markedly lower level than characterized the Great Depression, the rich nations of the world seemed determined to reenact that greatest of historic failures of economic and financial policy. In the United States, and not merely on the fringes of political debate, forces have been at work for a generation to delegitimize the state as an economic actor. To the extent their success persists, we will experience the consequences of the deconstruction of big-state capitalism in both the near and the long terms. In the near

---

[16] H. P. Minsky, *Stabilizing an Unstable Economy* (New Haven, CT: Yale University Press, 1986), pp. 21, 52.

term we will forgo growth, employment and income; in the long term we will retreat from leadership of the Innovation Economy as well.

This volume is the expression of the double life I have lived as a theorist-practitioner of financial economics, to recall the term that Minsky applied to me twenty-five years ago. The first half of the book is an inside-out narrative of my education in the dynamics of the Innovation Economy. It presents the perspective of a practitioner of venture capitalism operating on the frontier where financial specula-tion intersects novel technology. The second half offers the outside-in perspective of a theorist concerned with two phenomena that have conditioned the opportunities and rewards for all who are engaged in doing capitalism in the Innovation Economy: financial bubbles and the engagement of the state.

First, financial bubbles have been the vehicle for mobilizing capital at the scale required in the face of fundamental, intractable uncer-tainty. Second, the post-Second World War American state, extending a diverse history of underwriting economic and financial uncertainty in pursuit of national goals, built the technological platforms on which I and my fellow venture capitalists have danced for a long generation. Beyond the confines of conventional financial economics, this inter-action of speculative financiers and the state represented the Three-Player Game at its most productive. Exploring how it arose and how it worked may help reignite the essential engine of the Innovation Economy.

PART I

Learning the game

1   Apprenticeship

I came to Wall Street in 1970 while still finishing my doctoral dissertation for Cambridge University because I knew what I did *not* want to do. During the summers of 1965 and 1966, on either side of my first year at Cambridge, I had served as an intern for the Senate Finance Committee as LBJ's triumphant Great Society administration began its catastrophic dissolution. I emerged from the experience permanently immunized against Potomac Fever.

In 1968 and 1969, I had worked nine-to-five in the Public Record Office in London's Chancery Lane, conducting primary research on the economic policies of the Labour government of 1929–1931. I expected that I would return from Cambridge to pursue an academic career in economics in the United States, so the following Christmas vacation I interviewed my way from my alma mater, Princeton, by way of Yale, to Harvard and MIT just before the academic job market was submerged by the deluge of graduate students whose scholarly ambitions had been intensified by the Vietnam War. In those slack market conditions there was an opportunity available in each school's Economics department. The results of the interviews were uniformly positive, but each offer of employment came with a common curse that expressed itself in the suggestion that I might be more comfortable in a department of Politics or Government or History rather than Economics.

The discipline of economics was then accelerating its transition to formal methods, mathematical models and quantitative techniques. Practitioners who did not deploy the toolkit, and topics that did not lend themselves to quantitative analysis and mathematical rigor, were being nudged to the sidelines. In 1994, Paul Krugman, meditating on the marginalization of the great development economist Albert Hirschman, recalled how maps of Africa evolved beginning in the fifteenth century, when distances and coast lines were inaccurate but the interior was rich in details, some real (the great city of Timbuktu), some imaginary ("men with mouths in their stomachs"):

Over time, the art of map-making and the quality of information used to make maps got steadily better. The coastline of Africa was first explored, then plotted with growing accuracy, and by the 18th century that coastline was shown in a manner essentially indistinguishable from that of modern maps. Cities and peoples along the coast were also shown with great fidelity.

On the other hand, the interior emptied out. The weird mystical creatures were gone, but so were the real cities and rivers. In a way, Europeans had become more ignorant about Africa than they had been before ...

Between the 1940s and the 1970s something similar happened to economics. A rise in the standards of rigor and logic led to a much improved level of understanding of some things, but also led for a time to an unwillingness to confront those areas the new technical rigor could not yet reach. Areas of inquiry that had been filled in, however imperfectly, became blanks.[1]

My research agenda, the intersection of politics and economics at times of extreme financial crisis, lay in one of those blank spaces. It and I were both found wanting, informed as we were by Cambridge economics.[2]

I had been drawn to Cambridge in the first place by the magnetic power of Keynes (dead since 1946), whose legacy defined a distinctive approach to economic problems. In his preface to *The General Theory of Employment, Interest and Money*, Keynes wrote that "the composition of this book has been for the author a long struggle of escape"[3] from the "classical" paradigm of economics in which he had been educated. By the late 1960s, the classical paradigm had risen anew, now in formal mathematical garb, as neoclassical economics. But, committed to Keynes's thinking under the tutelage of his leading

---

[1] P. Krugman, "The Fall and Rise of Development Economics" (1994). Available at http://web.mit.edu/krugman/www/dishpan.html.

[2] More than thirty years later, I came to appreciate that there had been an opportunity to carve out an academic career that integrated economic theory, financial analysis and political history when I read the most significant work yet published on the sources and dynamics of the Great Depression: B. Eichengreen, *Golden Fetters: The Gold Standard and the Great Depression, 1919–1939* (Oxford University Press, 1992).

[3] J. M. Keynes, *The General Theory of Employment, Interest and Money*, in E. Johnson and D. Moggridge (eds.), *The Collected Writings of John Maynard Keynes*, vol. 7 (Cambridge University Press and Macmillan for the Royal Economic Society, 1976 [1936]), p. xxiii.

student, Richard Kahn, I had come to read a deep philosophical message behind the Keynesian revolution in economic theory and policy, one that represented nothing less than an alternative statement of the purpose of economics. This statement turned on a radically different understanding of the nature of the world with which economists and their discipline engage.

I summarize now what I understood forty years ago. Neoclassical economics concerns itself with analyzing how rational agents, endowed with relevant information, more or less efficiently allocate scarce resources. In this neoclassical reading of the world, time is an ahistorical index of sequence that merely indicates the order in which events occur. Keynes's economics, on the other hand, explores the decisions (and the aggregate effects of those decisions) made by people who know that they do not and cannot know enough about the future, but who will nonetheless suffer the consequences of whatever they decide. In Keynes's reading of the world, time past is problematically comprehended history, and time future is a world of contingency and chance – and at the core of a capitalist economy are investment decisions that incorporate that uncertain future. As Keynes emphasized in *The General Theory*: "The outstanding fact is the extreme precariousness of the basis of knowledge on which our estimates of prospective yield have to be made."[4]

Beginning in the mid-1950s, the "war of the two Cambridges" animated the discipline. By the late 1960s, as Krugman retrospectively observed, the war was over, unequivocally won by MIT and Harvard. Even to a research student in old Cambridge this was clear. My interpretation was that Paul Samuelson's neoclassical synthesis had accommodated the Keynesian revolution by sleight of hand. Success in the pursuit of economic efficiency by rational agents presumes that all available resources are fully employed at all times, and Keynesian macroeconomic policy was invoked to ensure that such would be the case. The Keynesian revolution, far from entailing the reconstruction of the foundations of economics, served as a handy footnote.

The "Bastard Keynesians" of new Cambridge, as Keynes's student Joan Robinson provocatively called them, had appropriated the mantle of Keynesianism while abandoning the ontological core of Keynes's thinking. Some fifteen years after I left academia, Hy Minsky

---

[4] *Ibid.* 149.

summarized his indictment of Samuelson's achievement: "the neoclassical synthesis became the economics of capitalism without capitalists, capital assets and financial markets."[5]

I returned to Cambridge at the start of 1969 determined to complete my thesis and earn my doctorate, whatever its apparent irrelevance to mainstream economics. Beyond that, I only knew that I did not want to return to a dysfunctional Washington, and at the age of twenty-six I certainly did not want to keep going to school. And so by unanticipated default I entered the world that Keynes had described with such telling insight in the essential chapter 12 of *The General Theory:* the world of the financial markets – that is, the world of Wall Street. I did not appreciate at the time that my four years at Cambridge had endowed me with an advantage of great prospective value.

Most obviously, I had been mentally living in the world of 1929–1931, a period that had demonstrated the interdependence of the financial system and the market economy, as well as the occasional need each could have for state intervention at times of extreme stress. Beyond consideration of the content and context of macroeconomic policy, my study of that period also forced my attention to the microeconomics of bubbles and crashes. I later came to appreciate that the stock market boom that culminated in the Great Crash of 1929, and the global financial crisis of 1931 that transformed a recession into the Great Depression, were previews for the movies we all lived through during the dotcom/telecom bubble of 1998–2000 and the global financial crisis that began in 2007.

Thus I was already equipped with a peculiar set of framing concepts and historical metaphors when, in 1970, I stumbled into F. Eberstadt & Co., one of the numerous investment banking partnerships that peopled Wall Street in those days. Those concepts and metaphors have shaped my professional career for over forty years, proving extraordinarily relevant at critical moments. They have also motivated me to observe and engage with the evolving disciplines of economics and finance, even while standing apart from the academic mainstream for a generation and while deploring the intellectual and

---

[5] H. P. Minsky, *Stabilizing an Unstable Economy* (New Haven, CT: Yale University Press, 1986), p. 120. Paul Davidson, the doyen of post-Keynesian economists, has developed this critique with vigor; see P. Davidson, *John Maynard Keynes* (New York: Palgrave Macmillan, 2007).

institutional chasm that opened up between economics and finance after Keynes's death.

From old Wall Street to new

In 1970, Wall Street was run by a generation who had grown up under the shadow of the Crash of 1929 and the Great Depression. In 1937, the New York Society of Security Analysts was founded; only three graduates of the Harvard Business School went to work on Wall Street; and Richard Whitney, recent past president of the New York Stock Exchange, went to jail for stealing his clients' money.[6] Thirty-three years later, the Generation of 1937 was in charge. They hardly noticed that 1970 was also the year when the National Association of Security Dealers agreed to create NASDAQ in order to automate the trading of stocks that could not qualify for the New York Stock Exchange.

The structure of Wall Street in 1970 reflected three institutional facts. First, prior to that year, all member firms of the New York Stock Exchange were required to be general partnerships, which entailed unlimited financial liability for their principals and limited access to external capital. Second, the New York Stock Exchange maintained a schedule of fixed brokerage commissions that all member firms were required to charge their clients. Finally, the Glass–Steagall Act of 1933, separating the business of commercial banking from that of investment banking, was the law of the land. As one relevant metric of that institutional landscape, when in 1970 I chose not to pursue the chance to start in the bullpen at Morgan Stanley (it would have meant giving up my pursuit of a Cambridge doctorate when it was almost within grasp), the firm had some 250 employees and total capital of $7.5 million; the equivalent numbers forty years later were 62,500 employees and $222 billion.[7]

Still sheltered from competitive pressures, the commercial bankers of the day were a dull lot, generally confined to taking deposits and making loans. The first signs of their awakening to new opportunities

---

[6] "Adam Smith," *The Money Game* (New York: Random House, 1967), p. 10.

[7] R. Chernow, *The House of Morgan: An American Banking Dynasty and the Rise of Modern Finance* (New York: Atlantic Monthly Press, 1990), pp. 585–586 and Morgan Stanley, Form 10-K for the year ended December 31, 2010, pp. 1, 42. Available at www.morganstanley.com/about/ir/shareholder/10k2010/10k2010.pdf.

could just be discerned in the unintended consequences of the Johnson administration's attempts to protect the dollar against the threats posed by the financial demands of the Vietnam War. As a direct response to US financial protectionism, the "Eurodollar" markets emerged in London. There, dollars that had accumulated offshore in consequence of growing deficits in the US balance of payments with the rest of the world could be freely borrowed and lent. In these markets, American commercial banks competed as underwriters of loans, unconstrained by domestic legislative and regulatory barriers.

The investment bankers of Wall Street served collectively as the agents for their clients – corporate, institutional and retail. They bought and sold securities and other financial assets, underwrote new issues of debt and equity, and advised on corporate strategy and merger and acquisition transactions. They were structured in a well-defined hierarchy. At the top of the heap were the white-shoe corporate advisory firms, led by the bulge-bracket lead managers of quality underwritings: Morgan Stanley; First Boston; Kuhn, Loeb; and Dillon, Read. These firms, in turn, enforced a strict ranking of status among their lesser counterparts that was published to the world in the order in which the firms appeared in the tombstone advertisements that accompanied every public offering of securities.

The retail-oriented firms, led by Merrill Lynch, distributed new securities and aggregated demand and supply for existing ones through more or less national networks of brokers; they were called wire houses because their branch offices were linked to the trading floor by telegraph (yes, still!) and telephone wires. The block trading firms – Goldman Sachs, Salomon Brothers, Bear Stearns – had the brains and the guts to put their own (still quite modest) capital at risk on behalf of their clients and themselves. They were below the salt, with the increasingly clear exception of Goldman, whose rise to respectability reflected more than thirty years of labor by Sidney Weinberg to overcome the taint left by its exploitation of its customers in the stock market bubble of the 1920s. And literally hundreds of niche partnerships thrived, subsidized by the NYSE commission schedule to compete for business by any means other than price.

As Chernow notes in *The House of Morgan*, the traditional "religious segregation" of Wall Street was "crumbling" but still visible.[8] By

---

[8] Chernow, *House of Morgan*, p. 581.

and large, the leading advisory firms in the Street remained WASP, with the exception of Kuhn, Loeb (whose past preeminence was plainly fading). The trading powerhouses were Jewish. Merrill, with its sales army known as "We, the People," was Irish. It was barely possible to meet an Italian-American outside the mailroom in any of them. Professional women were virtually nonexistent in the established firms: Muriel ("Mickie") Siebert was the first woman allowed to buy a seat on the NYSE, at the peak of the bull market in the late 1960s, and she had to start her own firm to have a place from which to trade.

The culture of Wall Street was a holdover from the days when the brokers were big and the clients were small. The canonical story went back to before the Great Crash, and every new entrant heard it. I was told it this way: In, say, 1928 a fellow from, say, Indianapolis came to New York with his wife and visited an old college pal in the latter's skyscraper office downtown. His friend escorted them to a window and showed them the sights: "There's Mr. Hutton's yacht; there's Mr. Dillon's yacht; and there, *there*, is *Corsair*, Mr. Morgan's yacht." "Yes," the visitor replied, "but where are the customers' yachts?"[9]

As late as 1967, *The Money Game* – an account of the great postwar bull market, that is in equal measure insightful and hilarious – depicted a culture that in its essence was recognizably continuous with that of generations past, despite such forced institutional intrusions as the Securities and Exchange Commission (SEC). In his focus on brokers doing well by servicing new institutional clients from a fee schedule that harked back to another era, author "Adam Smith" (George Goodman, a former Rhodes Scholar in disguise) identified the force that would obliterate old Wall Street.

After the Second World War, the architecture of finance in the United States was transformed by the rise of investing institutions. Institutional investors had existed since time immemorial: the trust departments of banks, the investing side of insurance companies, the investment trusts (closed-end funds) organized by brokers to aggregate

---

[9] Forty years later I discovered a chronicle of pre-Second World War Wall Street whose title demonstrates the persistent power of the joke: *Where Are the Customers' Yachts? or A Good Hard Look at Wall Street*. In his introduction to the 2006 edition, Jason Zweig backdates the story all the way to Newport, Rhode Island, on a "summer day, probably in the 1870s." J. Zweig, Introduction to F. Schwed Jr., *Where Are the Customers' Yachts? or A Good Hard Look at Wall Street* (Hoboken, NJ: John Wiley, 2006 [1940]), p. xv.

their clients' capital. What drove structural transformation was the postwar institutionalization of savings, first through the broad emergence of defined-benefit pension plans, encouraged by amendments to the tax code, for both private- and public-sector employees. In parallel, newly founded open-end mutual funds competed for retail investors who were gradually emerging from the shadow of the Crash and the Depression. This was the source of the growing weight of the block trading firms, who provided liquidity to customers who had to trade in scale.

The growth of the institutional equity market was the counterpart to the long bear market in bonds that set in after the Second World War. This was partly a function of the fact that, contrary to popular fears and the conventional wisdom of most economists, the end of the artificial demands of military mobilization did not return the world to the conditions of the Depression: rather, economic growth drove profits and real incomes into a golden age of broad-based prosperity.

Unlike the aftermath of previous great wars – the Napoleonic Wars, the Civil War and the First World War – in the United States, as in the United Kingdom and across Europe, the inflation of war was not followed by postwar deflation. In the first instance, this was directly the result of far wiser techniques of public finance in both the United States and Britain, which had relied on comprehensive rationing and direct industrial controls to divert resources to the war effort while protecting the build-up of voluntary and forced savings from dissipation by unconstrained price increases.[10] A commitment to full employment and sheer growth in the scale of the public sector to serve commitments to both social and – with the onset of the Cold War – national security were accompanied by a persistent, gradual inflation that continued after an uncorrected spike during the Korean War.

In 1959, anticipating and accelerating the future, three young men – Bill Donaldson, Dan Lufkin and Dick Jenrette – had started a firm (DLJ) to implement a great idea. As the post-Second World War bull market in common stocks increasingly drew investors out of the

---

[10] Arguably, the single most productive contribution to the formulation of public policy ever made by Keynes was through his 1940 pamphlet "How to Pay for the War: A Radical Plan for the Chancellor of the Exchequer," whose precepts were substantially followed in Britain and the United States. J. M. Keynes, *Essays in Persuasion,* in Johnson and Moggridge, *Collected Writings,* vol. 9, pp. 367–439.

extended, anti-equity trauma of the Depression, they all had to pay the fixed NYSE commissions. Previously, competition for business had involved a number of noneconomic factors – old school ties and the "three Bs" (booze, babes and baseball tickets) prominent among them. DLJ competed for business by offering documented recommendations for stock purchases and (less commonly) sales on the basis of fundamental investment research; this was novel and needed. It was the first firm to define itself as a research brokerage, and it was followed by many others. In 1972, *Institutional Investor* magazine, its own existence emblematic of the new structure of finance, inaugurated an annual "All America" ranking of institutional research analysts.

Between autumn 1973 and spring 1975, old Wall Street entered an accelerating process of irreversible change. The first shock came with the oil embargo of September 1973. Inflation rates and interest rates soared to levels not previously experienced in peacetime. By the summer of 1974, Watergate had paralyzed Washington just when Wall Street both needed help and knew that it did. Nixon was in the bunker, the Watergate Committee was closing in, and the Dow Jones Industrial Index, which had tried and failed three times to hold steady above the iconic 1,000 level, was falling back toward 500.

The bear market that began in the fall of 1973 provided the context for the structural reforms that would transform Wall Street over the next generation. But the underlying cause of these reforms was the reversal of position between the Street's agents and their customers. As brokers, Wall Street firms had become small relative to their institutional clients. And as investment bankers, they had become small relative to their premier corporate clients – AT&T, DuPont, GE, GM, IBM – which had become substantial enough to access the capital markets on their own. In the commercial paper market, the great business corporations created a new capital market as they lent their excess cash to each other.

The transformational reform for the brokerage business took place on May 1, 1975: May Day. The NYSE suspended its fixed commission schedule, and member firms were free to negotiate with their customers. For most firms, negotiating with a pension fund was easy: just say "yes" to whatever rate the client proposed. And so brokerage commissions began their monotonic descent from more than 20 cents per share on an institutional-size, 10,000-share block toward zero.

Seven years later, the SEC confirmed the transformation of the world of corporate finance by promulgating Rule 415, allowing shelf registrations for qualified issuers, who could thus avoid the expense of underwritten offerings by putting registered securities "on the shelf" to be sold when demand presented itself at an acceptable price. Each policy initiative reduced the rewards available for Wall Street firms from acting as agents and generated powerful incentives for them to reposition themselves as principals.

The narrative of Wall Street's evolution since 1970 confirms that one abiding law of history is the law of unintended consequences.[11] Deregulation of the capital markets beginning in 1975 achieved its intended result. It brought vastly improved transactional efficiency, represented most visibly by a radical decline in brokerage commissions and an enormous increase in trading volumes. But it also radically reduced informational efficiency. When the subsidy from brokerage commissions disappeared, fundamental investment research evolved from being a public good openly offered by the brokers and dealers on the sell side to become a proprietary asset of the buy side – among managers of financial assets, from pension funds and mutual funds to hedge funds.

Moreover, the changes revolutionized the institutional structure of the financial markets. Institutional investors who demanded the best execution from their brokers at the lowest net price spawned a set of bigger, smarter, tougher counterparties who made unimaginably more money as principals than they ever could have as agents. In parallel, under pressure from leading theorists and practitioners, the regulators unleashed capital market competition from its post-Great Crash shackles. Liberated from unlimited liability and more or less insured against liquidation by deposit insurance or the lender-of-last-resort powers of the Federal Reserve, Wall Street's banks enjoyed a position on the risk–reward spectrum never before experienced in the history of financial capitalism. Enabled by advanced computer technology and modern finance theory, they were free to construct an infinite web of derivative securities in which every player had the opportunity to become too systematic to fail lest the circle of issuers and purchasers be broken at any link.

---

[11] R. K. Merton, "The Unanticipated Consequences of Purposive Social Action," *American Sociological Review*, 1(6) (1936), p. 903.

Wall Street's transformation expressed itself through the progressive securitization of one asset class after another, beginning with mortgages around 1980. Financial instruments that had been held on the books of the originating creditor became tradable securities, so the prices at which they traded became subject to the same dynamics of bubble and crash that characterize all markets in securities. As principals in the markets they had invented, the players in the new Wall Street rendered themselves utterly dependent on the presumption of liquidity in the markets in which they dealt. That is, they had to rely on the ability to transform any asset into cash at a predictable, historically consistent cost (funding liquidity) and on the continuity of trading in the markets where the assets they held were priced (market liquidity).

Here is a critical instance of the dependence of practice on theory. Theory asserted that the statistical attributes of the instruments the Wall Street firms bought and sold – their average return, their volatility, the correlation of return and of volatility among different securities, and especially their liquidity – could be relied on to be stable over time, and that cash would always be available on predictable terms. My practice as an apprentice venture capitalist would teach me that Cash and Control – assured access to sufficient cash in time of crisis to buy the time needed to understand the unanticipated, and sufficient control to use the time effectively – is the joint hedge against the inescapable uncertainties of economic and financial existence. The big banks and their regulators chose theory over practice as long as they could and were validated by Alan Greenspan's Federal Reserve when market reality challenged them, as it did in the 1987 stock market crash; in the Asian Flu, the Russian default and the collapse of the hedge fund Long Term Capital Management in 1998; and in the bursting of the dotcom/telecom bubble in 2000.[12]

This intellectual construct enabled the excesses of 1929 to be emulated, even exceeded, eighty years later. The great financial institutions acted as though sufficient cash would always be available whenever needed, and in 2008, for the first time in three generations, they

---

[12] Perry Mehrling has published a deeply insightful analysis of the parallel development of the theoretical "economics" and "finance" views of how markets work, and of the abandonment of the practitioner's "money view," which emphasizes problematic access to liquidity as the hinge on which markets turn. P. Mehrling, *The New Lombard Street: How the Fed Became the Dealer of Last Resort* (Princeton University Press, 2010).

brought the capitalist system to its knees when they discovered that only institutions of the state could deliver the cash they needed to survive.

The transformation of F. Eberstadt

How Wall Street transformed itself from a private club of highly paid agents into an enormously more profitable band of dealers resonates with the narrative of how my colleagues at F. Eberstadt and I were forced to evolve from investment banking agents into venture capital principals. In each instance, competitive pressures forced innovation on those who had enjoyed the economic rents provided by membership in a closed cartel. One decisive difference, however, was that F. Eberstadt was not too big to fail. We knew that in time of need our survival would depend on access to the cash owned by our best clients. So we learned to do what we had to do in order to deserve access to that cash.

I lived through and, to some degree, led the transformation of the institutional research business during the ten years that followed 1975's May Day. The Eberstadt firm possessed a remarkable endowment with which to face the new era. It had been founded in 1931, just as the Great Crash turned into the Great Depression, by a great financier, Ferdinand Eberstadt. In the early 1920s, Clarence Dillon, the original "Wolf of Wall Street," had recruited Eberstadt to the investment banking firm of Dillon, Read. Eberstadt led Dillon, Read to play a major role in refinancing German industry after the losses of the First World War and the hyperinflation of 1922. As the peak of the bull market approached toward the end of the decade, he suggested to Dillon that his partnership share might be increased to reflect more closely his contribution to the firm's profits. According to Eberstadt, Dillon responded, "You're not happy here, are you?"

So, in 1928, Eberstadt was freed to play a leading role in the drafting of the Young Plan (named for Owen Young, then chair of General Electric), a collaborative, quixotic effort to reduce to manageable scale the burden of reparations established at the Versailles Peace Conference in 1919. Eberstadt completed this pro bono assignment and returned to Wall Street at the worst imaginable time. In 1930, he put his considerable capital into one of the then major wire houses, Otis and Company, which closed its doors less than two years later with unlimited liability to its partners. Eberstadt literally walked across the Street and, with $15,000 and some used furniture proffered by friends such as Averell Harriman, started his own firm, determined that no one else would ever again have the opportunity to lose his money.

During the Second World War, Eberstadt returned to the public sector, first as head of the Army/Navy Munitions Board and then as vice chair of the War Production Board. At the latter he directed the implementation of the Controlled Materials Plan, a conceptually brilliant and operationally effective tool for directing the mobilization of American industry for total war by controlling the physical allocation of three critical inputs: steel, aluminum and copper. After the war, the Eberstadt Report on America's national security architecture led directly to the founding of the National Security Council and the passage of the National Security Act of 1947 which created the Department of Defense.

In my father's chronicle of the industrial mobilization that led to Allied victory, *The Struggle for Survival*, Eberstadt emerges as the only heroic figure other than FDR himself. He was a

financier intimately acquainted with the workings of industry, a magnate frankly sympathetic with the claims and contributions of labor, a remarkably blunt and forceful character of scholarly attainments and penetrating intellect, an administrator able to master endless detail and yet to formulate comprehensive and workable over-all policy.[13]

With regard to Eberstadt the man, I had the best of both worlds. I knew him from my boyhood, and he was a mentor to me until his death. He instilled in me the idea that Wall Street and Washington were and are ever locked into mutual interdependence. The libertarian bankers who despise the idea of government interference in any economic or financial activity are as suicidally unrealistic as those political entrepreneurs who do not appreciate that every public policy is inevitably subject to the direct or indirect test of the financial markets' temperament.

It was Eberstadt who, in conjunction with my father, led me to focus my doctoral research on the formulation of economic policy in time of crisis. Eberstadt exemplified in one person the game played between the practitioners of financial capitalism and those who control the

[13] E. Janeway, *The Struggle for Survival: A Chronicle of Economic Mobilization in World War II* (New Haven, CT: Yale University Press, 1951), p. 312.

apparatus of the state. Through his firm, he operated effectively in the game played between the market economy and the sources of finance. On the other hand, I never actually worked for Eberstadt and so was never subject to his dictatorial rule.

By the time Eberstadt died, in 1969, at the age of seventy-nine, he was still managing partner of his firm. To the end he held a morning meeting every day, where each partner reported what he had done in the previous twenty-four hours and how he proposed to pass the next twenty-four. This was not an environment in which a new generation of entrepreneurial leaders was likely to thrive; indeed, many of his partners left to pursue their own destinies over the years. Fortunately, shortly before his death Eberstadt agreed to a recapitalization of the firm that created at least the opportunity for it to survive his own demise.

Because of his genius and despite his need for absolute control, Eberstadt left behind three franchises. The firm's investment banking team sponsored emerging companies that he liked to call his "baby blue chips." The team advised the companies on strategy, negotiated mergers and acquisitions on their behalf, and raised debt and equity capital for them in the financial markets. The second franchise, Chemical Fund, was a phenomenon. It was the first mutual fund to be started after the Crash of 1929 and the first to focus on science-based growth industries, starting with chemicals and moving on to pharmaceuticals, then electronics and computing. Not coincidentally, it was also the first mutual fund to reach $1 billion in assets under management. Through the mid-1970s, Chemical Fund's management fees could be counted on to cover the firm's basic operating expenses. Third, and least in prominence, was an institutional research brokerage business that had been spun off from Chemical Fund and had a similar focus.

Eberstadt also left behind a set of senior partners who proved unable to defend, let alone renew, the first two franchises. By the late 1970s, virtually all of the firm's inherited investment banking clients had been poached. And Chemical Fund, which had built its outstanding investment record on long-term holdings of the great postwar engines of growth and innovation – DuPont and Pfizer, IBM and Xerox – followed these and the other "Nifty Fifty one-decision" stocks over the cliff and into the abyss of the 1973–1975 bear market.

That the firm had a future at all was the work of two men. Pike Sullivan and Ed Giles had joined with Eberstadt's son-in-law in the early 1960s to launch the firm's institutional research business. The son-in-law gave up waiting for the succession, but Sullivan and Giles stayed on as Eberstadt's most junior partners in the part of the firm most removed from him. Sullivan built and ran the firm's sales and trading activities. He possessed a remarkable, if inarticulate, instinct for stock selection. He executed a simple analytical construct by dividing the world and its contents into a two-by-two matrix: one dimension ranged from the "simple" to the "complicated" and the other ran from the "real" to the "remote." The secret of management, whether of investments or of the firm, was to live to the maximum extent possible in the quadrant that was both simple and real, and to avoid all that was both complicated and remote.

Giles had joined Eberstadt as Chemical Fund's chemical analyst and had recruited the research team for the institutional business. He combined deep knowledge of the dynamics of the first science-based industry with insatiable curiosity about the context in which its industrial participants operated and in which their securities were valued. In contrast to Sullivan, Giles would habitually lead an audience through a complex and nuanced discussion of the global chemical industry or some particular segment of it and punctuate each stage of the argument by saying: "Do you follow me? Well, it's not that simple!" They made a formidable team.

As their seniors followed their failing franchises down and out, Sullivan and Giles inherited the opportunity to reinvent the firm around the research core. In 1979, they took the decisive step of selling the remains of Chemical Fund to Marsh & McLennan, owner of the Putnam Group of mutual funds. Those partners who went with Chemical Fund received compensation for their Eberstadt interest entirely in Marsh & McLennan stock. Those who were invited and chose to take the risk of a restart received a portion in such liquid form and the balance in the stock of "new Eberstadt," the first explicitly defined "research-based investment banking firm."

The idea was simple. Since the institutional clients would no longer pay us enough in commissions for us to earn a worthwhile return on our investment in research, we had to generate other income streams. Three were available. All depended on repurposing the research team from generating commissions on the trading desk to generating fees from corporate clients: strategy advice, mergers and acquisitions, and corporate finance. The tight focus of the firm's research on the "high IQ" industries meant that the small group of investment bankers, whose purpose was to leverage the knowledge and insights of the research analysts, had no choice but to go native into the chemical, health care and emerging IT sectors. At a time when the major Wall Street firms would not let analysts near their corporate clients for fear they might say something "smart" and undermine the relationship, our model turned on the analysts telling the bankers where to go and what to do.

During the half-dozen years of old Eberstadt's unwinding, I had been engaged in absorbing the basics of the business as an apprentice in the investment banking department. And the firm had enough business in the early 1970s to provide a comprehensive education in corporate valuations, public offerings of debt and equities, and merger and acquisitions transactions, including hostile takeovers. The most fundamental lesson arose from the most mundane of work: the valuation of private companies, a reliable fee-generating practice.

I learned to pursue parallel but methodologically independent approaches. First, one would project forward estimates of future cash flows, discounting them back at a rate judged to reflect an appropriate level of idiosyncratic risk specific to the perceived stability of the business and its competitive position, as well as to market rates of interest. In the language of the new finance theory just being propagated, this defined the "fundamental," as if only one such number could be generated and as if all interested parties would agree on it. In practice, alternative approaches were invoked. One would identify more or less comparable public companies, then introduce market metrics such as price/earnings and market/book value ratios, making appropriate adjustments to reflect the particulars of each company in question. Finally, one would estimate the likely net realization from a hypothetical sale of the business, having due regard for "what a willing buyer would pay a willing seller, neither under any compulsion to transact."

The layers of judgment embedded in each of these methodologies for valuating companies were as evident then as they are now. In a financial universe transformed institutionally beyond imagining from that of the early 1970s, the same techniques remain central to the discipline, and they are just as dependent on judgment as ever, regardless of the reservoirs of data and massive computing power brought to bear.

Such valuations were and are typically used in court or at least subject to legal review when they are needed to help settle an estate or for tax purposes. I learned that the professional goal was to manage each of the processes so the resulting numbers would be within approximately 10 percent of each other: farther apart, and the disparity would threaten the edifice of legitimizing objectivity; too close, and the coincident accuracy would raise suspicions. Practice drove any belief in a single, verifiable fair or fundamental value out of my brain long before I seriously thought through the theoretical impossibilities of the Efficient Market Hypothesis and its assertion that market prices could be relied on to represent accurately that fair and fundamental value.[14]

I was fortunate to learn so early in my career the value of viewing the "fundamental" – a central building block of modern finance theory and neoclassical economics alike – with suspicion. Application of such skepticism faced in two directions. With respect to financial assets, the anchor of a value around which prices are supposed to fluctuate is itself a problematic entity, subject to divergent opinions and estimates. The same stance applies to the calculations that rationalized investment in the physical assets of the so-called real economy – and more so to the extent that those assets embodied innovative technology.

Of course, individual cases are situated along a spectrum that runs from relative continuity and predictability to outright ignorance. At one extreme, in 1970, AT&T functioned as a legislated monopoly that controlled the pace at which essential services would be extended and new technology deployed. Because its revenue and cash flow grew monotonically, it could reliably forecast the return it would generate from any new investment. And its shareholders, informed by a stated and rigorously maintained dividend payout policy, could predict the return they would receive. At the other and more sporty end of the spectrum were, and are, the host of start-ups venturing into the economic and financial unknown and unknowable.

---

[14] For rigorous, analytical assaults on the Efficient Market Hypothesis that cover thirty years, see S. J. Grossman and J. Stiglitz, "On the Impossibility of Informationally Efficient Markets," *American Economic Review*, 70(3) (1980), pp. 393–408 and H. Pesaran, "Predictability of Asset Returns and the Efficient Market Hypothesis," in A. Ullah and D. E. Giles (eds.), *Handbook of Empirical Economics and Finance* (Boca Raton, FL: Chapman and Hall/CRC, 2010), pp. 281–312.

Years later at Warburg Pincus, I would instruct my team that they were allowed to run one instance of a financial model of a start-up to check for logical consistency, but if they insisted on running more instances in the hope of defining the prospective rate of return, we would not do the deal. The parameters of such a model were necessarily so soft that any net present value of expected future cash flows could readily be generated.

Understanding that the fundamental is an uncertain construct, even when applied to an established and ostensibly secure business, has strategic importance. At a systemic level, it forces recognition of the waste that must be generated by any process of economic development and growth through time. Schumpeter's process of creative destruction can only proceed by trial and error. We see that which is created through the lens of survivors' bias and ignore the "hopeful monsters" that economic evolution has spawned and left behind in metaphorical emulation of Darwin's process of natural selection. No doubt every one of them was launched on the basis of an exercise in forecasting future revenues, costs and an expected value to be compared with a rough estimate of the cost of capital. As Schumpeter well knew, the wastage is the measure of the inescapable uncertainty that attends the practice of doing capitalism:

We need only visualize the situation of a man who would ... consider the possibility of setting up a new plant for the production of cheap aeroplanes which would pay only if all people who drove motorcars could be induced to fly. The major elements in such an undertaking simply cannot be known ... Neither error nor risk expresses adequately what we mean.[15]

All of this seemed to be decoupled from the institutional research business through the mid-1970s. But, as impossible as it may be to conceive of today, it was possible then to live multiple professional lives in an investment firm like Eberstadt. So, while I was being paid as an apprentice, then journeyman, investment banker, I continued to write and lecture on the increasingly fraught state of the domestic and global political economies. In particular, during the winter of 1973–1974, when Wall Street generally held Watergate to be a partisan political

---

[15] J. A. Schumpeter, *Business Cycles: A Theoretical, Historical and Statistical Analysis of the Capitalist Process* (London: McGraw-Hill, 1939), vol. 1, p. 100.

sideshow, I was speaking and writing on its economic consequences. My thesis was that Nixon's loss of authority would cripple the government's ability to meet the need for political underwriting of the financial and economic risks that the first oil shock was generating. The game between the state and the market economy of 1931, which I had explored in depth during my years at Cambridge, had returned, if this time only as a shadow and a warning. The persistent relevance of that warning reaches forward as well as backward. Loss of authority by those charged with directing the state will always undermine the confidence of participants in the markets of financial capitalism: a lesson that was learned again in the autumn of 2008.

My work in this domain attracted the attention of Ed Giles around 1975. He asked me to produce regular research reports on the political economy, to be published as part of the firm's offerings to our institutional clients. In this back door manner, I had the opportunity to align myself with the "smart guys" in the firm as the old investment banking franchise into which I had been hired was fading away. By the time we split up the firm in 1979, I was working increasingly closely with key members of the research team on specific opportunities to generate investment banking deals, and with Giles and Sullivan on developing the business model for the new firm.

The most economically significant new business that we created in new Eberstadt was what we called post-venture private placements, the sale of unregistered securities by emergent companies to institutional investors. This business proved to be as good as the market for initial public offerings (IPOs) was bad. Understanding this dynamic is crucial. The public equity markets exist to provide liquidity to investors who can correct an investment error by selling the shares back to the market. But liquidity in any market is fragile and vulnerable. It is subject to two different threats: one-sided market opinion and the existence of categories of securities that are deemed too risky for trading.

If market opinion is heavily one-sided and investors are united in the belief that a given share or the market as a whole can move only in one direction – the conditions that enable a bubble or a crash – then the premium or discount that an investor must pay or can receive will be large. Under extreme conditions of panic, as in the autumn of 2008, the discount may become infinite. As Keynes wrote in *The General Theory*: "Best of all if we should know the future. But, if not, then ...

it is important that opinions should differ."[16] Precisely because no one can know the value of the fundamental for sure, markets offer liquidity as those with different opinions bid and offer prices that correspond to their differing views. So, at a fundamental level, uncertainty explains why financial markets exist in the real world.

As for the second threat, there have been repeated episodes when whole categories of securities – for example, debt securities of governments that have defaulted on their obligations – have been deemed too risky for trading. Most relevant to my own career and to the dynamics of the Innovation Economy, there are times when the common stock of new companies is judged unsuitable for introduction to the public market. Generally, when aversion to perceived risk is high and bear market conditions prevail, the IPO window closes. Such were market conditions after the oil shock of 1973 and through the remainder of the 1970s. During those years, the number of venture-backed companies that managed to go public was very small. A few names stand out: Cray Research (1976), Tandem Computer (1977) and Federal Express (1978).

At roughly the same time, we discovered at Eberstadt that we could mobilize large sums of capital – tens of millions of 1980-vintage dollars, worth some 2.5 times as much today – in order to fund the sort of emerging company that in normal times would have gone public. In 1980, when the first $100 million venture fund was just being raised (by my present firm, Warburg Pincus, as it happens) and when the typical IPO amounted to only $10 million in aggregate proceeds, this was real money. The basis of the business was the relationship of trust that Eberstadt had established with a highly diverse set of our best institutional clients: ranging from the State Farm Insurance Company, to private investment advisory firms around the United States, to various branches of the big Swiss banks and members of the private banking confraternity in Geneva, to the Scottish investment trusts. These relationships, in turn, reflected underlying economic self-interest: because these investors were so important to the overall revenues of our firm, they knew that we could not afford to exploit them.

The terms of these private placements reflected a balance of issues. On the one hand, by sponsoring a company, we were certifying its post-venture status as a revenue-generating business delivering (or soon

[16] Keynes, *General Theory* (1936), p. 172.

to deliver) positive cash flow from operations. This was instantiated by the form of the equity securities our clients bought: straight common stock, underneath the convertible preferred shares typically purchased by venture capitalists. Of course, this subordination was powerfully attractive to the entrepreneurial founders and the venture capital backers of the issuers. On the other hand, the price our clients paid reflected the scarcity of capital and the lack of liquidity.

One of our early successes was a medical device company called IMED, a leader in computer-based pumps to control the intravenous infusion of fluids and drugs. When we sold shares to our clients, the company already had annual revenues of $35 million, and it was growing at some 30 percent per year with an operating profit margin of 20 percent. We valued the company at $50 million, perhaps half or less of the valuation freely traded shares of a comparable company would have received in the public market under less stressed conditions. Barely two years later, Warner–Lambert bought IMED for $465 million in cash.

An echo of the Eberstadt post-venture financing business could be heard in the pseudo-market that emerged in 2010 around the most visible exemplars of the consumer-oriented internet that were still privately held. The purchase of secondary shares by passive investors without SEC registration has a passing resemblance to our innovation of more than thirty years ago. The one clear link is the absence of an active IPO market. The primary difference is valuation: the buyers of these shares were paying premium prices, as if they had the certainty of liquidity that only a deep trading market can provide. These private placements need not end in tears for the purchasers, but it should not be a surprise if one of them does. As I learned from my apprenticeship on old Wall Street, when liquidity is available, escape from error is available, even if a loss must be accepted. When liquidity is not available – whether by reason of contract or law or an adverse change in market conditions – the path to redemption is laborious work, at best (as Virgil said of the return from hell). I would have the opportunity to learn this lesson, too, at first hand.

2   Discovering computers

Early in my apprenticeship at Eberstadt, when I was splitting my time between being a political economist and being a trainee investment banker, I discovered computers. That is to say, I discovered why computers are interesting. This came about as an unexpected result of the collapse of the post-Second World War golden age. From the autumn of 1973, under the impact of the oil embargo and energy crisis triggered by the Yom Kippur War, both political and market processes broke down, nowhere more definitively than in the United States. Making sense of the new economic environment in which the financial markets were functioning was as challenging as it was necessary.

By the early 1970s, the macroeconomics of Samuelson's neoclassical synthesis, universally and misleadingly termed Keynesian, had come to be intimately associated with large-scale econometric models. Otto Eckstein's DRI (Data Resources, Inc.) Model, based on his research at Harvard, led the field, with competition in the commercial world from Michael Evans's Chase Econometrics and Lawrence Klein's Wharton Model. Every major central bank had its own version, as did the Treasury Department. Derived from the work that had won Jan Tinbergen his share of the first Nobel Prize in Economics, these models all deployed a statistical methodology intended to define consistent relationships between variables, using the correlations between time series to establish predictable patterns of systemic behavior.

From the beginning of the econometrics enterprise in the late 1930s, Keynes had raised objections to the whole procedure, even though he had championed the development of the national income statistics that populated the models.[1] Tinbergen himself emphasized the practical promise of econometrics:

---

[1]   R. Frydman and M. Goldberg correctly point out that Keynes's critique was shared by F. A. Hayek. R. Frydman and M. Goldberg, *Beyond Mechanical Markets: Asset Price Swings, Risk, and the Role of the State* (Princeton University Press, 2011), p. 250.

The establishment of a system of equations compels us to state clearly hypotheses about every sphere of economic life and, in addition, to test them statistically. Once stated, the system enables us to distinguish sharply between all kinds of variation problems. And it yields clear-cut conclusions. Differences of opinion can, in principle, be localised, i.e., the elementary equation in which the difference occurs can be found. Deviations between theory and reality can be measured.[2]

Keynes, in response, identified a number of technical issues that infest any attempt to derive causal relationships from statistical correlations. He then turned to the core structural issue: the instability of behavioral relationships through time. This is what undermines Tinbergen's project at the most fundamental level and renders econometrics finally unable to serve Tinbergen's second purpose: to test the validity of alternative economic theories. Fifty years later, Pesaran and Smith evaluated the prewar argument between Tinbergen and Keynes:

Given that there were not strong *a priori* reasons for believing economic relations to be stable over time, and the fact that estimated equations are prone to structural change, one is forced to agree with Keynes that at a logical level econometric inference, like other forms of inference, is unsupportable.[3]

In practice, Keynes himself had emphasized that in the face of uncertainty

we have tacitly agreed, as a rule, to fall back on a *convention*. The essence of this convention ... lies in assuming that the existing state of affairs will continue indefinitely, except in so far as we have specific reasons to expect a change.[4]

As David Hume had asserted some 150 years before Keynes, reliance on the convention of continuity underlies the observable stability of behavioral relationships in "normal" times, even though the "precariousness" (Keynes's term) of such foundations can also be observed in

---

[2] J. Tinbergen, *An Econometric Approach to Business Cycle Problems* (Paris: Herman & Cie, 1937), p. 73, cited in H. Pesaran and R. Smith, "Keynes on Econometrics," in T. Lawson and H. Pesaran (eds.), *Keynes' Economics: Methodological Issues* (London: Croom Helm, 1985), p. 136.

[3] *Ibid.* 147.

[4] J. M. Keynes, *The General Theory of Employment, Interest and Money*, in E. Johnson and D. Moggridge (eds.), *The Collected Writings of John Maynard Keynes*, vol. 7 (Cambridge University Press and Macmillan for the Royal Economic Society, 1976 [1936]), p. 152 (emphasis in original).

the drastic regime shifts represented by bubbles and crashes.[5] And so, as Pesaran and Smith conclude, "it does not follow that econometrics is useless." Indeed, it was their "practical usefulness in decision-making and policy formation" that drove the proliferation of econometric models in the postwar decades.[6]

In the winter of 1973–1974, however, Keynes's attack on "the promise of structural stability" resonated.[7] For the energy crisis drove all the key variables of the models – interest rates, inflation rates, unemployment rates and, with the contemporaneous collapse of the Bretton Woods international financial system, exchange rates – beyond the ranges that had been observed during the mere quarter century in which national economic statistics had been systematically collected. The functional relationships that had been defined on the data from this period and that constituted the guts of the models were left floating in air, decoupled from empirical observation.

In a series of papers written for Eberstadt's institutional clients, I defined this as "the database problem." The econometric models represented a statistical economy whose behavior was supposed to evolve in close emulation of the underlying complex networks of agents and institutions, stocks and flows, goods and services, money and credit. But beginning in 1973, the world economy was ejected from the models. We were living outside the database. Whether or not a given dependent variable would exhibit the same relationship to the supposedly relevant independent variables was an entirely arbitrary judgment once the latter moved to levels never before observed. So, quite apart from the econometric models' standing in economic logic, as practical tools for prediction they had broken down as thoroughly as the political economy they were supposed to represent.

Agent-based simulation models

In 1975, my persistent search for alternative tools with which to evaluate global economic discontinuity led me to a warehouse off

---

[5] D. Hume, *An Enquiry Concerning Human Understanding* (Oxford University Press, 2007 [1777]), pp. 4.19, 4.21.
[6] Pesaran and Smith, "Keynes on Econometrics," p. 137.
[7] Keynes, *General Theory*, p. 146.

Kendall Square in East Cambridge, Massachusetts. There I found a band of academic refugees, led by a young scholar named Nathaniel Mass. They had been students of Jay Forrester, renowned first for his leadership of MIT's pioneering "Whirlwind" computer project and then for his development of a methodology for representing the behavior of complex systems by capturing both the positive feedback effects that amplify initial movements and the negative feedback that dampens them.

At the end of the 1960s, in collaboration with Donella Meadows, Dennis Meadows and others, Forrester applied his system dynamics to economic systems, an effort that culminated notoriously in the fiasco of *The Limits to Growth: A Report for the Club of Rome's Project on the Predicament of Mankind.*[8] Forrester's design goal was to represent complex systems with parsimonious models that would reveal the systems' modes of behavior, and he did so with the discipline of an engineer. But the system dynamics model deployed in *The Limits to Growth* was so parsimonious that it lacked a price mechanism. As a result, increasing demands on resources, driven by population growth and rising incomes, led monotonically to resource exhaustion, since rising consumption and stretched supply generated no price signals to ration demand and divert investment toward the development of alternatives.

Under assault from economists of all persuasions, the younger members of the team had learned the appropriate lessons. Now isolated from MIT's engineering and economics departments, they set about constructing a national economic model piece by piece, from the bottom up, incorporating both price mechanisms and actions by financial institutions. Their goal was to simulate the behavior of a monetary economy by tracking the collective behavior of agents that were realistically defined with respect to the data they could observe, the instruments they could control and the constraints to which they were subject. This was the opposite of the reductionism of neoclassical economics, and therefore all the more appealing. The work was an early exercise in what have come to be known generically as agent-based

---

[8] D. H. Meadows, D. L. Meadows, J. Randers and W. W. Behrens III, *The Limits to Growth: A Report for the Club of Rome's Project on the Predicament of Mankind* (New York: Universe Books, 1974).

models: comprehensive, alternative approaches to understanding how a market economy evolves through time.[9]

When I learned what Mass and his colleagues were up to, a very large penny dropped in my mind. I realized that the transformational function of computers went far beyond their ability to perform arithmetic and statistical operations on ever larger quantities of data. Computers could serve as simulation engines, making it possible to address problems too complicated to solve analytically and enabling analysts to represent the behavior of systems too complex to model by hand. My immediate response was to engage actively with the System Dynamics National Modeling Project as its practitioners moved from specification of the production sector to construct the financial and government sectors of their model.

In the spring of 1977, I attempted to lay out for our clients how agent-based simulation models differed from econometric models driven by statistical correlations. Econometrics generated prediction models that were valued to the extent that they yielded accurate forecasts of economic and financial variables. The experience of the previous few years had shown how unreliable such tools could be in the face of radical discontinuities. The MIT agent-based simulation project, by contrast, was an exploration model whose explicit microstructure offered the prospect of being able to trace the nonlinear, disequilibrium consequences of the behavior of the participating agents.

It is true that agent-based simulation had limited immediate utility as a prediction model, but the opportunity to follow the simultaneous evolution of individual behaviors and emergent systemic phenomena was novel and provocative. Writing more than thirty years later, Doyne Farmer and Duncan Foley expressed the promise I saw then:

To understand what such a model would be good for it is useful to make a comparison to climate models. We specifically compare to climate rather than weather because we think that it will be a long time before such models will be useful for short term forecasting (though this is not impossible). We think the main utility of such models will be to model the equivalent of the economic climate: For example, when the economy is at

[9] See J. M. Epstein, *Generative Social Science: Studies in Agent-Based Computational Modeling* (Princeton University Press, 2006) and J. D. Farmer and D. Foley, "The Economy Needs Agent-Based Modeling," *Nature*, 460 (2009), 685–686.

a given point in the business cycle, what central bank actions tend to be most effective?[10]

My hope that agent-based simulations would develop into a full-blown methodological alternative was frustrated in the field of economics, even though it has thrived in such fields as epidemiology and climate studies. Lately they have resurfaced in economics because of the deep dissatisfaction – within and outside of the discipline – with the failure of academic macroeconomics to comprehend the possibility that wretched excess on the part of financial capitalism could freeze the market economy.[11] Back in the 1970s, Mass and his team took their project out of MIT on a quixotic venture to apply their model precisely as a tool for macroeconomic forecasting, with the predictable (and predicted) result: the assertion of a superior methodology was irrelevant to potential clients whose sole criterion of merit was the short-term accuracy of the model's prediction of such variables as GDP growth rates and market interest rates.

The demise of the MIT Systems Dynamics National Model in no way inhibited my determination to learn more about the uses of computing. This, in turn, required learning as much as I could digest about the range of contributing disciplines, including semiconductor physics, digital logic and software engineering. It also involved constructing access to the commercial activities that were emerging not only within the behemoth of IBM but also on the Route 128 periphery north and west of Boston and, barely discernibly, in the potato fields south of Palo Alto.

Along the way, I discovered a history – still living then, now all but forgotten – that represented perhaps the most productive collaboration ever in the game between the American state (or, indeed, any other state) and the market economy. Understanding how the US government's unprecedented investment in fundamental science and related technologies fostered the emergence of computers and all things digital is central to understanding, first, the emergence of a venture capital industry focused predominantly on information technology and, second, the creation of the new digital economy that venture capitalists and the financial markets have funded over the past generation.

---

[10] Farmer and Foley, "The Economy Needs Agent-Based Modeling," p. 686.
[11] See, for example, the discussion of the work of Giovanni Dosi and colleagues in Chapter 12 of this book.

Government investment in science and technology

During the Second World War, the United States had followed the
United Kingdom's example in mobilizing science for war. In addition
to funding the development and procurement of advanced technological products, from radar to the atomic bomb, the US government
invested in the scientific sources of technological innovation. At war's
end, Vannevar Bush, who had served FDR as founder and director of
the Office of Scientific Research and Development (OSRD), delivered
to President Truman a prospectus for continuing this investment of
public funds. In *Science, the Endless Frontier*, Bush argued:

The Government should accept new responsibilities for promoting the flow
of new scientific knowledge and the development of scientific talent in our
youth. These responsibilities are the proper concern of the Government, for
they vitally affect our health, our jobs and our national security. It is in
keeping also with the basic United States policy that the Government should
foster the opening of new frontiers and this is the modern way to do it. For
many years the Government has wisely supported research in our agricultural colleges and the benefits have been great. The time has come when
such support should be extended to other fields.[12]

Bush explicitly advocated funding basic research, calling it the "scientific capital" that "creates the fund from which the practical application of knowledge must be drawn,"[13] and he argued for making
the results of scientific research broadly available to industry and the
public at large.

For five years, implementation of Bush's vision for permanent programs of state investment in fundamental science was delayed by
arguments over the extent and manner of political control. Into the
institutional vacuum moved the more entrepreneurial agents in the
public sector, which took control of elements of the OSRD's domain:
the newly created Atomic Energy Commission assumed responsibility
for nuclear research; the National Institute of Health pluralized its
name and took over OSRD's programs of extramural grants for life
sciences research; and the Office of Naval Research emerged as the

---

[12] V. Bush, *Science, the Endless Frontier: A Report to the President on a Program
for Postwar Scientific Research* (Washington, DC: US Office of Scientific
Research and Development, 1960 [1945]), pp. 8–9.
[13] *Ibid.* 9.

vanguard of the newly formed Department of Defense, focusing on the range of sciences and technologies that supported the development of microelectronics and digital computing. In 1950, the outbreak of the Korean War finally induced the creation of the National Science Foundation, a relatively modest version of the all-encompassing National Research Foundation envisioned by Bush.[14]

The National Science Foundation was endowed with a broad mandate across both the natural and the social sciences, but the Office of Naval Research's initiative pointed the way. National funding of the basic research that enabled the IT revolution emerged largely from the Defense Department. The Soviet threat, crystallized in the years following 1945 and amplified by the Korean War in 1950 and the launch of Sputnik in 1957, was the context for the US military's massive commitment to renewing its wartime role as the principal financier of IT research and the principal customer of the products generated therefrom.[15] Indeed, the fact that various arms of the Defense establishment had become sophisticated purchasers of advanced digital technology may have been more significant than the government's direct funding of research, for it both enabled substantial investments in productive capacity and know-how by the industrial side of the military-industrial complex and encouraged the sharing of expertise by requiring second sources of supply and cross-licensing of patents.[16]

Kira Fabrizio and David Mowery summarize the essential elements of federal policy:

The IT sector, which scarcely existed in 1945, was a key focus of federal R&D and defense-related procurement spending for much of the postwar period. Moreover, the structure of these federal R&D and procurement programs exerted a powerful influence on the pace of development of the

---

[14] For a thorough analysis of the competing priorities, rationales and policy entrepreneurs out of which the Cold War consensus emerged, see D. M. Hart, *Forged Consensus: Science, Technology and Economic Policy in the United States, 1921–1953* (Princeton University Press, 1998), pp. 145–205.

[15] The role of the Cold War in legitimizing novel state interventions is evident in the names of two signal acts of legislation that passed during the Eisenhower administration with overwhelming bipartisan support: the National Interstate and Defense Highways Act (1956) and the National Defense Education Act (1958).

[16] D. C. Mowery and N. Rosenberg, *Technology and the Pursuit of Economic Growth* (Cambridge University Press, 1989), pp. 126–128, 143–146.

underlying technologies and the structure of the industries that developed these technologies for defense and civilian applications.[17]

And the scale was substantial: for twenty-five years through 1978, federal sources accounted for more than 50 percent of national R&D expenditures and exceeded the R&D expenditures of all other OECD governments combined.[18] As Henry Kressel, my partner and collaborator at Warburg Pincus, would write in retrospect, drawing on his own entry into the digital research enterprise at RCA's Sarnoff Laboratory around 1960: "The real visionaries in the early days were to be found in U.S. defense organizations."[19]

The computer industry in the 1980s

By 1980, the world of computing had stabilized. IBM dominated commercial data processing across the corporate world. The "seven dwarves," including the BUNCH companies (Burroughs, Univac, NCR, Control Data and Honeywell) plus the computer divisions of GE and RCA, all knew that IBM was more than a mere competitor. IBM defined and managed the environment in which they sought to survive. Digital Equipment Corporation (DEC) led the minicomputer industry. At the peak of that segment there were some 200 companies focused on automating manufacturing management and financial reporting for smaller companies and for divisions of large ones.

All the computer companies were vertically integrated: that is, the core processing engines were built according to proprietary designs that ran proprietary operating systems often bundled with their own application software and peripheral devices. The goal was to manage complexity for the customer – an important need given the novelty of the technology and the scarcity of trained personnel. The cost was laggardly innovation and customer lock-in. The resultant profit margins were too good to last.

---

[17] K. R. Fabrizio and D. C. Mowery, "The Federal Role in Financing Major Innovations: Information Technology During the Postwar Period," in N. R. Lamoreaux and K. L. Sokoloff (eds.), *Financing Innovation in the United States, 1870 to the Present* (Cambridge, MA: MIT Press, 2007), p. 283.

[18] *Ibid*. 283 and Mowery and Rosenberg, *Technology and Economic Growth*, p. 125.

[19] H. Kressel, *Competing for the Future: How Digital Innovations are Changing the World* (Cambridge University Press, 2007), p. 13.

The disruption of the vertical, centralized computer industry into a horizontally layered, distributed industry was the work of two decades. The developments unfolded on multiple fronts. One was in computer-aided design, manufacturing and engineering software. Here, the technical members of staff required the continuing, dedicated power of a machine that could run complex engineering algorithms. The engineering workstation, networked to specialized servers, challenged and defeated the minicomputer: Sun Microsystems defeated DEC. It was especially significant that the software technologies deployed by the victors embodied open standards. Although the software was customizable by particular vendors, who were subject to competitive pressure to experiment and innovate, the interfaces were collectively agreed and were accessible to all. Thus, products from different vendors could be integrated into a working system.

The UNIX operating system was developed in the Bell Laboratories of AT&T and licensed to the world as a consequence of the 1956 consent decree with the US Department of Justice that precluded AT&T from competing in the nascent commercial computing markets. The Ethernet networking protocol was developed at Xerox's Palo Alto Research Center (PARC) and successfully promoted as an open standard, in collaboration with DEC and Intel, in competition with IBM's proprietary offering. The profit margins of the new players who used these open standards were distinctly lower than their entrenched competitors', but their growth was positive and accelerating.

Client–server computing was proven in niche technical applications where the scale of the addressable market was measured by the number of "seats" occupied by distinct categories of engineers. In time, as the technology matured and as the performance of general-purpose microprocessors grew to match and then to exceed the custom hardware at the core of IBM's mainframes, client–server systems would penetrate the enormously larger commercial markets, IBM's home environment. The manner in which I was educated to appreciate the economic and investment significance of this revolution came by way of an abstruse academic exercise.

Real lessons from artificial intelligence

A persistent interest in innovative applications of computing had led me to the frustrating frontier of artificial intelligence (AI). Around

1980, Phil Meyer, a colleague of mine at Eberstadt who had followed the oil boom from the electronics industry to the sophisticated end of the oilfield equipment and supply industry, discovered that the chair of the oilfield services company Schlumberger, Jean Riboud, had recruited the entire team of AI researchers from the Stanford Research Institute. On the simple premise that if Schlumberger was interested in AI then we should be as well, Phil set out to learn all he could, in the style of the unreconstructed, old-fashioned investment analyst that he was. Riboud's immediate purpose was relatively easy to discern. The core of Schlumberger's extraordinarily profitable business was the generation of data from proprietary instruments inserted into oil wells to enable analysts to estimate the likelihood of finding hydrocarbons and to assess the magnitude of any find. The data were being interpreted by human experts; if their work could be even partially automated, then the productivity of the process and Schlumberger's profits would rise in tandem.

Phil correctly read Schlumberger's project as indicative of a broader potential. And so he set out, with me in tow, to explore the broad world of academic and industrial AI research. MIT's Artificial Intelligence Laboratory, established in 1970 and managed by Pat Winston, was the first stop. MIT was the logical place for us to start because of its early engagement with the field and because we had already built a relationship with its Industrial Liaison Program. But the range of relevant research establishments was broad, covering a multitude of academic and industrial labs and a growing number of start-ups staffed therefrom. Projects included primitive exercises in machine learning of the physical and the definitely more problematic metaphysical worlds that humans find it natural to navigate. The center of gravity of these research endeavors lay in "expert systems," software programs populated with relevant rules for decision making in specified domains, from medical diagnosis (University of Pittsburgh) to management of shipboard propulsion systems (Bolt, Beranek and Newman). That the researchers in the field had their own chosen language, LISP, and required specialized workstations optimized to run LISP added a certain esoteric allure and exemplified the cult nature of the enterprise.

Over the course of a year or more, we visited all the labs and met all the start-ups. We managed not to lose any of our own or our clients' money in the process largely because along the way we had met a legendary figure on the West Coast who, we were persistently informed, was a radical critic of the AI research agenda and who spoke from a position of authority within the world of computer science. At the suggestion of Howard Austen, a knowledgeable, credible and connected consultant whom Phil had retained, one evening after dinner I found myself knocking on the door of a small, nondescript building on a side street off Page Mill Road in Palo Alto. Eventually I was admitted and escorted to a conference room, where I was joined by a tall, bearded man. This was John Seely Brown, or JSB as he had already come to be known. JSB was still an independent scientist and not yet director of Xerox PARC, but he was already a figure with extraordinary reach across the entire space of information technology, from the physics that constituted its foundation to the epistemological issues that attended its applications. For the next two hours, he and I set out to discover what we were talking about – which meant discovering *how* to find out what we were talking about.

JSB and I bonded over the impossibility of deriving semantic information – "meaning," that is – from the syntactical rules of language. The purportedly expert systems could replicate only the most simplistic of intelligent behaviors, those following well-defined rules. Genuine expertise, by contrast, is a function of, first, perceiving patterns that distinguish possible signals amid a world of noise and, next, bringing experience to bear in order to interpret them. Meaning, that is to say, is relative to context, and reading context adequately is a lifetime's work. The ability of computers to track the evolution through time of the elements of complex systems, like their ability to estimate correlations across ever larger sets of data, make them increasingly useful tools for extending the application of human intelligence. However, the expectation that they could be developed into autonomous substitutes for human intelligence was doomed.

JSB offered me informal access to PARC, where I got to play with the Xerox Star, the first PC that could run a graphical user interface and be managed by a mouse, and where I had the opportunity to be a naive guinea pig for the assertedly intuitive directions for operating the holy grail: the digital copiers that would transform Xerox's core business. At this frontier of digital innovation, a future of intelligent client computers distributed across networks and drawing on the power of dedicated servers could be lived in real time.

This was some years before Xerox finally learned how to earn a return on PARC's extraordinary innovations in the architecture, technology and application of digital systems.[20] The profitability of Xerox's patented position in the copier market meant that no start-up business could compete with the economics of the existing business, so the company was passively watching entrepreneurs depart to start new companies when headquarters refused to commit the funds required to turn invention into commercially significant innovation. This was a powerful lesson in how the innovator's dilemma expresses itself in action, crippling the ability of a company with surplus resources to exploit commercially the innovations generated by research funded with those resources.[21] Warburg Pincus would benefit hugely from such corporate paralysis when it came time, more than a decade later, to challenge IBM's core engine of monopoly profit. As for Xerox, it finally began earning a return on PARC's innovations years later by taking minority stakes in planned spin-off ventures.

In March 1983, we at Eberstadt sponsored a colloquium on artificial intelligence at MIT. One of my assignments was to induce JSB to participate in what was bound to be a festival of promises that he profoundly disbelieved could be kept. His lecture, on the high road and the low road of AI research, stays with me to this day. The high road was the project to give computers the ability to think like human beings. When that project had failed, as JSB correctly anticipated it would, we would be rewarded nonetheless for having, of necessity, followed the low road of incrementally improving how human beings and computers interact. Three years later, the Dreyfus brothers nailed the lid on the pretensions of the first generation of AI research with their definitive work, *Mind over Machine.*[22]

My engagement with Xerox PARC provided an education at the frontier of innovation in information technology. More than twenty years later it would pay an exceptional dividend by validating our shared critique of the initial, fundamentally misguided approach to AI. As JSB had anticipated, the work "wasted" on AI would contribute to

---

[20] For the history of Xerox's failure to exploit PARC's innovations, see D. K. Smith and R. C. Alexander, *Fumbling the Future: How Xerox Invented, then Ignored, the First Personal Computer* (San Jose, CA: Excel, 1999).

[21] The canonical text on the subject is C. Christiansen, *The Innovator's Dilemma: When New Technologies Cause Great Companies to Fail* (Cambridge, MA: Harvard University Press, 1997).

[22] H. Dreyfus and S. E. Dreyfus, *Mind over Machine* (New York: The Free Press, 1986).

the integration of computers into the working and social lives of human beings for three decades and more. Paul Ricci was a young member of the PARC staff when JSB introduced us in 1983. In September 2000, he left Xerox, where he had risen to the role of group vice president of marketing, to become CEO of one of Xerox's family of sponsored spin-offs, Scansoft. Endowed with Xerox's optical character recognition technology, which is used to scan paper documents into digital formats, Scansoft was struggling to reach profitable scale as an independent public company. Once Paul had acquired Scansoft's principal competitor and established a sustainable – albeit slow-growing – base of cash flow from operations, he decided that the time was ripe to address automatic speech recognition, a domain of technological invention that seemed to be persistently a decade from commercial maturity.

Automatic speech recognition was one of those fields of AI research where the rules-based approach had failed to produce adequate results. Paul's bet succeeded largely because research and development in speech recognition was turning toward the application of increasingly sophisticated statistical techniques to ever larger data sets using ever more powerful computers to identify ever more subtle correlations. In other words, researchers broke the code in speech recognition by using computers as computers, not as pathetically inadequate simulacra of the human mind. It should come as no surprise that much of the underlying science and technology was funded by the Defense Department and other arms of the government.[23]

The first time Paul approached me at Warburg Pincus to ask me to consider backing his vision was in 2002. I listened with academic interest and minimally restrained skepticism. But within two years Paul had purchased relevant technology, and Scansoft had begun to demonstrate both step-function increases in the accuracy of speech recognition and meaningful revenue from a variety of applications of the

---

[23] The Defense Advanced Research Projects Agency (DARPA) remains an active funder of advanced speech recognition and natural language understanding through a number of programs, including Global Autonomous Language Exploitation (GALE), Multilingual Automatic Document Classification, Analysis and Translation (MADCAT), Robust Automatic Transcription of Speech (RATS), and the Spoken Language Communication and Translation System for Tactical Use (TRANSTAC). See "Our Work" on the DARPA website www.darpa.mil/our_work.

technology. Moreover, Paul understood that the critical factor was not the raw accuracy of the recognition engine but, as always, customer satisfaction. Unlike the techno-geeks who had been driving the technology for decades, Paul recognized that turning automatic speech recognition from a laboratory curiosity and a science fiction fantasy into a large-scale commercial solution required taking seriously the delicate process of engineering human beings into the system as back-up and for quality control.

Warburg Pincus acquired Xerox's residual ownership of Scansoft in March 2004, when annual revenues were somewhat above $100 million. We subsequently funded several strategic acquisitions while the company was on its way to approximately $1.5 billion in revenues in 2011. One of those acquisitions was the Stanford Research Institute's entry in the game, Nuance Communications, which had a far more relevant name for the leader in speech recognition than Scansoft. As Nuance, the company established leadership positions in a range of major markets: voice control of mobile devices; automation of enterprise call centers; dictation, both general purpose under the Dragon brand and with specific applications, such as medical transcription. Extension of the statistical approach to automatic speech recognition led Nuance to computerized natural language understanding, applicable not only to digital transcripts but to all media of human communication.

The return of the IPO market

The passage from PARC in the early 1980s to Nuance in one professional and multiple technological generations illustrates the continuity available from human relationships through discontinuous shifts at the frontier of technology. Long before I reconnected with Paul, when I was still in the microworld of Eberstadt's research-based investment banking practice, the first hint of a major shift in the capital market context came in the autumn of 1980, when the hugely successful offerings of Genentech and Apple signaled the end of the IPO drought in which we had thrived. The Volcker credit crunch that broke inflation with double-digit interest rates postponed the revival, but by the autumn of 1982 the writing was on the wall or, rather, the growl was in my ear.

The year before, we had financed Daisy Systems, a pioneer in computer-based electronic engineering software. Daisy's lead venture capital investor was a remarkable individual named Fred Adler. With extraordinary analytical powers and intense purpose, Fred had worked his way from poor Jewish Brooklyn through Harvard Law School to a leading Irish Catholic law firm in New York. From that base, he had put his talents to work as a turnaround artist, taking operational control of troubled businesses and driving them to positive cash flow. His successes reached from Loehmann's, a chain of discount women's clothing stores, to a Silicon Valley semiconductor company backed by some of the Valley's venture capital elite. Fred's motto, displayed on needlework pillows in his office, was: "Corporate Happiness Is Positive Cash Flow."

Fred had made his decisive step to become a venture capitalist in 1969 by mobilizing the capital to back a brilliant engineer, Ed de Castro, who had left DEC to start Data General, one of the top tier of minicomputer companies that emerged in the 1960s and 1970s. By 1980, Fred had built a substantial venture capital firm, based in New York, with a portfolio that extended from Israel to Silicon Valley. Daisy Systems was one of his most promising investments when I proposed that we do a second private placement to fund its growth. Specifically, I proposed using roughly the same valuation metrics as the year before, despite hints that the IPO window might be finally opening. My argument was that returning to our institutional clients, long-term equity investors who already knew the company and owned the stock, was a safety play for which a substantial discount from a hypothetical future IPO was appropriate. I knew the game had changed when, on a cold evening in November, I stopped at a pay phone in Columbus Circle on the way home to catch up with Fred, who reported, "Sandy Robertson just told me he'll do Daisy at Janeway-plus-10 percent!"

Fred and Daisy stayed with Eberstadt for this financing despite the offer of a higher valuation, but the game had indeed changed. As the window opened with breadth and depth and even some speculative excess, both the institutions and the bankers woke up. The latter were led by the "Four Horsemen" of the venture capital ecosystem: Alex. Brown, Hambrecht & Quist, Robertson Stephens (Sandy Robertson's firm) and Rothschild, Unterberg & Towbin. Even the major firms, such as Morgan Stanley and Goldman Sachs, were drawn to the new business opportunity represented by financing venture-backed IT and biotech companies in the public equity market. And all recognized that pairing research analysts with investment bankers was the way to win the business and to market the stock.

What only some fifteen years before had been a marginal, hardly respectable activity – peddling shares in speculative, early stage companies to risk-seeking retail investors – had become a worthy and substantial line of business. In what seemed like a heartbeat, our innovation of the late 1970s, research-based investment banking, had become business as usual, although in the generic model it was the bankers who told the analysts where to go and what to do.

By 1984, it had become clear that fundamental investment research as a product of the "sell side" of the market had two possible futures that were emphatically not mutually exclusive: commoditization and prostitution. As food for institutional investors, the path forward was toward commoditization. By the mid-1980s, commission rates on large institutional blocks of shares had fallen more than 50 percent from their former fixed levels, breaking through ten cents per share ("a dime a dance") with no bottom above zero in sight. In the absence of a cartel-based subsidy from brokerage transactions, sell-side research could not pay for itself: why would any institution pay for an investment idea if the vendor was simultaneously offering it to all others? In economists' jargon, the output of sell-side research was a nonexcludable, nonrivalrous good that, once published, any number of competitors would own simultaneously without the protection that copyright or patent law offered other forms of intellectual property.

No wonder, then, that the migration of talent from the research departments of the Wall Street brokers in search of ways to monetize the value of their knowledge commenced almost as soon as commission rates began to fall. By 1980, two of the leading analysts of the computer industry had shown the way. Gideon Gartner had left Oppenheimer & Company to start his highly successful, eponymous information business, advising corporate clients on their IT purchasing decisions. And Ben Rosen had left Morgan Stanley to start his newsletter and conference business before he cofounded the most successful new venture capital firm of the 1980s.

The alternative path, the one toward prostitution, was already apparent fifteen years before the revelations that followed the dotcom/telecom bubble. A direct example of how economic incentives constantly threatened analytical objectivity came in our corporate advisory business. Ed Giles, in addition to serving as president and research director of Eberstadt, continued to function as the best ever investment analyst of the chemical industry. In the mid-1970s he had hired arguably the second best analyst out of a provincial trust department. One of the chemical companies with whom they had built a close and rewarding relationship was Hercules. There came a day when number two came into Giles's office with the news that the numbers did not add up to what Hercules was forecasting. So Giles called the Hercules CEO, whose response was: "Ed, ignore it. You're a president and I'm a president. We have people who worry about the numbers."[24]

Research-driven investment banking existed in a sea of conflicting interests. When we first met with the management of an interesting company, we would begin by explaining that we had no idea whether we would end by proposing to sponsor the company to our institutional clients (and join them in buying the stock), or propose a merger or acquisition or invite them to put us on retainer to provide strategic advice. We did intend to demonstrate that we understood their business better than any other financial firm. I used to say, "Conflicts of interest exist; the difference between children and grown-ups is that the latter know how to manage them." Perhaps it should not be surprising that when the stakes increased exponentially during the bubble, many senior bankers and analysts proved themselves to be children. But by then we had long since declared victory and sold our firm.

---

[24] After 2000, the major banking firms' abuse of our innovative alignment of research analysts with investment bankers would become notorious during the dotcom/telecom bubble and result in the "Global Settlement," which established a regulatory wall between the two.

3 Investing in ignorance

At Eberstadt, before fleeing from the dual dooms to which the research business was fated, we attempted to escape by moving upstream, incrementally shifting our role from that of investment banking agent to venture capital principal. In 1981, I had hired Jack Lasersohn into our investment banking group. Jack had been top of his class at Yale Law School and was an associate at Cravath, Swaine and Moore when he decided that he needed a more entrepreneurial career path than that available at one of the most prestigious corporate law firms in Wall Street.

Having been an undergraduate student of physics at Yale, Jack was fascinated with computers and computing and was determined to participate more directly in the industry. When we responded as a firm to persistent requests to establish a conventional limited partnership to serve our clients who wanted to be able to make a single decision in committing to our stream of private placements, Jack took the lead in managing Post-Venture Capital, LP, which was chartered to invest broadly in venture opportunities, not just in the deals we originated.

This shift in our center of gravity was not entirely voluntary. Not every one of the companies we backed as investment bankers performed like IMED and Daisy. Given our commitment to our institutional clients, when a company performed badly, we had no choice but to intervene. As I said regularly to our investors, "If we ever lose one of these companies, I will be in the emergency room with my thumb on the carotid artery, covered in blood."

In such circumstances, our challenge was to work our way out of the role of hired gun in order to sit on the venture capitalists' side of the table. This was not an easy task, especially given that we had sold and our clients had bought common stock that carried neither preferential rights nor board representation. But in critical circumstances our relationship with our institutional clients provided the necessary source of leverage. Before we came to establish our own modest venture capital funds and beyond any commitments our clients made to them, our clients had deep pockets, far deeper than those of any venture capitalist or all of them in combination. In practice, these funds were accessible only with our active support and on terms we recommended, which endowed us with the ability to act as principal by proxy.

So I learned the venture business by coming in the back door as a sort of cross between a police officer and a garbage collector. By far the most effective mentor I had in this career-changing transition was Fred Adler, that same lead investor in Daisy Systems. When he was operating under the guise of a venture capitalist, Fred's excellence lay in his ability to take a business apart analytically and dissect the interaction of its functional operations and its financial cash flows. He was a notoriously difficult human being, treating CEOs as subordinates and subordinates as trash. I used to tell him that the greatest compliment he ever paid me was that he never offered me a job. But it was through two collaborations with Fred that I learned the substantive consequences of taking responsibility as a financier for the economic life of an operating business.

Bethesda Research Laboratories

The first of these collaborations concerned Bethesda Research Laboratories (BRL), a pioneering producer of enzymes and other biological products needed by all who were active in the nascent field of molecular biology and the technologies of genetic engineering. Eberstadt's involvement with BRL began as a legacy of the firm's old investment banking franchise. One of BRL's cofounders was married to an heir to one of Ferdinand Eberstadt's baby blue chips, the medical device manufacturer Becton, Dickinson.

At new Eberstadt, we had become intrigued with biotechnology in the late 1970s. In 1977, Bob Swanson, the business cofounder of Genentech and a former Wall Street analyst, had called me to introduce his start-up. After some serious exploration of the emergent science of molecular genetics and its potential to deliver clinically effective, commercially significant therapeutic and diagnostic products, we decided not to participate as financiers. Despite the government's growing support for research in the life sciences through the National Institutes of Health (NIH), the time line from laboratory to clinic was certain to be so long, and the rate of attrition from candidate molecule to

FDA-approved drug was certain to be so high, that investment returns were bound to be hugely speculative. No biotech start-up could be expected to reach positive cash flow from operations during the lifetime of the venture funds that launched it. Investment success across the prospective new industry would be far more dependent on the varying state of the public equity markets, for both primary financing and ultimate liquidity, than on the scientific and operational success of the ventures.

Here was a signal example of the game played between financial capitalism and the market economy; in this example, we discerned the dubious odds correctly at the outset.[1] Thirty-five years later, I do not regret the decision, despite the several windows of opportunity for early investors to exploit transient waves of investor enthusiasm and despite the handful of start-ups (including Genentech) that beat the odds to transform themselves into durable businesses.

We had also decided at the time to remain engaged as students of the science and its long-term potential to influence and even transform the pharmaceutical industry. We hired Scott King, a young Ph.D. biologist out of Harvard, who would be dedicated to the nascent domain, and we developed a collaboration with MIT's Industrial Liaison Program that resulted in a symposium titled Biotechnology: Status and Prospects. The conference brought our investment clientele together with scientific leaders in the field. It took place on October 15, 1980 – by coincidence the day after Genentech's IPO brought the genetics revolution to the investing public's attention.

Beyond our work with MIT on the research side of our business, we were also attuned to the potential for a "Levi Strauss opportunity." Rather than backing any of the host of start-ups panning for gold, we wanted to find a business that delivered what all of the prospectors needed to do their work, including those still ensconced in Big Pharma and in academia. This is what BRL did, offering a growing range of the molecular tools needed to conduct genetic engineering. With the National Institutes of Health as its anchor client, BRL was growing fast and had already attracted a major venture capital investor. Given our demonstrable understanding of the company's market and technology and a growing track record of success in bringing institutional

---

[1] See G. Pisano, *Science Business: Promise, Reality, and the Future of Biotechnology* (Boston: Harvard Business School Press, 2006).

equity to support the sort of company that BRL appeared to be, in 1981 Eberstadt was hired to execute a private placement that would carry the company through the estimated two years needed to reach the promised land of positive cash flow from operations. And this we did, selling some $20 million worth of common stock (more than $50 million in today's money) to our best institutional clients.

In barely three months, we learned the truth of the adage "No business is so good that it cannot be destroyed by incompetent management." The cofounder's father-in-law, although not a member of the board of directors, had prudently mandated BRL's choice of outside counsel, thereby maintaining oversight of his financial and familial investment. This was how, in January 1982, we discovered that the young entrepreneur and his scientific partner, despite the presence of that major venture firm on the board, had gone mad. The capital that was to fund BRL over the better part of the two years needed for the achievement of sustainable cash flow had disappeared in a spending spree on people and equipment and facilities unconstrained by any business discipline at all.

I recall hearing the news on a Friday. The initial shock expressed itself in preemptive regret for the loss of what had been a promising business: not BRL, but our own post-venture corporate finance business – and with it, of course, my own career as an entrepreneurial financier. Through the ensuing sleepless weekend, however, I worked my way through the pragmatic logic of the situation. BRL was indeed a promising business with more than $10 million of annual revenue, and it was growing rapidly in a rapidly growing market. In other words, it was worth saving. To save it, however, was going to take time and money: money to buy the time needed to cut costs and stabilize operations. Our clients had ample additional resources from which to fund the turnaround, but we could not ask them for more cash unless we could do so in partnership with new leadership whom we and they could trust to use their money effectively. But, of course, we were hired agents with no seat on the board, and our clients owned common stock with no defensive protections against just such circumstances.

The order of action resolved itself into a conceptually simple sequence of events, each of which had to occur so that BRL – and our business and my career – might be saved. First, we had to secure the commitment of an experienced, credible, operational war leader who would join forces with us. Then, in partnership with this leader, we had to secure effective control of the company, subject to raising the needed new capital. In turn, we would bring our new leader and an agreed turnaround plan to our investors as a trustworthy steward of the requisite incremental investment. Subsequent to the radical surgery necessary, we would jointly recruit long-term successor management. On Monday morning, with the unanimous support of my partners, I called Fred Adler.

Fred had substantial capital in his Venad fund, but I began by explaining that we had no need for his fund's cash. In fact, it was critically important that we clear the way for our investors to be the sole funders in the turnaround operation in order to maximize their opportunity to recoup the loss on their original investment. Rather, I told Fred, we wanted to hire him to plan and execute the turnaround, and to this end I offered him 10 percent of BRL's equity if, as, and when we secured effective control and refinanced the business. Of course, at the time of the offer it was not yet legally or practically possible for us to deliver on it. I subsequently learned that Fred's acceptance of our proposal generated intense conflict with his junior partners, who understandably objected to the obvious conflict of interest with his own obligations to his firm and the fund he had raised. At the time, both issues proved to be blessedly irrelevant to his decision to join the project.

The next step was for Fred and me to invite the principals of the incumbent venture firm to meet us in New York for what proved to be a remarkably efficient confrontation with reality. The process was helped by the fact that the venture capitalists knew they did not command the resources required to save BRL. Their choice was clear: immediate and very public bankruptcy and loss of all of their investment, or surrender of their protections against the substantial dilution that our investors' refinancing of BRL was bound to entail. They acquiesced completely.

The following step was more melodramatic. We had to secure complete agreement to our plan by the two founders of BRL, who still owned effective control of the company. My partner John Hogan and I arrived at the company's building in Gaithersburg, Maryland in the afternoon, knowing that if we did not get a signed agreement by that evening to the terms of an emergency bridge loan, which carried with it transfer of control, BRL would not meet its payroll on the following day. Fred was in New York, available to join us by phone at any time.

The founders' incompetence as business people was easily matched by their powers of denial and evasion. Fred's extensive repertoire of threats and promises was not prevailing until, long after nightfall, a telephone message was delivered to the office where we were meeting. BRL's products, restriction enzymes and nucleic acids and other molecular tools of biotechnology, physically existed inside inoculated eggs that were held in a special-purpose rented warehouse. The owner of the warehouse now advised that if he were not paid his overdue rent by the next morning he would literally pull the plug on BRL's eggs, which meant pulling the plug on all its inventory of products for sale, which meant pulling the plug on the company itself. This, finally, was the catalyst for capitulation.

Within twenty-four hours, Fred had become chair of a newly created executive committee of the board. Within weeks he directed a substantial restructuring of the business, while we brought in $5.5 million of new capital from our investors. My own transition from agent to principal was confirmed as I, too, joined BRL's board. By June 1982, Jim Barrett had been recruited from SmithKline to lead BRL, and the company was back on track.

One year later, Ed Giles and I led a strategic process to merge BRL with the GIBCO life sciences division of the Dexter Corporation (which, not coincidentally, had been the first strategic advisory client of new Eberstadt's research-based corporate business). This merger created Life Technologies, a strongly profitable business with $100 million in revenue – indeed the Levi Strauss of the biotechnology industry. And Fred had succeeded in constructing an outstanding group of scientific advisors including, most notably, Richard Axel of Columbia, who had already pioneered recombinant DNA technology for application in mammalian cells and who would, some twenty years later, share the Nobel Prize in Physiology or Medicine for elucidation of the genetic basis of the sense of smell. Life Technologies completed an IPO in June 1986 on a basis that provided liquidity on attractively profitable terms to Eberstadt's investors.

The BRL saga was an intense education in the financial economics of uncertainty at the micro level. Despite our research into the emergent biotechnology industry and into BRL's own operations, we had made investments while we were fundamentally ignorant of the competence and integrity of the company's management. Unlike investors in a public company, when we began to learn what we had not known, our clients could not get out: the illiquidity discount was infinite.

Hedges against uncertainty

Could we and our investors have hedged against our necessary ignorance? From a pre-2008 point of view – but definitely not from a post-2008 perspective – it is tempting to imagine a derivatives market in which we could have purchased that hedge. In neoclassical economic theory, the central notion of general equilibrium depends on the existence of just such a market. In that fantastical virtual space, rational agents protect themselves from the ontological uncertainties of life by trading Arrow–Debreu securities (named for Kenneth Arrow and Gerard Debreu, both winners of the Nobel Prize in Economics).[2] These securities are conceived to provide exactly the state-contingent insurance for which all of us yearn. Markets for goods and services and assets are made complete by the supposition that at any point in time one can buy and sell insurance over every possible future state of the world.

In the spirit of Arrow–Debreu, let us suppose that an active market in credit default swaps – insurance against the bankruptcy of a company, which evolved in the first decade of the twenty-first century – had existed in 1981. Could we have bought protection so we would have been indifferent to the failure of a business on whose quality and prospects we had bet our reputation? Even at the peak of the credit bubble in the first half of 2007, there were only a limited number of corporations against whom it was possible to purchase single-name credit insurance. Any institution prepared to write such a contract on a company at BRL's stage of development would either have had to charge a premium so huge as to make the hedge uneconomic on its face or would itself have been so obviously incapable of evaluating and pricing risk as to be utterly unreliable as a counterparty.

In other words, a market mechanism for hedging the sort of ontological uncertainties that proliferate where entrepreneurial innovation meets emerging commercial opportunity has never existed, is unlikely ever to exist, and will not persist if someone is foolish

---

[2] K. J. Arrow and G. Debreu, "Existence of an Equilibrium for a Competitive Economy," *Econometrica*, 22 (1954), pp. 265–290.

enough to create it. Here is another aspect of the game between the market economy and financial capitalism: however stationary the processes of the market economy may appear to be, contracts that will guarantee the persistence of such stability through time will never be valid under all the limitless alternative states of the world that may obtain.

Does the specific instance of BRL's rescue convey some more general lesson? It does. The conjunction of available surplus cash and our success with Fred in leveraging access to that cash to wrest effective control of the company from its founders constituted a retrospective hedge against the adverse consequences of having incompetent managers and inattentive directors. But the succession of contingencies on which our improvised rescue mission depended was terrifyingly tenuous. How much more efficient (as well as less emotionally arduous!) it would have been to hold effective control in the first place so that, if needed, the surplus cash could have been deployed without the necessity of the face-off with the venture capitalists and the late-night cliff-hanger with the founders.

Ever since BRL, I have known that Cash and Control represent the sole conjoint hedge against the radical uncertainty that comes with the opportunity to seek outsize returns from making illiquid investments. This is a more complex proposition than venture capitalists' clichéd Golden Rule, "Whoever has the gold makes the rules," which addresses the straightforward, bilateral game between the venture capitalist and the entrepreneur. Cash and Control relates to the open-ended, multidimensional game we are doomed to play with the universe at large, addressing the infinite range of possible threats to continuity from outside the frontiers of the enterprise.

My experiences in discovering how to construct defenses against the vagaries of living in this uncertain economic world are far from unique. The most successful venture-backed companies typically hold cash reserves far in excess of what conventional economic theory can rationalize as efficient. To pick at nonrandom four companies, as of late 2011, Apple held $26 billion in cash and short-term investments, plus no less than an additional $56 billion in long-term investments; Cisco held $44 billion; Google held $43 billion; and Microsoft held $57 billion. Having accepted radical technological risk in the development of novel products and services, along with radical market risk to discover whether there are customers for their inventions, even the most outstanding winners in the Innovation Economy understandably choose to accept no financial risk whatsoever. And although the context was different, the same strategy expressed itself in the fortress balance sheet that Jamie Dimon succeeded in building at J. P. Morgan Chase in anticipation of the Crisis of 2008. At the global level of the game, the turn toward aggressively mercantilist policies by the nation-states of East Asia, led by China, in direct response to the destruction wrought by the International Monetary Fund (IMF) in the late 1990s, has the same pragmatic motivation.[3] To avoid the threat that the IMF would again impose severe reductions in spending and increases in taxes, thereby accelerating and deepening the contraction of their economies into recession, these nations were determined to achieve the autonomy that Cash and Control ensures.

At the national level there is a reason why policies aimed at accumulating cash and ensuring autonomy of action are termed protectionist, whether they are implemented by way of an undervalued currency or legislated tariffs and subsidies. Of course, political leaders in these instances are also serving the economic interests of those in the market economy who export and thrive on protectionist policies at the expense of the mass of consumers who suffer at the margin from the adverse shift in the terms of trade with the external world. And, of course, the intensely focused interest of the few whose wealth buys access to those in power always tends to trump the diffuse interests of the many.

The political economy of protection extends far beyond the narrow confines of the efficiency of markets. Only nations that are the most competitively productive and that hold substantial net balances of international assets can afford to implement the pieties of free trade without fear – think Great Britain in 1846 or the United States in 1945. Friedrich List put it succinctly some 170 years ago: "Any power which by means of a protective policy has attained a position of manufacturing and commercial supremacy can (after she has attained it) revert with advantage to a policy of free trade."[4] All other participants

---

[3] E. G. Mendoza notes: "Self-insurance in response to Sudden Stops justifies large increases in foreign reserves, as observed in the past decade." E. G. Mendoza, "Sudden Stops, Financial Crises and Leverage," *American Economic Review*, 100(5) (2010), p. 1966.

[4] F. List, *The National System of Political Economy*, trans. Sampson S. Lloyd (New York: Augustus M. Kelly, 1966 [1841]), p. 11.

on all the fields on which the game is played are on notice to develop strategies of self-insurance.

MicroPro International

The second collaboration with Fred provided an education at a more granular level. Through working with him to save MicroPro International, I learned how to exercise operational control during crisis – how, that is, to play the role of turnaround expert. The collaboration also represented Eberstadt's most salient engagement with the PC revolution.

By the early 1980s, the killer applications for the PC had been discovered: tools for automating office work. The most visible was the electronic spreadsheet, and the first electronic spreadsheet to hit the market was VisiCalc, a product that rapidly became a brand. It was made by a company called Personal Software, which changed its name to VisiCorp, gained backing from venture capitalist Arthur Rock and from Venrock (the venture capital arm of the Rockefeller family) and hired a senior manager from Intel as CEO. VisiCorp appeared to be unstoppable. We at Eberstadt had built a relationship with Arthur Rock. According to legend, Rock had followed the New York Giants west to San Francisco and become a founder of Silicon Valley venture capital. He had orchestrated the start-up capital for Intel; had been an investor in Scientific Data Systems, the first computer company to be acquired for $1 billion (by Xerox in 1969); and, before VisiCorp, had joined with Venrock in funding Apple.

Second only to VisiCalc as an early winner was the leading word processing software program, WordStar, spawned by MicroPro International, whose venture capital investor was none other than Fred Adler. My partner Jack Lasersohn and I set about creating the opportunity to finance these two leaders in this most dynamic market at a time when access to the public IPO market was still uncertain. VisiCorp was undoubtedly the class act, with its premier venture capital backing and professional leadership. Yet we chose to commit to MicroPro, pushed in good part by a valuation of VisiCorp that its board insisted should reflect the quality of its brand above and beyond its operating results. In addition, with BRL we had already experienced first hand Fred's distinctive ability to cross over from independent investor to operational leader. This provided a substantial degree of insurance for making an illiquid investment in the immature and volatile world of the PC. It was an insurance policy on which we would have to make a claim.

In early 1982, MicroPro was riding a rocket. Revenues, at $4.2 million in the fiscal year ended August 31, 1981, were on the way to $22.3 million for the new fiscal year. Seymour Rubenstein, MicroPro's founder, had possessed the vision as early as 1977 to imagine a word processing program that would run on any of the new wave of personal computers, at a time when the term "word processor" referred to a closed, dedicated and expensive machine from IBM, Xerox or Wang. Rubenstein had teamed up with a genius programmer named Rob Barnaby to produce the first version of WordStar in 1979. When it took off in 1981, he accepted an investment from Fred.

In June 1982, Eberstadt completed another in our succession of post-venture private placements, delivering on the order of $10 million (close to $25 million in 2010 dollars) in return for unregistered, illiquid shares of common stock. And then, with extraordinary speed, MicroPro proceeded to blow up. Revenue forecasts proved as ephemeral as the growth in expenses was inexorable. In the quarter ended November 30, 1982, the company managed to lose $1.5 million on only $6.3 million of revenue.

Fred became an effective ally of us and our abused clients – a circumstance that was made more likely by the fact that one of our lead investors, General Electric's pension fund, was one of his lead limited partners. Fred's intervention was needed not least because it turned out that Rubenstein, along with a number of his followers, was a devotee of Werner Erhard and his self-empowerment movement EST. As I came to learn, ESTies (or "EST-holes" as they were called by those who knew them well) believed that "we are each responsible for our own self." This could all too readily be translated into the maxim: "If I screw you, it's your own fault."

As it turned out, Fred convinced Rubenstein that if the latter wished to avoid litigation, a price adjustment to our financing was in order. It was duly delivered by way of 250,000 additional shares issued to our investors at no additional cost. Along with negotiating this compensation, Fred took over operational control of the company, and I joined him as a sort of adjutant with Jack at my side. Fred called for a detailed structural layout of the company, with every employee tagged with her or his direct compensation and placed in the appropriate functional role and reporting relationship. We were assisted by Henry Montgomery, an experienced finance professional whom Fred had managed to convince Rubenstein to hire and who had no interest whatsoever in denying reality or in resisting the need for drastic action.

Being immediately on hand, Fred was able to reduce headcount by some 20 percent while maintaining operational continuity of the business and without needing any additional capital. More broadly, he showed me how to implement his dictum, "There is no such thing as a fixed cost; what matters is how much time and money it takes to turn what appears to be a fixed cost into a variable one."

The deep lesson I learned from Fred in this case was to understand the internals of a business by following the cash. He liked to deploy a time-worn anecdote to explain how he learned the fundamental importance of cash flow. Every morning his father would count the currency and coins on his bureau before putting them into his pocket. Every evening, his father would return home from work, empty his pockets and again count the cash. If he had more than he had started with, it had been a good day.

Fred's emphasis on the primacy of cash flow took on progressively greater significance in years to come. Generally accepted accounting principles (GAAP) seek to match costs with sales by accruing expenses and deferring recognition of revenue independent of the actual transfer of cash between buyers and sellers. The consequent disparities between cash flow and reported profits used to be relatively easy to track. But, by the turn of the millennium, accountants had fallen in love with the economics of efficient markets. They began to require that assets and liabilities on the balance sheet be "marked to market" at "fair value," as if the latter bore a necessary and consistent relationship to the prices generated from time to time in the inevitably less than perfectly efficient markets of the real world. This meant that ever more experience and expertise were required to reverse engineer the GAAP financial statements in order to expose the actual underlying cash flows. Thus, as with the elimination of fixed brokerage commissions a quarter century earlier, an initiative motivated by an explicit commitment to increasing economic efficiency had perverse consequences. In this case, too, the financial markets were rendered less informationally efficient, to the significant benefit of professional investors with the time, skill and motivation to undo the accountants' work.

Fred fixed MicroPro. After that disastrous first quarter, the full fiscal year ending August 31, 1983 showed revenues doubling to $45 million and net after-tax profits in excess of 10 percent. The next problem was to convince Rubenstein that he had to turn over managerial control to a professional CEO and yield ownership control if he were to be able to realize a return on his entrepreneurial vision through an IPO. Rubenstein had accumulated sufficient legal baggage to make his appearance in a prospectus as CEO and controlling stockholder problematic. Fred and I recruited Glenn Haney from Sperry-Univac (not yet merged with Burroughs to create Unisys) as CEO. And Kit Kaufman of the Heller Ehrman law firm came up with a creative solution to the control issue, known as Founder's Common Stock. This had the peculiar attribute that so long as it represented 10 percent or more of the total common shares it could only be voted to elect one member of the board. It would convert to full voting common stock, share for share, at the time of a merger or sale of the company or when it was transferred to a party entirely independent of Seymour Rubenstein.

MicroPro went public in March 1984 at a valuation of $125 million, and Rubenstein got to sell some $8 million of stock at the offering. The stock held up for a year or so, allowing all of the investors to achieve liquidity before the entry of new competitors, first WordPerfect and then Microsoft Word, cut off WordStar's growth. Its transient market leadership had been based on code that was necessarily written in a low-level software language called assembler in order to generate acceptable performance from the primitive 8-bit microprocessors that served as the engines for the first generation of PCs. The new competitors had been designed from scratch to run on the next generation of PCs, with 16-bit microprocessors, whose far greater processing performance and addressable memory enabled them both to support a graphical user interface and to deliver WYSIWYG ("What You See Is What You Get") renderings of text on the screen. By the time MicroPro's new management sought to join in the process of making its own core product obsolete, it was too late. This was another lesson to be learned and retained.

MicroPro had performed well enough long enough to deliver liquidity to all of its stockholders, not just Rubenstein. The contrast with VisiCorp was stark. There, management and board alike had been blindsided when Mitch Kapoor, a top developer, left to start his own company and launched Lotus 1–2-3, a product that integrated charts and graphs with numerical spreadsheets to deliver killer competition-not-in-kind. VisiCorp never managed to go public, and its investors were entirely liquidated, not liquefied.

Only years later did I realize that in our idiosyncratic collaboration with Fred we were reinventing a wheel originally fashioned by J. P. Morgan himself. Naomi Lamoreaux and her co-authors summarize the process:

> Morgan had worked out a technique for building investors' confidence when he reorganized bankrupt railroads during the 1890s, putting his own people on the boards of directors to reassure stockholders that the business would be run in their interests. The railroads' return to profitability enhanced his reputation, and Morgan used the same method to promote the securities of the giant consolidations he orchestrated at the turn of the century. Studies ... suggest that stockholders responded by flocking to buy the securities of "Morganized" firms and also profited handsomely from their purchases.[5]

Institutional revolution

The context in which Eberstadt reinvented itself from agent to principal was one of industry-wide institutional revolution. The man who had offered me the chance to give up my doctoral ambitions and join the Morgan Stanley bullpen back in 1970 was Fred Whittemore. "Father Fred" was the longtime head of syndicate at the number one investment banking franchise in the Street, and thus the chief arbiter of its hierarchy of status. In 1979, Whittemore dismissed Dillon, Read and Kuhn, Loeb from the bulge bracket and replaced them with Merrill Lynch, Goldman Sachs and Salomon Brothers. National distribution and trading muscle trumped tradition. Also in 1979, Morgan Stanley itself had a painful moment when IBM required, not requested, that the firm share leadership of a $1 billion debt offering with Salomon. Morgan Stanley refused to surrender its traditional sole manager role, and the upstart Salomon got the business on its own.[6]

---

[5] N. R. Lamoreaux, K. L. Sokoloff and D. Sutthiphisal, "Reorganization of Inventive Activity in the United States during the Early Twentieth Century," National Bureau of Economic Research Working Paper 15440 (2009), p. 9.

[6] R. Chernow, *The House of Morgan: An American Banking Dynasty and the Rise of Modern Finance* (New York: Atlantic Monthly Press, 1990), p. 626.

As corporate clients learned to use their power, the old traditions of relationship banking faded away. Merger and acquisition advice had been a free service offered by bankers to long-term clients. Beginning in the mid-1970s, it rapidly became a transactional service, with every deal standing on its own and every firm charging what the traffic would bear on a deal-by-deal basis. Lewis Bernard of Morgan Stanley remarked in 1978, "Clients will do more for themselves. Our principal competition is our clients."[7] In turn, the major firms, led by Goldman Sachs and Morgan Stanley, began to invest in the people and the computer systems necessary to compete effectively against their clients – institutional and corporate – from the trading desk. This reversal of position was the fundamental change that defined the business of the investment banks, both the independents and those captive inside the universal banks such as Citibank and J. P. Morgan, in the run-up to the Crisis of 2007–2009.

During the 1980s, two developments confirmed the irreversible transformation. To obtain the capital necessary to compete as principals, the investment banking firms had to go public. In 1970, the NYSE had relaxed its generations-old prohibition to make this possible, but the opportunity had only been taken by the major retail wire houses. They had gone public to fund their investments in their branch office networks and in the first generation of the computer systems forced on them by the paperwork crisis of the late 1960s, when stock trading choked on rising volume. Now the wholesale banks followed, leveraging advanced computer systems to trade against their clients with the first generation of mathematical models for pricing financial assets.

At the same time, the Federal Reserve and the Securities and Exchange Commission began to let the commercial banks creep back into the investment banking business. Glass–Steagall had been established fifty years before to protect the retail depositors of commercial banks against the volatility of the financial markets and against the greed of bank managements intent on exploiting that volatility. The contemporaneous creation of the Federal Deposit Insurance Corporation meant that Glass–Steagall also protected the taxpayers generally by insuring them as depositors. These actions condemned the commercial banks to the slow-or-no-growth business of lending to corporate customers that were not substantial enough to access the capital markets directly.

---

[7] *Ibid.* 595.

The most aggressive of the commercial banks had historically been the most conservative: J. P. Morgan, the commercial banking side of the House of Morgan, which Glass–Steagall had divided from Morgan Stanley. By 1987, with Glass–Steagall still nominally in force, J. P. Morgan's fee revenues exceeded its income from the net interest spread on its lending business. The opportunity to play across all of the wholesale financial markets in London, with the growth of the Eurodollar markets, was a training experience not only for J. P. Morgan but for its commercial banking competitors as well. Appropriately, it was also in 1987 that Dennis Weatherstone, a working-class Brit without a university degree, who had grown up on the foreign exchange trading desk, became the bank's president.[8]

Wall Street was becoming open to new talent and, with more than a little lag, so was the City of London. There, hard on the heels of the Big Bang of 1986, which eliminated restrictive practices and longstanding guild-like monopolies, the "barrow boys" on the trading desks were generating more profit and taking home more money than the public school and Oxbridge-educated blue bloods of corporate finance and advisory services. As brokerage commissions declined in all markets, volume rose more than proportionately, and trading activity as a source of revenue and profit rose with volume. Moreover, the accelerating proliferation of computers, moving from routine back-office accounting functions toward the trading desk on the front line, created space for new players with new skills.

The combination of intellectual and temperamental qualities that make for successful trading – intense focus, infinite patience for haggling, a propensity for gambling – had always earned a return in the market, albeit a highly volatile one. Now those skills became ever more central to the economics of both banks and brokers. Further, the ability to analyze market data and to devise innovative trading strategies began to generate value. Those with such expertise, whether traders or trading strategists, tended not to be heirs of old Wall Street and the City of London. Relationships yielded to transactions as the source and measure of value, and the sociology of the financial markets was transformed. As more and more classes of financial assets were transformed into tradable securities – from residential and commercial mortgages, to corporate and credit card receivables, to student

---

[8] *Ibid.* 656.

loans, and on and on – there were ever more transactions and ever more opportunities for the dealer banks to earn attractive spreads versus their less-informed clients.

Analytical skill, the mastery of quantitative techniques, and an all-consuming work ethic – these were required to populate the vast expansion of investment banking practices. First-class credentials that testified to such abilities now trumped family and old school ties. But something was lost as well. There was not much room for eccentricity in the new Wall Street. Perhaps that was merely an aesthetic loss. But formulaic finance and the computers that enabled it made it easy to substitute an algorithm for judgment. When I was learning how to value private companies in the early 1970s, the tools at hand were a Monroe electromechanical calculator and a book of logarithms: it took half a day to run a case, and the analyst thought long and hard about the assumptions employed. Barely ten years later, when I addressed the artificial intelligence colloquium at MIT on the valuation of ventures, the Hewlett-Packard digital calculator had already made it possible to generate innumerable cases at the push of a few buttons, so it was easy to construct whatever model was needed to rationalize the prospect of earning the required rate of return. "And then," I said at the colloquium, "came VisiCalc."

The lessons I learned from collaborating with Fred Adler to generate positive returns from start-up ventures that had seemed destined to go bankrupt cut against the grain of how modern finance theory instructs investors to manage risk – namely, by diversifying. For the venture capital investor, a fund portfolio typically consists of no more than twenty-five positions, usually in no more than two or three industrial sectors and often concentrated in only one; this is hardly an opportunity for substantial diversification. Moreover, each position is definitionally immature as a business and is subject to failure along any of several dimensions, including managerial competence, technological efficacy and market acceptance. In a venture capital portfolio, that is to say, idiosyncratic risk is both very great and quite homogeneous. And, as in the case of BRL, it cannot be hedged through any sort of transactions in markets that either do not or cannot exist. Thus, the counterpart of learning the game of venture capital in the trenches was learning that modern finance theory is largely irrelevant to its practice.

My collaboration with Fred not only defined a technique for addressing the chances and contingencies that face the venture capitalist.

Fred's mentoring also represented a case study in what Perry Mehrling calls "the money view," which focuses on the continuously evolving present moment in which "cash flows emerging from past real investments meet cash commitments entered in anticipation of an imagined future."[9] In fact, as I discuss at length in Chapter 8, what Fred taught me at the level of practice corresponds exactly with what Hy Minsky was teaching me concurrently at the level of theory. Minsky's "survival constraint" binds at the point at which currently due obligations cannot be met from operating cash flow, from new borrowings or from asset sales. So I had the opportunity twice over to absorb the core of Minsky's extension of Keynes to encompass the "Financial Instability Hypothesis" more than twenty years before the world would have its Minsky moment in September 2008.[10]

While I was making my professional transition from investment banker to venture capitalist, it was becoming clear that the Eberstadt firm as a whole could not succeed in similarly transforming itself. To try would have entailed dismissing more than half of our partners. Not even Fred could have worked out how we could reduce costs to where they could be covered by the management fees from two modest post-venture funds plus investment banking and corporate advisory fees while we maintained our distinctive competitive position. The relationships that the brokerage business had created with our institutional clients were crucial to the research-based investment banking model even as the brokerage business generated ever less direct revenues. We were facing a contradiction in our operating environment that we lacked the power, not the understanding, to resolve. So, in September 1985, we were fortunate to learn that Robert Fleming & Company, a global investment manager and bank and a major institutional client of the firm, was seeking an American link between its London base and the hugely successful Asian joint venture it had established with Jardine Matheson in Hong Kong. As we walked back from closing the sale of Eberstadt to Robert Fleming, Pike Sullivan remarked: "Well, we got rid of the black queen."

---

[9] P. Mehrling, *The New Lombard Street: How the Fed Became the Dealer of Last Resort* (Princeton University Press, 2010), p. 4.

[10] H. P. Minsky, "The Financial Instability Hypothesis," The Levy Economics Institute of Bard College Working Paper 74 (1992).

PART II

Playing the game

4   The financial agent

The sale of Eberstadt to Robert Fleming & Company in the autumn of 1985 represented release from an intractable dilemma. But as a senior partner of Eberstadt I had perforce signed on to a three-year contract with Flemings, although neither my brain nor my heart was in it. Flemings was rigidly structured between an asset management business and an investment banking (still called merchant banking) business. I had spent some fifteen years in the internal migration from investment banker to principal investor within Eberstadt's loose framework; within Flemings I was placed irrevocably in the agency business of corporate finance. Working my way up to running four marathons per year on a training base of seventy to eighty miles per week provided one outlet during this time. Reading economic theory and engaging with Hy Minsky's maverick economics provided another.

The near-death experiences of Bethesda Research Laboratories (BRL) and MicroPro prepared my mind to understand in a deeper and more connected way what I had formerly experienced only as anecdotes: access to cash in case of crisis is the only effective hedge against ontological uncertainty. This resonated with what I had learned at Cambridge, at the theoretical level from Keynes and at the level of empirical analysis from the failure of economic policy in the face of financial crisis and economic collapse in 1931. It was also the central message of Minsky's post-Keynesian work.

Furthermore, engagement with the world of computing had introduced me to a crucial institutional aspect of the Innovation Economy. This was the upstream dependence on prior investment in the enabling science, investment that was necessarily made independent of any concern for quantifiable return. The role of the Defense Department remained evident in the IT sector, and the National Institutes of Health (NIH) were sponsoring the emergence of biotech as a second focus for venture capitalists. Through these instrumentalities the federal government funded research whose economic relevance could be discovered only in retrospect.

To understand how such economic relevance is revealed in practice by repeated trials and errors, I found an unlikely guide in the great French historian Fernand Braudel. I encountered Braudel and his three-volume discourse *Civilization and Capitalism, 15th–18th Century* in 1985, just after my partners and I sold the Eberstadt firm in the face of a changing competitive environment that we could neither control nor evade. Braudel's meditations on what capitalists do generated a shock of recognition that I can still feel. Although the domain and context in which Braudel's financiers operated is vastly different from the world of today's working venture capitalist, yet the activity remains recognizable: putting surplus cash to work, again and again, wherever the potential return is unlimited by either institutional structures or competition.

The financial capitalist at the venturesome frontier

I have found it useful to interpret the doing of capitalism at the venturesome frontier within Braudel's frame – a frame that intersects other salient analyses of the core drivers of capitalism at the scale of the human agent, those of Marx, Schumpeter and Keynes.

In Braudel's comprehensive view, the "unlimited flexibility" of capitalists in their search for profit is the "essential feature" that established "a certain unity in capitalism from thirteenth century Italy to the present day West":

One's impression … is that there were always sectors in economic life where high profits could be made, *but that these sectors varied*. Every time one of these shifts occurred, under the pressure of economic developments, capital was quick to seek them out, to move into the new sector and prosper.[1]

The telling point is Braudel's grasp of the capitalist's unchanging goal: to escape from the "world of transparence and regularity," as he defines the market economy, where the potential for profit is constrained by the regulations of the traditional market or the competition

---

[1] F. Braudel, *Wheels of Commerce*, trans. Sian Reynolds, vol. 2 of *Civilization and Capitalism, 15th–18th Century*, 3 vols. (New York: Harper & Row, 1982), pp. 433–434; emphasis in original.

of the emerging free market. In the premodern, preindustrial era that is Braudel's subject, "the capitalist game only concerned the unusual, the very special, or the very long distance connection."[2] It was in long-distance trade that Braudel's capitalists flourished:

Long-distance trade certainly made super profits; it was after all based on the price difference between two markets very far apart, with supply and demand in complete ignorance of each other and brought into contact only by the activity of middlemen ... If in the fullness of time competition did appear, if super-profits vanished from one line, it was always possible to find them again on another route with different commodities.[3]

Unlimited flexibility to arbitrage across vast geographical space: this is Braudel's defining attribute of the premodern capitalist. The notion of arbitrage as the essence of the capitalist transaction has powerful resonance. For the modern venture capitalist, the arbitrage is typically between a technological innovation and the commercial product or service that can be derived from it. My own experience suggests that too much weight is often given to management of the process of technical transformation – "research and development" – and too little to the selection of the target market and the establishment of a channel to that market. For Braudel's capitalist, the question asked of the sea captain would be: Why are you setting your course there? For the modern venture capitalist interrogating the entrepreneur, the corresponding question would be: Whose problem are you proposing to solve? It took me twenty years to absorb this principle fully.

In Marx's vision of the capitalist project, the entrepreneur and the financier are one. The capitalist directs the process of accumulation by inverting the circulation of commodities from commodity–money–commodity (selling in order to buy) to money–commodity–money (buying in order to sell).[4] The concept of the capitalist as the embodiment of accumulation crosses the nominal phases of economic evolution:

Buying in order to sell, or more accurately, buying in order to sell dearer, M-C-M′, appears certainly to be a form peculiar to one kind of capital alone, merchants' capital. But industrial capital too is money that is changed into

---

[2] *Ibid.* 456
[3] *Ibid.* 405.
[4] K. Marx, *Capital*, vol. 1, trans. S. Moore and E. Aveling (Moscow: Foreign Language Publishing House, 1964 [1887]), pp. 152–153.

commodities and by the sale of those commodities is re-converted into more money. The events that take place outside the sphere of circulation, in the interval between the buying and the selling, do not affect the form of this movement.[5]

But those events decisively do affect the substance of the movement: they constitute the very reason for the circulation of industrial capital. The increase in money arises from the capitalist's purchase and exploitation of that alone which can create value in the world of classical economics that runs from Smith through Ricardo to Marx – namely labor. So the capitalist exists as the omnipotent human link in the endless chain of accumulation, converting cash into "means of production and labor-power" in order to produce commodities that the capitalist then sells for cash "over and over again."[6]

The power that Marx's capitalist enjoys to command labor power in order to create surplus value distinguishes him from Braudel's capitalist, who finances a venture that literally sails beyond his control. Yet on the frontier of capitalist evolution, where "the law of the tendency of the rate of profit to fall"[7] asserts itself, Marx finally allows entry to the uncertainty inherent in the capitalist process of investment and production. There is in *Capital* one remote yet intriguing reference to what might dimly be recognized as venture capital, albeit in most unflattering guise:

If the rate of profit falls ... there appears swindling and a general promotion of swindling by resource to frenzied ventures with new methods of production, new investments, new adventures, all for the sake of securing a shred of extra profit which is independent of the general average and rises above it.[8]

Behind the potential for speculative excess, Marx's simple and profound dialectic remains: from money to commodity to more money. Substitute "company" for "commodity" and you have, in brief, the charter of the professional venture capitalist.

For Schumpeter, the entrepreneur is the driving force of capitalist development, freed more or less completely from the responsibilities

---

[5] *Ibid.* 155.   [6] *Ibid.* 564.
[7] K. Marx, *Capital*, vol. 3 (Moscow: Foreign Language Publishing House, 1962 [1894]), p. 207.
[8] *Ibid.* 253–255.

of the financier. As Carlota Perez has written of the Schumpeterian tradition:

In Schumpeter's basic definition of capitalism as "that form of private property economy in which innovations are carried out by means of borrowed money," we find his characteristic separation of borrower and lender, entrepreneur and banker, as the two faces of the innovation coin. This is not, however, as his legacy has been interpreted and enriched by the great majority of neo-Schumpeterians. The accent has almost invariably been on the entrepreneur to the neglect of the financial agent, no matter how obviously indispensable this agent may be to the innovation.[9]

Overstated as this emphasis by his followers may be, it is there in Schumpeter's work. Innovation – "any 'doing things differently' in the realm of economic life"[10] – drives the course of economic evolution. And innovations, in turn, are embodied in new plants, new firms and, above all, new people, the entrepreneurs who carry out innovations:

The entrepreneur may, but need not, be the person who furnishes the capital … In the institutional pattern of capitalism there is machinery, the presence of which forms an essential characteristic of it, which makes it possible for people to function as entrepreneurs without having previously acquired the necessary means. It is leadership rather than ownership that matters.[11]

The capitalist, in the prime role of owner of surplus cash available for investment, is relegated in remarkable fashion:

Risk bearing is no part of the entrepreneurial function. It is the capitalist who bears the risk. The entrepreneur does so only to the extent to which, besides being an entrepreneur, he is also a capitalist but *qua* entrepreneur *he loses other people's money*.[12]

Now here was a message – a warning – to which I could relate after surviving the BRL and MicroPro dramas. Those experiences prompted me to formulate what I call the First Law of Venture Capital: "All

---

[9] C. Perez, "Finance and Technical Change: A Neo-Schumpeterian Perspective," in H. Hanusch and A. Pyka, *Elgar Companion to Neo-Schumpeterian Economics* (Cheltenham: Edward Elgar, 2007), p. 776.

[10] J. A. Schumpeter, *Business Cycles: A Theoretical, Historical and Statistical Analysis of the Capitalist Process*, 2 vols. (London: McGraw-Hill, 1939), vol. 1, p. 84.

[11] *Ibid*. 103.　[12] *Ibid*. 104 (emphasis added).

entrepreneurs lie." That is, entrepreneurs begin by proposing to change the world through their own efforts. The promises they make to their financiers, customers and employees are sufficiently unlikely to be realized that confident assertion that they will be realized challenges any conventional definition of reasonable truth.

Even when there is no dishonest act of commission on the part of the entrepreneur, the Second Law of Venture Capital obtains: "No news is never good news." After forty years, I have yet to meet the entrepreneur who dallies in delivering word that "the product works" or "the sale has closed." When communication ceases, then the venture capitalist can expect to discover that "the product needs another rev" or that "we lost the order." The venture capitalist's responsibility, therefore, is to follow the cash with intense focus in order to observe in timely fashion when the entrepreneur's vision and the recalcitrant reality of the market deviate too far from each other.

Schumpeter himself was aware of "how important it is for the functioning of the system … that the banker should know and be able to judge what his credit is used for." And Schumpeter also understood the challenge presented by innovation, whether the financial agent is a banker or a venture capitalist:

It is but natural that since such failure primarily shows in dealing with novel propositions – where judgment is most difficult and temptation strongest – an association has developed between financing innovation and miscarriage or misconduct.[13]

Schumpeter is at pains to separate the entrepreneurial function from the variety of individuals who may fill the role. In the old "competitive capitalism," it was easy to find the entrepreneur "among the heads of firms" – as, indeed, remains the case in the start-ups that populate the Innovation Economy, where venture capitalists live. But in the modern capitalism of "giant concerns," the entrepreneur's identity as manager or salaried employee or major stockholder becomes problematic. Schumpeter extends his search further, finally touching on what appears to be the proto-venture capitalist:

Although company promoters are not as a rule entrepreneurs, a promoter may fill that function occasionally and then come near to presenting the

---

[13] *Ibid.* 116–117.

only instance there is of a type which is entrepreneur by profession and nothing else.[14]

The very process that transforms, historically and conceptually, the aggressive owner of surplus wealth into the passive candidate for entrepreneurial exploitation creates the space into which the professional venture capitalist can move.

Against the grain of decades of work, Schumpeter came to imagine that the maturation of capitalism would entail the death of the entrepreneur:

On the one hand, it is much easier now than it has been in the past to do things that lie outside familiar routine – innovation itself is being reduced to routine. Technological progress is increasingly becoming the business of teams of trained specialists who turn out what is required and make it work in predictable ways …

On the other hand, personality and will power must count for less in environments which have become accustomed to economic change …

The perfectly bureaucratized giant industrial firm not only ousts the small or medium-sized firm and "expropriates" its owners, but in the end it ousts the entrepreneur.[15]

Schumpeter was not wholly wrong. There are domains of innovation where only the large-scale enterprise has the resources to develop innovative technology to the point of commercial readiness and to discover relevant commercial applications. The realm of materials science offers examples. From the iconic plastics of *The Graduate* to nanotechnology, the cost in money and time to reduce innovative manufacturing processes to reliable and low-cost practice and to find applications where new materials offer competitive advantages of compelling economic significance has meant that companies such as General Electric and DuPont – not venture-backed start-ups – have been the pioneers. But all too often the broad-based firm with multitudes of established market positions has failed to lead, even when its own laboratories have been primary sources of the very innovation in question. In my world of information technology, this has been the predominant condition.

---

[14] *Ibid.* 103.
[15] J. A. Schumpeter, *Capitalism, Socialism and Democracy*, 4th edn. (London: Allen & Unwin, 2010 [1943]), pp. 132–134.

For Keynes, the maturing of capitalism is represented by the distance between the entrepreneur's investment decision from that of the financier, mediated by markets in which titles to ownership and to debt can be traded. The consequent separation of ownership and control has turned the capitalist into a passive investor, and the way in which securities markets work has almost invariably turned the investor into a speculator. Against speculation, "the activity of forecasting the psychology of the market," stands enterprise, "the activity of forecasting the prospective yield of assets over their whole life."[16] For the capitalist engaged in financing enterprise,

the outstanding fact is the extreme precariousness of the basis of knowledge on which our estimates of prospective yield have to be made ... If we speak frankly, we have to admit that our basis of knowledge for estimating the yield ten years hence of a railway, a copper mine, a textile factory, the goodwill of a patent medicine, an Atlantic liner, a building in the City of London amounts to little and sometimes to nothing; or even five years hence.[17]

Embedded in a market infused with "imperfect knowledge," Keynes writes, investors must be

largely concerned, not with making superior long-term forecasts of the probable yield of an investment over its whole life, but with foreseeing changes in the conventional basis of valuation a short time ahead ... For it is not sensible to pay 25 for an investment of which you believe the prospective yield to justify a value of 30, if you also believe that the market will value it at 20 three months hence.[18]

Derived in response to the failure of capitalist enterprise to spur economic recovery from the Great Depression, Keynes's characterization of the investor who is constrained to operate within the casino of the stock exchange has remarkable resonance for the

---

[16] J. M. Keynes, *The General Theory of Employment, Interest and Money*, in E. Johnson and D. Moggridge (eds.), *The Collected Writings of John Maynard Keynes*, vol. 7 (Cambridge University Press and Macmillan for the Royal Economic Society, 1976 [1936]), p. 158.

[17] *Ibid.* 149–150.

[18] *Ibid.* 154–155. A useful interpretation of Keynes's nuanced understanding of the context of "imperfect knowledge" in which investors function is provided by R. Frydman and M. Goldberg, *Beyond Mechanical Markets: Asset Price Swings, Risk, and the Role of the State* (Princeton University Press, 2011), pp. 121–127.

modern venture capitalist. In fact, the entire process out of which the activities of a small number of professional venture capitalists emerged as an industry between 1980 and 2000 is intimately entangled with and ultimately driven by the greatest bull market in the history of capitalism.

Evolution of the venture capital industry

In 1980, following amendment of Employee Retirement Income Security Act (ERISA) regulations to permit pension funds to invest in such risky assets as venture capital, the total capital committed to member firms of the National Venture Capital Association (NVCA) was $2 billion, about $5 billion in 2010 dollars. Twenty years later, in 2000, the flow of funds to venture capital peaked at no less than $105 billion, having risen to that level from a relatively stable range of $5–10 billion (in then-current dollars) from 1985 to 1995. Access to the stock market for new, venture-backed companies was almost continuous, punctuated by several hot IPO markets and culminating in the great dotcom/telecom bubble of 1999–2000. To provide some sense of scale, the total amount of capital raised in all venture-backed IPOs in the mini-bubble year of 1983 was $3.8 billion, slightly less than $9 billion in 2000 dollars. The amount raised in 1999 and 2000 was $21 billion and $26 billion, respectively.[19]

Here we have a flag for identifying the factor that has dominated venture returns over past generations, namely, the state of the public equity markets. Looking across the entire span from 1980 to the post-bubble era, the dependence of venture capital returns on access to the IPO market is clear. My own research, in collaboration with Michael McKenzie of the University of Sydney, characterizes each quarter since the start of 1980 by the number of venture-backed IPOs and the proportion of them that were for companies not yet profitable; McKenzie and I employed these figures to generate an index of IPO market speculation. We found that when distributions back to the investors coincided with IPO market conditions characteristic of a bubble, the median internal rate of return for the funds in our sample

---

[19] National Venture Capital Association, *2010 Yearbook* (New York: Thomson Reuters, 2010), pp. 15, 19, 28, 43–46, 49–54.

was 76 percent; when exits occurred under poor IPO market conditions, the median return was only 9 percent.[20]

Necessary dependence on the public equity markets creates perverse incentives. Perhaps the most tempting path to perdition for a modern venture capitalist has been to attempt to read from current market signals the appropriate loci for new venture investments. Keynes explicitly cites the "inducement" to invest an "extravagant sum" if the project "can be floated off in the Stock Exchange at an immediate profit."[21] But almost invariably, the latency in the venture investment process is too great. New ventures were conceived and offered to the public market within the span of the bubble of 1999–2000, but the reckoning generally came too soon for the venture investors to liquefy their paper gains before first the shares and then the project they represented collapsed.

Yet the impact of the bubble and its aftermath on the profile of venture capital returns is enormous. From the incipient emergence of a venture capital industry in 1981 through funds launched in 1994, the aggregate distributions of venture capital firms to limited partners (net of fees and carried interest) amounted to 3.24 times the capital they had committed to the funds. For the 1995 vintage, the multiple reached 6.19 times, and it was 4.97 for the 1996 vintage. However, the 1998 vintage, at 1.38 times, was the last to generate a positive cash-on-cash return to limited partners. The ten-year return on the US Venture Capital Index turned negative as of the end of 2009 and declined at a compound annual rate of 2 percent through December 31, 2010, before turning modestly positive (2.6 percent) through the third quarter of 2011.[22]

It was the herd-following movement of the major state pension funds that generated the approximately tenfold increase in the value of funds under management by members of the NVCA between the early 1990s and the mid-2000s, from an average of $22 billion in

[20] M. D. McKenzie and W. H. Janeway, "Venture Capital Funds and the Public Equity Market," *Accounting and Finance*, 51(3) (2011), pp. 764–786.

[21] Keynes, *General Theory*, p. 151.

[22] Cambridge Associates LLC and National Venture Capital Association, "Difficult Q3 2011 Did Not Slow Improvements in Long Term Venture Performance," press release, January 24, 2012. Available at www.nvca.org/index.php?option=com_content&view=article&id=78&Itemid=102.

the years 1989–1992 to a peak of $240 billion in 2006. An immediate consequence was a comparable inflation in the scale of individual venture funds: firms went from raising $100 million funds to raising $1 billion funds. Sufficient opportunities to put that amount of capital to work in the classic venture capital model were simply not available, but a tenfold increase in management fees provided a powerful incentive against returning to pre-bubble scale.

A number of firms have extended their mandate from funding early-stage ventures to acquisition of minority positions in established businesses and even to participation in leveraged buyouts. Each of these strategies has distinctive characteristics, and success in each depends on quite different disciplines that can be mastered only the hard way, through extended periods of learning by doing. Other firms have sought and found investment opportunities of sufficient scale to absorb multiples of the capital traditionally committed to start-ups: the ranks of failed alternative-energy ventures are testimony to their efforts.

A growing number of venture capitalists have reckoned that in the prolonged absence of an active IPO market accessible by emergent companies prior to their reaching sufficient scale to launch a $100 million issue, the rational strategy is to scale back both resources and commitments in order to focus on funding distributed research and development for large companies, with the explicit intent to hold an auction as soon as a venture has proven its concept, and to forgo the risk and the opportunity entailed by trying to build a sustainable, independent business. Yet other firms have scaled back even further, backing consumer-oriented web start-ups whose odds of sustainable success may be very low but whose capital requirements for launch are also minimal, given the availability of free open-source software, clouds of rentable computing resources, and the web itself as the channel for marketing and distribution.

After a post-bubble rebound in the mid-2000s, new commitments to venture funds have declined sharply: to $16 billion in 2009, $14 billion in 2010 and $18 billion in 2011.[23] Mark Heesen, president

---

[23] Thomson Reuters and National Venture Capital Association, "Venture Capital Firms Raised $5.6 billion in Fourth Quarter, as Industry Continued to Consolidate in 2011," press release, January 9, 2012. Available at www.nvca. org/index.php?option=com_content&view=article&id=78&Itemid=102.

of the NVCA, summarized the state of the industry when he presented the data on 2011 fundraising:

This past year we saw more venture capital money raised by essentially the same number of firms, a sign that consolidation within the industry is continuing. We also continued to invest more money in companies than we raised from our investors. Both of these trends – if they continue – suggest that the level and breadth of venture investment is starting to recalibrate to reflect a concentration of capital in the hands of fewer investors. Our cottage industry is indeed getting smaller still and that will impact the startup ecosystem over time.[24]

Venture capital's dependence on speculation and the state

The bubble of 1999–2000 revealed the financial dynamic of the downstream phase of the Innovation Economy at its most extreme. The host of hopeful monsters, the vast majority of which failed, could be funded precisely because those who provided the financing needed to have only minimal concern for the fundamental economic value of the ventures. The investment decisions, by the founding venture capitalists as by the willing IPO purchasers, were not informed by evaluation of the future cash flows of the projects. The decisions were driven by the hope, indeed the expectation, that well before any cash flows would be generated, the shares would be sold to yet more hopeful – or foolish – buyers. Here too, as with upstream investments in scientific discovery and technological invention, the Innovation Economy turns on the ability of the economic system to tolerate waste. The systemic cost is less to the extent – as was largely the case in 1999–2000 – that speculative excess is limited to the equity markets and does not spill over to infect the credit system on which routine economic activity relies.

Since 2000, there has been a sharp and prolonged decline in the IPO market, from an average of 547 IPOs per year during the 1990s to 192 per year since 2001.[25] This decline is not only a function of the bursting of the dotcom/telecom bubble. Since the end of fixed brokerage commissions in 1975, a series of reforms aimed at improving the

[24] *Ibid.*
[25] IPO Task Force, "Rebuilding the IPO On-Ramp: Putting Emerging Companies and the Job Market Back on the Road to Growth," presented to the US Department of the Treasury, October 20, 2011.

transactional efficiency of the equity markets succeeded in reducing the profit from trading stocks to a minimum – especially in the case of thinly traded stocks with relatively small market capitalization. Not only was the subsidy to fundamental investment research eliminated, a core source of revenues for independent investment banks was liquidated.

The post-bubble imposition of enhanced reporting and accounting requirements on public companies has increased the cost of going and staying public. The more fundamental transformation has been in the architecture of the equity markets: consolidation of the investment banking industry reflects in good part the fact that the business model for the venture-focused investment banking firm no longer exists. The cutely named Jumpstart Our Business Startups ("JOBS") Act, passed into law in March 2012, will not reverse this institutional reality. By reducing regulatory oversight and transparency while sanctioning retail "crowd-sourcing" to finance speculative start-ups, however, the JOBS Act does have the potential to regenerate the unethical dynamics that characterized the IPO market prior to the 1970s.

The dependence of venture capital returns on the state of the IPO market at time of exit is one of four stylized facts about venture capital. The second one, widely recognized, is the extraordinary skew in such returns: a very small number of venture capital funds and firms drive the aggregate returns for the industry as a whole. In the database of 205 venture funds that McKenzie and I analyzed, the mean internal rate of return was 47 percent. However, the mean rate of return realized by the top decile of funds was 215 percent; excluding these twenty funds from the sample dropped the mean return to 27 percent.[26]

Even with the top funds included, the returns realized by the funds McKenzie and I studied were broadly comparable in statistical measure with the returns available from the public equity market. Because we had access to the actual, dated cash flows between the limited partners (who provided us with the data) and the funds in which they invested – a rare circumstance – we were able to compare the returns realized by these funds to what an investor would have received by investing in the public market. For this part of the study, we needed to limit our sample to the 136 funds that were fully terminated, with all

[26] McKenzie and Janeway, "Venture Capital Funds and Public Equity Market," p. 8.

realized returns distributed, thus excluding the distorting impact of the dotcom/telecom bubble. We created a synthetic alternative fund for each actual fund by "investing" the same number of dollars that went into that fund on each date into the NASDAQ index and withdrawing from the index the amount distributed back to the limited partner at each distribution date. The result was striking: while the *mean* return to the 136 actual venture funds was 1.59 times what would have been realized by investment in the index, when the top decile was excluded, that figure dropped to 1.02 times. And the *median* return of the entire sample of 136 funds, including the top decile, was exactly identical to what the public market would have delivered – and delivered with complete and continuing liquidity to the investing limited partner.[27]

The third stylized fact of venture capital is that – in contrast with all other asset categories – persistence can be detected in the returns of individual managers. Analysis of our data confirmed the findings of a survey of a broader sample of funds conducted by Steven Kaplan and Antoinette Schoar: performance of a given fund is a significant predictor of the returns realized by the next fund of the same managers.[28] Persistence in the success rate of serial entrepreneurs can also be discerned,[29] confirming the intuition that superior venture capitalists and superior entrepreneurs establish a self-reinforcing positive feedback loop.

The fourth stylized fact of venture capital (largely neglected in the academic literature, unlike the first three) is that professional venture capitalists have concentrated their activities and earned their returns in a very small number of industrial domains. In the three decades since 1980, the ICT sector has accounted for 50 percent to 75 percent of all dollars invested by members of the NVCA, with its average share usually hovering around 60 percent.[30] The ICT and biomedical

[27] This methodology was developed by Steven Kaplan and Antoinette Schoar to characterize a large database of venture capital funds with comparable results; it was published in S. V. Kaplan and A. Schoar, "Private Equity Performance: Returns, Persistence and Capital Flows," *Journal of Finance*, 60(4) (2005), pp. 1791–1823.

[28] M. D. McKenzie and W. H. Janeway, "Venture Capital Fund Performance and the IPO Market," Centre for Financial Analysis and Policy, University of Cambridge Working Paper 30 (2008), p. 21 and table ix.

[29] P. A. Gompers, J. Lerner, D. Scharfstein and A. Kovner, "Performance Persistence in Entrepreneurship and Venture Capital," *Journal of Financial Economics*, 96(1) (2010), pp. 18–32.

[30] The standard deviation of the time series is only 0.09 over the period.

sectors together have consistently accounted for 80 percent of all dollars invested by venture capitalists.[31]

In Chapter 2, I discussed the extraordinary endowment that federal funding of scientific research and technological development provided to the nascent venture capital industry, with the Defense Department as a customer for the products of ICT. Biotechnology, too, was fostered by research funding from the NIH. This history is central to addressing a question that should have been confronted – but very rarely has been – by anyone who evaluates the phenomenon of the venture capital industry of the past generation. Just why has it been in the world of information technology and, secondarily, biomedicine that venture capitalists have been so successful, in striking contrast with the nearly continuous record of failure across so many other frontiers of scientific discovery and technological innovation? In brief: only in these sectors of research did the state invest at scale in the translation from scientific discovery to technological innovation. Through the Defense Department and the NIH, that is, the federal government funded construction of a platform on which entrepreneurs and venture capitalists could dance.

Biotech demonstrates most clearly the critical role for venture capitalists of access to the public equity markets and confirms the distinctive persistence in returns. As my partners at Eberstadt and I realized at the birth of the industry in the late 1970s, the prospective fate map of a biotech start-up is very different from that of a new software or semiconductor company: it is not possible to imagine how a biotech venture will generate revenues from the sale of products (versus from the sale of rights to those possible revenues) within the lifetime of the investing venture fund. The industry's historical economic performance has manifestly fulfilled this expectation.

Gary Pisano provides an authoritative analysis of the biotech industry over its thirty years of existence:

From 1975 to 2004 … while revenues have grown exponentially … profit levels essentially hover close to zero throughout the life of the industry. Furthermore, the picture becomes even worse if we take the largest and most profitable firm, Amgen, out of the sample. Without Amgen the industry

---

[31] National Venture Capital Association, *2010 Yearbook*, p. 31. The ICT sector includes Media and Entertainment, which did not become a significant category until the mid-1990s. By that time (for venture capitalists, at least) it was embedded in the world of the internet.

has sustained steady losses throughout its history ... The analysis includes no privately held firms, almost all of which lose money. Therefore, the data presented here are just for the most profitable part of the industry populations.[32]

Pisano calculates that "the average time to first year of positive cash flow" for public biotech companies "was approximately eleven years," and this lag was from the date of their IPO, not from their actual inception as enterprises some substantial number of years earlier.[33] But he overstates our intuition when he writes:

It is virtually impossible to find other historical examples, at least at the industry level, for which such a large fraction of new entrants can be expected to endure such prolonged periods of losses and for which the vast majority may *never* become viable economic entities.[34]

For there are other sectors where comparably long and variable time to positive cash flow has stunted venture capital activity. For example, there is no successful record of venture investment in industries derived from materials science. Plastics, that touchstone of entrepreneurial possibility, was no place for a venture capitalist, however patient. As I learned from Ed Giles at Eberstadt, it took DuPont and General Electric each at least twenty years and more than $1 billion of then-current dollars to commercialize the new generation of engineered plastics. That history is in the process of repeating itself in the domain of nanoscience and nanotechnology: again, it will require the ability to mobilize very large financial resources over decades to identify what potential applications serve economic needs and to work down the learning curve to reliable and efficient production – both tasks appropriate for established businesses and simply not available to start-ups. And the premature efforts by venture capitalists to promote clean tech and green tech ahead of the required public investment in the enabling science and technologies have failed to ignite the desired speculative response from the financial markets.

The question remains: Why have venture capitalists continued to fund biotech ventures despite their disappointing prospective and realized operating performance, and done so in increasing absolute

---

[32] G. Pisano, *Science Business: Promise, Reality, and the Future of Biotechnology* (Boston: Harvard Business School Press, 2006), p. 117.
[33] *Ibid.*   [34] *Ibid.* 118; emphasis in original.

amounts? Commitments to biotech ventures were approximately $500 million per year from 1985 through 1994 and rose with the scale-up of venture capital generally to $4 billion at the peak of the bubble. Since 2001, venture capitalists have invested more than $3 billion in biotech companies every year through 2010, with investment peaking above $5 billion in 2007. In 2009, the $3.7 billion invested in biotech represented 17 percent of all venture capital investments.[35]

The puzzle is resolved by the fact that through the early years of this century the returns venture capitalists have earned from biotech compare reasonably well with the returns from ICT. And, unsurprisingly, these returns have been a function of access to the IPO market. There have been more than ten IPOs for biotech companies in fifteen of the thirty years since 1980, with hot activity clustered in 1983, 1991–1993, 1996–1997, and 2000. Remarkably, from 2004 to 2007, relatively dismal years for venture-backed IPOs, there were seventy-seven biotech IPOs, substantially more than the aggregate of all the ICT sectors combined.[36] This helps to explain why the rates of return to funds concentrated on biotech have approximated those of the venture capital industry as a whole.[37]

Why have public investors stood ready to buy into such IPOs? Pisano offers an explanation:

While the aggregate returns to biotechnology are poor, investors are focusing on the "tails" of the distribution. The phenomenal stock returns for a company like Amgen provide a beacon for investors ... Never mind that the probabilities are very low and, on a risk adjusted basis, it may not be a good bet. The promise is there.[38]

There is another, deeper reason. When a target molecule is identified as a potential therapeutic response to a disease state, the population of potential patients – the "addressable market" – is known. So is the approximate charge per treated patient based on drugs already in the market. And because demand is funded by third party payers and is consequently inelastic, a plausible projection of revenue can be projected contingent, of course, on successful clinical trials and approval by the Federal Drug Administration. Thus, a biotech start-up

---

[35] National Venture Capital Association, *2011 Yearbook* (New York: Thomson Reuters 2011), table 3.10 (p. 31).
[36] *Ibid.* 51. [37] Pisano, *Science Business*, p. 113. [38] *Ibid.* 129.

is unique: only in this instance is it possible to estimate a fundamental value, the present value of the net cash flows from the investment – *if*, and it is a huge if – the scientific and regulatory hurdles to market entry are overcome. The fact that investors have repeatedly chosen to bet on that contingency demonstrates, as well, the weight that the risks of marketing bear versus scientific and technological risks: the biotech exception exemplifies the value attached to the minimization of marketing risks in a domain where scientific and technological risks are enormous.

Against the odds, in biotech there are a few repeatedly successful venture investors: Brook Byers of Kleiner Perkins and Tony Evnin of VenRock have established extraordinary track records over more than thirty years. Their records confirm my lived experience and the weight of my own and others' academic research. Rather than allocate capital to venture funds as if they were an independent asset class that can be expected to yield returns reliably and significantly higher than those available in the public equity market, investors should seek access to that small number of professional venture capitalists who have demonstrated their distinctive skill over multiple funds and across diverse market conditions. If such access is not available, the lesson is simple and absolute: move on.

In the late 1980s, my academic research into venture capital returns was two decades in the future, as was, of course, the evidence on which it would be based. But the underlying intuition, informed by practical experience of the contingent nature of venture returns, was becoming established in my mind. The central focus of my investment activity was the computing complex, broadly defined. There, dependence on the haphazard processes of the public equity markets was not as decisive as elsewhere because it was plausible that positive cash flow from operations could be achieved within the investment horizon of the founding venture capital funds – largely because the government's sunk investment in the underlying science and technology positioned venture investments far enough along the road from invention to commercially realized product or service.

And so at that very specific intersection of professional experience and techno-economic evolution, the dynamic of the Three-Player Game as applied to the Innovation Economy could be already discerned, even if the words to express it were yet unknown to me. The effort to extract Braudel's super-profits from technologically driven disruption in the market economy was subsidized by the state's unprecedented commitment to the sector. The realization of such gains, however, would be a function of speculative interest, even excess, on the part of the broader financial markets.

Starting at Warburg Pincus

I joined Warburg Pincus on July 5, 1988, soon after completing my obligation to Flemings. I had known John Vogelstein, the firm's president and chief investment and operating officer, for almost a decade. By far the largest member of the NVCA, Warburg Pincus had always appeared on the list of potential investors for the post-venture private placements that had been the core of Eberstadt's corporate finance business. But the firm's investment strategy cut right across the grain of what we were offering. Never a passive investor in any situation, Warburg Pincus always sought to act as the strategic financial partner of management, generally buying senior securities with governance rights and protections and invariably securing a seat on the board of directors. I had grown to admire John's extraordinary investment acuity from afar as, time and again, he would analyze a proposed deal in depth and explain why – as attractive as it was as a business – it was not an investment opportunity for Warburg Pincus.

Since the 1960s, Warburg Pincus had been a pioneer in the professionalization of what had been known as the "deal business" in old Wall Street. Investment banking firms had long constructed private, illiquid investments for themselves and their clients, the substance ranging from oil wells to movies to black box antigravity machines that cured cancer, also known as high technology. The deal business was very much a hit-or-miss activity, although there were some stand-out practitioners, including Laurance Rockefeller, Benno Schmidt of J. H. Whitney, André Meyer of Lazard and Ferdinand Eberstadt. As a young investment banker in the early 1960s, Lionel Pincus had imagined the possibility of building a firm exclusively dedicated to such investments and had enticed his friend John Vogelstein to join him in the endeavor.

Lionel enjoyed a critical jump start in implementing his vision because of his association with Eric Warburg, son and heir of the great Max Warburg, Germany's leading financier from the end of the nineteenth century through the 1920s. By the time the Nazis seized control of M. M. Warburg & Company, Eric was established in New York. His family ties there were deep: one uncle, Paul Warburg, had been a leading architect of the Federal Reserve System, and another, Felix Warburg, was in the process of establishing an international network of philanthropies from his mansion at 92nd Street and Fifth Avenue, now the Jewish Museum. The two brothers had forged a dynastic alliance through marriage with the daughters, respectively, of Solomon Loeb, founder of New York's leading Jewish investment bank – Kuhn, Loeb – and Jacob Schiff, the bank's dominant force.

In 1971, Warburg Pincus had made the critical transition from ad hoc deal-making to establishing an institutional base. Lionel and John raised their first fund, EMW Ventures, with $41 million in capital. "It seemed like all the money in the world," Lionel used to say. Through shrewd reading of a stock market whose valuations were being undermined by the financial and economic consequences of the Vietnam War even before the first oil shock in September 1973, they kept their powder dry. In the subsequent bear market, the firm made strategic investments in deeply discounted public companies, notably Twentieth Century-Fox and the predecessor to Humana, and funded the construction of a major waste-disposal business.

Overcoming the mathematical burden of having taken down all its capital at inception, EMW Ventures delivered a net internal rate of return of 15 percent over a decade (half of the 30 percent it would have earned had the funds been taken down as needed, in line with what shortly became standard practice). Lionel and John also managed to ignore the increasing frustration of Eric Warburg's second cousin Siegmund Warburg. Even as he constructed the leading investment bank in London, Siegmund never reconciled himself to the reality that there was an American firm with equal right to his family name but in whose success he played no role and over which he exercised no influence.

Lionel and John built on their investment success to scale the firm's resources substantially. The first ever $100 million fund in 1980 was followed by a $341 million fund in 1983 and the first ever $1 billion fund in 1986. Throughout, the firm remained true to its core strategy: bringing active but patient equity capital to back exceptional operating executives in order to build or rebuild significant and sustainable businesses. With this broad investment mandate, Warburg

Pincus was prepared to operate across the life-cycle of the enterprise, from funding early stage start-ups, to making minority investments in growth companies, to acquiring part or all of established but undervalued businesses. Always on the side of Keynes's enterprise in working to evaluate "the prospective yield of assets over their whole life," the firm also had a powerfully contrarian view relative to speculation.[39] With the decade-plus life of its funds, Warburg Pincus could afford to invest against the current mood of the market. By the late 1980s, the firm had become a master player of the game between financial capitalism and the market economy.

As the firm grew and matured, it began to develop deep expertise in selected industry sectors where early investment success fostered an understanding of the longer-term industry dynamics. The first of these, following on the success of Humana, was in health care services, broadening out progressively into medical devices and biotechnology. But even though the firm was the largest founding member of the NVCA, Warburg Pincus kept its distance from high-technology ventures. This was the one sector where it was a follower, taking positions in later rounds behind such leading venture firms as Kleiner Perkins and Asset Management. Now, with a $1 billion fund to invest, John had decided, with Lionel's support, that it was time to explore whether the firm could invest successfully in the most rapidly growing sector of the economy in its own distinctive fashion, not as a secondary member of a syndicate but as the lead – even the sole – investor.

In conversation over lunch in April 1988, John and I spontaneously discovered a shared sense of opportunity. Over the previous fifteen years, evolving as a hybrid investment banker and venture capitalist, I had extracted several strategic lessons. The first began as an observation: at any point in time, there is more technology available than anyone knows what to do with. Its corollary was that merely contributing to the stock of available technology creates no economic value. Identifying market needs and delivering products and services that would meet those needs – that was the source of value. Contrariwise, if a market need was obvious and the technology was available, multiple products from multiple ventures would surely be launched simultaneously. I had observed the notorious disk drive battle of the early 1980s from afar: twenty venture-backed start-ups attacked the

---

[39] Keynes, *General Theory*, p. 158.

market, of which no more than two delivered a positive return.[40] This was followed closely by the JAWS ("just another workstation") war, in which a dozen start-ups competed and from which only Sun Microsystems and Silicon Graphics emerged as winners.[41]

A second and closely related lesson was that the best technology was not destined to win; in fact, there were precedents for believing that it was likely to lose. At three critical turning points, the companies that had developed the best implementation of state-of-the-art information technology were run over by those who solved the business challenges of marketing and sales. Too often those who had developed the best technology – and knew it was the best – acted as if they believed that the commercial components of the business were of secondary significance. In their path-breaking work in evolutionary economics, Nelson and Winter had modeled the competition between innovators and imitators: "In our model world, an imitative strategy may, if supported by luck early in the industry's evolution, be a runaway winner. And certainly imitators will have good luck at least some of the time."[42]

At the end of the 1970s, Zilog Semiconductors, which had owned the market for first-generation microprocessors that handled data eight bits at a time, designed the best microprocessor for handling data sixteen bits at a time. But the new Z8000 was incompatible with the host of software applications programmed to run on the Z80. As Zilog stranded its customer base, both Motorola and Intel invested in building technically inferior sixteen-bit microprocessors that were compatible with their respective previous-generation devices. Intel especially exemplified the triumph of marketing: its Operation Crush campaign not only won position as the engine of the IBM personal computer but established Intel's x86 architecture as the standard for a generation to come.

As it happened, Zilog's loss became our opportunity: a decade later, one of our first successful IT investments at Warburg Pincus was to back a management team that knew how to apply Zilog's legacy technology to low-cost consumer electronics. Jointly we constructed the first

[40] P. A. Gompers and J. Lerner, *The Venture Capital Cycle*, 2nd edn. (Cambridge, MA: MIT Press, 2004), p. 165.
[41] H. Kressel and T. V. Lento, *Investing in Dynamic Markets: Venture Capital in the Digital Age* (Cambridge University Press, 2010), p. 24.
[42] R. R. Nelson and S. G. Winter, *An Evolutionary Theory of Economic Change* (Cambridge, MA: Belknap, 1982), p. 344.

ever leveraged (actually, very underleveraged) buyout of a technology company when Exxon, Zilog's original sponsor and then owner, completed the liquidation of Exxon Enterprises, its utterly failed effort to divert excess cash flow from oil and gas to information technology.[43]

The second example of the best technology losing was also centered on the IBM PC, when IBM belatedly recognized the controlling significance of the operating system, the software that manages the resources within a computer. In its rush to market with its original PC, IBM had sanctified Microsoft's Disk Operating System (MS-DOS), itself kludged together from the work of others. Now IBM developed its own proprietary alternative, OS2, with robust features informed by a long generation of advanced research and operational experience from operating systems built for mainframe and midrange computers. But Microsoft's hold on the PC market was never shaken, rooted as it was in the enormous and ever-growing base of third-party tools and applications and user-implemented extensions tied to DOS and to its fragile but compatible successor, Windows.

Third, by the late 1980s, it was becoming apparent that Oracle was winning a dominant position in the market for relational databases. This technology, initially conceived at IBM but with a variety of implementations emerging from university computer science departments, was becoming the software platform of choice for business applications developed outside the centralized mainframe data centers dominated by IBM. Again, Oracle's version was generally recognized as technically inferior to other implementations of the relational model. But Oracle combined a determination to adapt its technology to every existing computer and operating system with a uniquely aggressive domestic sales force and an imaginative and highly successful approach to building an international presence. In the USA, Oracle succeeded in cutting off the oxygen – that is, cash receipts – of its competitors, while overseas the company learned how to integrate consulting services with technology to deliver working solutions to customers.

The overriding lesson went back to BRL and MicroPro. The lesson could be relearned through the problematic maturation of every start-up. In information technology, just as much as in the life sciences and every other industry, corporate happiness is positive cash flow.

---

[43] For a summary of the Zilog investment experience, see Kressel and Lento, *Investing in Dynamic Markets*, pp. 148–155.

Mainstream venture capitalists focused on launching projects to build the fastest, cheapest, best version of what the underlying science and technology would allow, one or possibly two of which might develop legs as a sustainable business. But an alternative model and strategy offered itself. This involved reading major markets for discontinuities, then looking backward to identify the relevant components of a business dedicated to exploiting the discontinuity. In this context, technology and the products and services it enabled were only one set of needed components. Also important were a customer base, channels to market, marketing itself, and customer implementation and support services. Given the goal of reaching positive cash flow from operations as rapidly as possible, my mantra was "Buy what you can; build what you must."

This investment philosophy fit extraordinarily well with Warburg Pincus's approach. From its beginning the firm had refused to limit the scope of its investment activities to any one style: by 1988 it had made money from start-ups, from buyouts and from all manner of investments in growth and turnarounds. Its strategy was as eclectic as that of Braudel's canonical capitalist. From my perspective, this opened the door wide to exploring alternative approaches for exploiting market discontinuities. If an existing business with an established competitive position, positive cash flow and strong operational management were available for acquisition at an attractive valuation, we had the mandate to do so. On the other hand, the firm possessed both the financial resources and the cultural discipline to commit to building a business from scratch, knowing that it could take three to five years for it to achieve the intermediate goal of positive cash flow and as many as another three to five years for the firm to realize the rewards from the investment.

This prospectively allowed for resolution of what I had come to think of as the start-up paradox. On the one hand, as I had learned more than once, start-ups suck. So much work has to go into so many ancillary activities – leasing space, creating a chart of accounts and on and on – that create no distinctive value. And the layers of uncertainty are daunting. Will the product light up when you plug it in, as Pike Sullivan used to ask? Will anyone pay for it if it does? Will management exercise minimally requisite levels of discipline and judgment? And yet, on the other hand, there are markets so compelling that one must participate, even if there is no mode of access other than a start-up. In direct contrast to the classic venture capital model, from my perspective doing a start-up is a last resort. But now in such a project, as in all others, I would be aligned with a firm that possessed the resources to assure access to cash and maintenance of control at the outset and throughout the life of any investment.

5   The road to BEA

In 1988, the once-in-a-generation investment opportunity in information technology that was to unfold over the next decade was hardly visible. IBM still dominated commercial computing. It remained the environment in which other participants, whether vendors of hardware or software or services, all subsisted. In this context, I was the beneficiary of an education in innovative scientific and technical computing, courtesy of engagement with such Eberstadt clients as Daisy Systems. And I had developed a transcendentally valuable relationship with John Seely Brown and his colleagues at Xerox PARC. Together, they had introduced me to networked and distributed computing architectures and novel applications that required sophisticated workstations.

Technical computing, as distinct from commercial data processing, where IBM was dominant, constituted a set of niche opportunities where market segments were quantified in hundreds of millions of dollars and potential users could be physically counted as occupants of functionally defined seats. A series of investments launched shortly after I joined Warburg Pincus illuminated a path forward. Not without stumbling, we incrementally conducted our own series of trials and errors, and along the way constructed a narrative of what it means to do capitalism on the frontier of technological innovation.

ECsoft: an educational failure

The first exercise, ECsoft, proved to be a highly educational failure. It came to us by way of Lee Keet and Jack Pendray, two consultants from the world of commercial computing, whom we had met in 1989. They had introduced us to an interesting – albeit limited – opportunity: TSI International had been spun out of Dun & Bradstreet to provide software that enabled electronic data interchange (EDI), the exchange of formatted messages between corporate buyers and sellers to allow the automation of commercial transactions. This first-generation exercise in electronic commerce depended on the painfully arduous process of negotiating protocols transaction type by transaction type, industry by industry. Worse, deployment of EDI was driven by super-hub companies such as Ford and Procter & Gamble, who understandably believed that their market power to force use of EDI by their vendors should be recognized in the split of economic benefit with such marginal providers of enabling software as TSI. For a decade TSI struggled until it reinvented itself by developing a general-purpose tool for mapping data between different formats, renamed itself Mercator after its product, and did both in time to be swept up in the dotcom/telecom bubble. We wound up making a satisfactory return on our investment, more or less by accident and after a very long wait.

As TSI struggled for scale, Lee and Jack introduced us to what appeared to be a more attractive and far grander investment concept. While consulting across corporate Europe, they had identified a substantial hole in the market and had hatched a timely strategy for addressing it. Corporate computing had come to be dominated by IBM in Europe almost as much as it had in the USA. To the extent that corporations' operations were automated, they ran software applications on IBM computers. In the United States, a derivative industry had arisen to provide tools for developing and managing such applications. This industry had benefited hugely from the ease of identifying the specific customer in the data center within virtually every significant company. However, these innovative vendors of tools for the world of IBM were typically too small and narrowly focused to build sales, marketing and support operations in Europe.

To address this opportunity, Lee and Jack envisioned the construction of ECsoft, a pan-European company that would command access to data centers and acquire the right to market and sell a portfolio of tools. ECsoft's start-up would begin with the acquisition of carefully selected providers of professional services in each of the major geographical markets: companies that provided skilled programmers to help corporate customers develop and maintain their software applications and the computers that ran them. Headquarters would identify and license the chosen software from the United States and repackage the products for the operating subsidiaries. The timing for all this was keyed to the contemporaneous elimination of restrictions on the movement of goods, services and people within the European

Union. For the purpose of geographical centrality, headquarters was established in Lyons, France, where it was supported by the excellent TGV rail service and, perhaps more importantly, by the outstanding local cuisine.

Ironically, the magnitude of ECsoft's failure as a business and an investment was a direct consequence of the initial success of its founders. The launch acquisition in April 1990 was of a Norwegian services company that exactly matched the ideal profile, not least because of its entrepreneurial leader, Terje Laugerud. Second, Léo Apotheker joined ECsoft as chief operating officer, coming from Europe's leading enterprise software company, SAP, whither he would return on a path that would lead him to become CEO there in 2008 and of Hewlett-Packard in 2010. The combination of the successful Nordic exemplar and Léo's extraordinary operating skills and sheer tenacity kept ECsoft going in the face of mounting challenges. Unfortunately, the evidence did not become dispositive until we had invested some $40 million over four years in addition to the initial $5 million, both to add far less ideal acquisitions around Europe and to fund stubbornly persistent operating losses.

ECsoft's failure was due to three fundamental flaws, each of which alone would likely have proved fatal. The first was that Terje's exceptional success was just that: exceptional. We learned that there is a fundamental distinction between selling services on a project-by-project basis and selling products. When a project is done, the customer owns the result in every way; the vendor has no ongoing responsibility. But a product requires support by the vendor so it will continue working as the computing environment evolves around it. Further, projects are custom-built to the customer's specifications; products, to succeed, must distill the needs of numerous potential customers, needs that can be served only approximately and by way of successive releases over time. The mindset inherent to each of the business models is critically, radically different. Outside of Scandinavia, none of the acquired companies mastered the melding of the two business models, except to the extent that Léo was present and directing operations.

The second flaw related to ECsoft's relationships with its US licensees. A licensor could meet one of several possible fates, none of which would be helpful to ECsoft. The company could succeed so well that it would demand the right to take back its European distribution. It could fail, leaving ECsoft with the responsibility of supporting its customers without the technical resources of those who had designed and developed its products. Or it could muddle along until it was acquired by one of the rapidly growing and highly aggressive aggregators of such companies, like Computer Associates. None of these outcomes promised anything but grief to ECsoft. We experienced at least one of each.

Finally – and of strategic significance that transcended ECsoft as a company or an investment – it turned out that by the early 1990s the IBM data center was no longer the rich and stable market for innovative tools that we and ECsoft's founders had supposed. A growing portion of corporate IT budgets was being siphoned off from the center to the periphery. Dissatisfaction with the lengthy delays in creating new applications and enhancing existing ones coincided with the availability of cheaper and more accessible computers that could be bought and deployed at the subsidiary and even the departmental level. These factors combined to feed a new open and distributed model and market for commercial computing.

And so, in 1994, we stepped back to allow ECsoft to retreat to its profitable Nordic base, where it was successful enough to return about half of our cumulative investment. We assuaged the pain of our financial loss with recognition of our gain in strategic understanding. Immersion in this most dynamic segment of the market economy provided information to us as financiers at a crucial breakpoint in the history of computing: it was as if we had been able to feel the seismic precursors of a world-class earthquake.

IMI and SHL: positive lessons

While ECsoft was still a promising experiment, Lee Keet introduced us to yet another investment opportunity. Martin Leimdorfer, an entrepreneurial Swedish engineer with experience in the United States, had improvised his way to building an enterprise application software company in Stockholm, Industri-Matematik (IMI), one of the first companies anywhere to deliver mainframe-class performance and functionality on Oracle's software platform. The critical innovation was a function of IMI's success in selling its software to Sweden's largest plumbing supply company on the basis of Oracle's promise that Version 6 of the Oracle database would support 1,000 simultaneous active users. When the Oracle software failed to support even

100 users with adequate response times, IMI's engineers worked out how to multiplex transaction calls to the database in order to deliver adequate performance while ensuring that the transactions were reliably captured and accurately recorded. This imaginative technical fix would resonate powerfully a few years later when I began the conversation that led to the creation of BEA Systems.

In the meantime, IMI offered a classic arbitrage opportunity. Its shares were languishing on the Stockholm Stock Exchange even as, in New York, NASDAQ had matured as the chosen venue for technology driven entrepreneurial companies, whatever their state of origin. And so, in the second half of 1991, we joined with the founder to take IMI private, one of the first such transactions executed on the Stockholm Stock Exchange. In 1996, after investing in the company's overseas growth, especially in the United States, we took IMI public at a multiple of the valuation of the former transaction. Even though IMI failed to maintain its competitive position in the face of SAP's far broader enterprise application solution, access to the liquidity of the NASDAQ market enabled us to realize more than four times our $33 million investment.

IMI represented a positive lesson in the accelerating transformation of enterprise computing that reinforced the negative one delivered by ECsoft. The lesson was further driven home by a parallel haphazard, challenging and ultimately rewarding engagement with SHL Systemhouse. SHL was the Canadian national champion of information technology. Our investment opportunity was created indirectly by the personal bankruptcy of its excessively entrepreneurial founder, whose shares had been pledged to the Royal Bank of Canada (RBC) and to the national telephone company, Bell Canada. As joint controlling stockholders, RBC and Bell Canada recruited John Oltman, a driven and visionary senior partner of what was then Andersen Consulting (now Accenture), as CEO. I had met John some years before. He was one of the first knowledgeable practitioners to be convinced of the pending demise of IBM's environmental control of commercial computing. At SHL, he recruited a like-minded set of young stars from Andersen and other leading IT consulting firms.

The core strategy was called transformational outsourcing: SHL would purchase the computing resources and operations of corporate customers, securing the financing to do so on contracts to move them

from the expensive and rigid world of the mainframe to the cheaper
and more nimble world of open and distributed systems. SHL was
a pioneer in client–server computing, whereby relatively cheap but
increasingly powerful computers provided data processing and stor-
age services to intelligent client computers – personal computers –
across networks. In this architecture, servers could be dedicated and
optimized for particular functions, while users of the system could use
their desktop computers for local applications, like word processing
and spreadsheets, when they were not accessing the enterprise applications. The contrast with large mainframes, where all functions were
centralized and accessed by dumb green-screen terminals, was stark.

Within two years, John and his team had sold the vision so effectively that SHL had run out of both the ability to deliver on its commitments and the cash to pay its bills. SHL was a public company in
Toronto, and its public standing in Canada heightened its visibility.
Its board included a former foreign minister of Canada and a former
prime minister of Ontario. In March 1993, as the company worked to
backfill its operational commitments, we made an initial investment
through the private purchase from the company of $32 million of con-
vertible preferred stock.

At this point, SHL gained access to its own transformational
opportunity: a $1 billion contract to take over the IT operations of
the Canadian Post Office. The only snag was the Post Office's insistence that SHL have skin in the game, some material risk of loss if it
failed to deliver. I retain a craftsman's pride in the construction of a
unique investment vehicle to enable SHL to win the contract. Warburg
Pincus deposited $15 million in an account at the Royal Bank that was
secured by the first tier of revenues to SHL under its contract, the "hell
and high water" payments that the Post Office could suspend only in
the case of proven fraud on SHL's part. In turn, we received warrants
to buy common shares in SHL equal in aggregate exercise price, at the
then price of the stock, to the amount of our deposit. In this case, our
own cash served as the hedge against loss, while the warrants gave us
an infinitely leveraged upside opportunity to share in the profits if SHL
delivered.

On the back of the Post Office contract, SHL led the market in demonstrating that enterprise-class application software could be built and
deployed on client–server computer networks outside the glass house

of the IBM data center. But its business model as a public company was compromised by the fact that the senior consultants John Oltman had hired came from their private partnerships with very high cash compensation and minimal orientation toward stock-based rewards. Here was a disconnect: the compensation system that John had to use in order to mobilize outstanding talent at the Schumpeterian frontier of the market economy entailed appropriating value from the public stockholders who financed the company. With my active support, John organized and led a major internal exercise to reconstruct the expense base of the company by convincing his team that they should trade their existing employment agreements for much lower cash salary and bonus provisions, offset by significant stock options. The shift was not trivial: it offered to improve SHL's operating profitability by as much as ten percentage points and to align the incentives and rewards of the talent with the returns to the stockholders.

Not every owner of equity was happy with the outcome. It happened that the second largest stockholder of SHL after Warburg Pincus was the State of Wisconsin Investment Board (SWIB). SWIB was a pioneer in seeking to impose good governance principles and practices on its portfolio companies. Among these was an absolute limit on the percentage of a company's outstanding shares that could be represented by employee stock options. SHL's new compensation plan exceeded SWIB's ceiling by a modest amount, a violation that turned out to be life-threatening to the company because the moment at which SWIB announced that it would vote against the new compensation plan coincided with a critically needed infusion of cash through a rights offering to SHL's stockholders. This offering, underwritten as to 35 percent by Warburg Pincus, was substantively justified by the increase in profitability promised by the new compensation system.

SWIB's decision hit the market as the SHL board was meeting at dawn in Mexico City to authorize the rights offering. On the way into the hotel from an early morning run I managed to stumble and cut my knee. So I joined in contemplating the unpleasant alternatives before us while still in my running gear with blood streaming down my leg. The transaction held together long enough for me to shower, change, get bandaged and join John Oltman on a mission to Madison, Wisconsin. With the clock ticking, we offered SWIB the alternatives of compromising its principles or seeing SHL go bankrupt. Common sense prevailed.

The rise of equity-based compensation

The argument over modalities of compensation at SHL has a broader significance. The 1990s was the decade when equity-based compensation plans proliferated. In 1976, two academics, Michael Jensen and William Meckling, had written a highly influential article that identified the "agency problem" between the owners of a corporation and its senior executives, who were nominally responsible to the stockholders but were motivated by their own incentives, which were distinct from the returns received by their ostensible principals.[1] In this, Jensen and Meckling were explicitly redeploying the insights Adolf Berle and Gardiner Means offered in their 1930s study *The Modern Corporation and Private Property.*[2] By 1994, seven out of ten chief executives of American corporations had received stock options, up from one in three in 1980.[3] The manner in which enormous one-way options incentivized stupendously excessive risk-taking in the banking sector, and outright fraud at such companies as Enron and WorldCom, has become conventional wisdom. But there is another aspect to the role of stock incentives.

The Innovation Economy by definition is saturated in unquantifiable uncertainty. The emergence of a venture capital industry focused on funding start-up companies was supported by recognition of the need to offer abnormal rewards for success. The goal was to construct an economic asset in the hope of eventually monetizing it in the public equity markets. The possible returns had to be abnormally high, given how very rarely it was reasonable to expect such success to be realized. By 1980 or so we were calling equity-based compensation "Silicon Valley socialism": every employee in a start-up, from the CEO through the technical architects and programmers to the receptionist was entitled to participate. In return for leaving behind the predictability of the established franchise players in the market economy – Digital Equipment Corporation, IBM, Hewlett-Packard – volunteers for the

[1] M. C. Jensen and W. H. Meckling, "Theory of the Firm: Managerial Behavior, Agency Costs and Ownership Structure," *Journal of Financial Economics*, 3(4) (1976), pp. 305–360.

[2] A. Berle and G. Means, *The Modern Corporation and Private Property* (New York: Macmillan, 1932).

[3] J. Cassidy, *How Markets Fail: The Logic of Economic Calamities* (New York: Farrar, Straus and Giroux, 2009), p. 292.

frontier received tickets to a lottery in which the odds were hugely skewed against them. And not only start-ups faced these odds. I and my partners at Warburg Pincus had been drawn to SHL Systemhouse in the first place by its potential for reinvention as an agent of innovation in the transformation of commercial computing architectures. We were going up against IBM on its most central home ground. This was what SWIB emphatically did not get.

The displacement of Silicon Valley socialism to the major commercial banks, whose acceptance of risk and tolerance of uncertainty was legally underwritten by the Federal Deposit Insurance Corporation, was an error of private and public policy with enormous negative consequences. It went hand in hand with the radical withdrawal of regulatory oversight, from the IRS to the Securities and Exchange Commission, from the Reagan administration through that of Bush II. One of the lessons of life as a venture capitalist was drilled into me by Tom Connors, a remarkable operating executive turned independent consultant and director, with whom we at Warburg Pincus built a close and collaborative relationship: "Don't expect what you don't inspect," Tom used to say.[4]

Venture capitalists were and are positioned and motivated to inspect their agents through intimate engagement, of which board membership is a formal expression. As Berle and Means had discussed as early as 1932, public stockholders are neither positioned to exercise such vigilance nor motivated to do so: discomfort with management is expressed through the friction-free action of selling the stock. The accountability problem is compounded by the fact that executive management has the ability to select its own overseers, the board members who are supposed to represent the owner or principals. These factors explain how the players in the market economy manage to structure the governance aspect of the game with financial capitalism to their benefit. In one of the most ludicrous examples of misguided good-governance reform, the federal government has barred any owner of more than 10 percent of a public company from sitting on its audit and compensation committees, as if those who had the most to lose

---

[4] Tom was a tough guy. When one of the business unit managers of Zilog sought a measure of understanding for failure to meet budget, Tom's response was: "You want sympathy? You can find it in the dictionary, somewhere between shit and syphilis."

could not be trusted to assess whether management was cooking the books or excessively feathering its own nest.

The IBM environment starts to open up

As SHL was surviving its own extended soap opera, IBM was beginning to wake up under its new CEO, Lou Gerstner. The first stirrings came in its invigorated services business, where IBM's very low cost of capital allowed it to fund outsourcing contracts on a basis with which SHL could not hope to compete. In the autumn of 1995, as John Oltman and I contemplated possible business combinations that might strengthen the company's competitive position, I received an unusual voice message that addressed our concerns definitively. It was from the head of business development of MCI, then the old, original AT&T's leading competitor in long-distance telephony. "We have decided we want to buy SHL," the voice said, thus initiating the easiest negotiation of acquisition terms I have ever enjoyed – a negotiation that began with my response: "What makes you think SHL is for sale?"

Less than three years with SHL had convinced me that IBM, for all of its financial might and technical prowess, was a crippled giant, a prime example of the innovator's dilemma. Although its services business was beginning to assert itself, its proprietary product lines were so profitable that it could not afford to undercut them by pursuing growth opportunities that carried the much lower margins of computers leveraging open interfaces and open standards. Moreover, IBM had suffered from a double psychological trauma. First, its comprehensive effort from the late 1970s to invent an entirely new, next-generation computing architecture known as Future System – in emulation of its defining success twenty years before in establishing System 360 as the world's standard for commercial computing – had failed. IBM was left with one hugely successful but entirely closed product, the AS400 midrange computer. Second, the seemingly endless antitrust assault by the Justice Department during the 1980s had diverted management's attention and frozen the company's once ferocious competitive instincts.[5]

---

[5] For a thorough analysis of how IBM became stuck, see P. Carroll, *Big Blues: The Unmaking of IBM* (New York: Crown, 1993).

IBM's reluctance to compete with itself was illustrated by an anecdote that I heard when I was attending one of Esther Dyson's PC Forum conferences in the late 1980s. I was walking back from dinner with John Seely Brown when we were accosted in friendly fashion by a brilliant computer engineer whose name I had heard but whom I had never met. Andy Heller had a tale he had to tell. He was based in Austin, Texas, where he had led IBM's program to develop an open competitor to the highly successful computer servers being delivered by Sun Microsystems. It was called the RS6000. As the technical effort reached fruition, Heller was summoned to IBM's Armonk headquarters to present his business plan, which anticipated establishment of a cash-generative business on the order of $600 million in three years, an ambitious goal by almost any standard.

It turned out that the details of the plan were entirely irrelevant because Heller had been bushwhacked. When he entered the conference room, he found that the team from Rochester, Minnesota, responsible for the AS400 was already there. In the previous year, as I recall the orders of magnitude, the proprietary AS400 had delivered no less than $14 billion of revenue to IBM and $10 billion of operating cash flow. The RS6000, identified as a threat to the monopoly profits of the AS400, was dead on arrival. Heller's career at IBM ended when he resigned to turn venture capitalist himself.

Whatever its apparent vulnerabilities, for a generation IBM had conditioned the marketplace about what to expect from an enterprise-class computing system. It was clear that if the open technologies being delivered by a host of innovative vendors were to be successfully sold and deployed on IBM's turf, they would need to deliver the mainframe levels of scalability, reliability, availability and security (collectively known in the trade as the "-ilities") that IBM's customers had come to take for granted. It was in this context that I renewed an acquaintance with a remarkable sales executive out of the heart of the commercial computing universe.

Mike Fields never went to college. The son of West Indian immigrants, Mike had discovered early on that he was a killer salesperson. He advanced from Burroughs, through Applied Data Research (ADR, one of the many companies selling software tools for IBM mainframes), to Oracle. Mike and I first met when he was leading a team of second-tier ADR executives on a quixotic quest for funding to enable a management buyout. I was particularly impressed that in doing so he was directly competing with his boss and the other top-tier executives who were trying to put together their own deal as the company was in the process of being divested by Ameritech.

As it turned out, ADR was purchased not by one of its competing management teams but by Computer Associates. Mike moved to Oracle. In 1992, he approached me with a very interesting idea, one that matched the lessons I had been absorbing. The proliferation of computing systems outside the corporate data center was creating both a major business problem and a major investment opportunity. Initially installed in sales offices and subsidiary production and distribution facilities to provide local managers with timely reports, they were increasingly being devoted to doing real work – that is, to managing business processes that involved cash obligations and receipts. At the core of these computer systems were the relational databases that Oracle and its competitors sold. These had been developed as flexible report generators. But they were maturing – somewhat haphazardly, as IMI had discovered – into software platforms for business applications that captured transactions of all kinds.

Distributed not merely in technical terms but also across business geographies, these client–server systems were barely visible to central IT management staff, let alone subject to their disciplined management. Moreover, the increasingly standard operating system running the hardware underneath the database was some variant of UNIX, developed in AT&T's Bell Labs and licensed widely in line with the rules according to which AT&T had been allowed to maintain its monopoly in telecommunications. UNIX itself was maturing as an alternative to IBM's proprietary systems software but was alien to the expertise of IBM-centric staff. And the client–server architecture that linked servers and PCs across networks was entirely different from the centralized mainframe supporting arrays of dumb terminals. Finally, all of these hardware components and the software that ran on them came from a variety of vendors who neither in principle nor in practice could deliver the seamless integration of IBM.

Addressing the need for "distributed systems management," as Mike laid it out, required building a business from the assembly of two types of components. The first comprised software: products that would deliver the sort of utility functions, like data backup and recovery, that were taken for granted in the mainframe world. On this score, my mantra was apt; there was indeed more technology around than anyone knew what to do with. Every vendor of computing hardware that was competing around the periphery of IBM's empire was providing all sorts of ancillary systems software to support its version of UNIX. In addition, numerous start-ups were entering the various niches in the emergent market. The availability of relevant technology was not the constraint.

What was also required was a new sort of dedicated sales force. The mainframe systems software industry had grown up in symbiotic relationship with IBM and had enjoyed easy access to its customers. With corporate computing resources concentrated in the data center, finding the customer had been so easy that vendors of the simpler sort of tools relied on telephone representatives dialing for dollars to generate leads and close sales. But the new distributed computing systems were just that: distributed. Oracle made the most widely adopted database and application platform, one that could run on just about every computer in production anywhere in the world. Its sales force had a unique ability to find the target customers.

OpenVision Technologies

In simplest form, Mike's proposition was to acquire a portfolio of systems management products to feed a direct sales force that he would recruit largely, of course, from Oracle. In June 1992, Warburg Pincus agreed to back Mike and his immediate team, and we launched OpenVision Technologies with a commitment to fund up to $25 million on terms agreed in advance. If this line of equity were fully drawn, we would own a share of the company determined up front, the founders would own their agreed share, and both would be diluted by a pool of stock options reserved in advance for future employees.

The structure was an innovation, constructed in direct contrast to the traditional venture capital funding model of multiple rounds of investments with multiple firms investing per round. The conventional model was rationally designed to spread risk across investing firms and through time. At start-up, typically two or more funds would invest in the A Round, with no contractual commitment to make a follow-on investment. Each subsequent round would be priced on the basis of then-current conditions: both internal progress against benchmarks, such as product development and customer acquisition, and the state of the external economic and financial environment. And each round would be open to new investors, although preemptive rights to invest would likely have been secured by the venture capitalists in previous rounds. Furthermore, some degree of protection against dilution by subsequent funds coming in at lower prices would almost always be in place.[6]

The standard model had multiple flaws relative to the strategy we were adopting. Designed to fund the development and commercial launch of a new product, an essentially linear process, it mapped poorly to a hybrid strategy that contemplated opportunistic acquisitions from the start. From management's point of view, the ability to execute such a strategy would be radically compromised if every initiative had to wait on a successful exercise in incremental fundraising. In addition, given my own history of crossing the boundary from agent to principal in time of stress, I was uncomfortable with the distribution of control across different tiers of investors, each with a different cost base of investment. This source of potential conflict was compounded by the fact that each venture firm in whatever tier was bound to be at a different phase in the life-cycle of its own fund and firm. In today's environment, characterized by an IPO market that is hardly accessible to any ventures that actually need the money, the relevance of a venture strategy whose focus is the achievement of positive cash flow at the earliest possible date is obvious.

Warburg Pincus had the cash to fund a venture such as OpenVision, but it only made sense to do so if we had unequivocal control. Delivery of funds under our commitment had to be entirely at our discretion. Our approach did give up the external market test represented by the willingness of other firms to invest, but it was subject to the regular scrutiny of all of the partners of the firm, each of whom had a keen economic interest in the state of play. As is common among venture capital firms, but vanishingly rare among private equity firms, all Warburg Pincus partners eat off the same plate. That is to say, each partner's interest in the firm applies to all of the investments the firm makes: a 1 percent partner based in New York and investing in health care, for example, has the same 1 percent interest in IT deals in Silicon Valley and energy deals in Texas. This structure motivates and rewards

---

[6] The standard text that documents and analyzes the conventional venture capital model is P. Gompers and J. Lerner, *The Venture Capital Cycle*, 2nd edn. (Cambridge, MA: MIT Press, 2004).

a culture of collaboration; it also provides a powerful incentive across the partnership to monitor the portfolio. In the case of OpenVision, strict scrutiny would be exercised at the time of each additional funding decision and not less often than quarterly.

By the summer of 1994, two years into the investment, three facts were clear relative to the hypotheses on which OpenVision had been founded. The first two were positive at first blush. There was indeed a surfeit of software tools to acquire from the indicated sources. OpenVision had bought no fewer than eighteen of them, too many for its technical team to integrate and support. And the perceived market for the sort of utilities OpenVision was created to provide was evident and growing, but the company's ability to serve the market effectively was undermined by the distractingly large and unintegrated product portfolio. Along a third critical dimension, operational integration of the acquired business and products, OpenVision's performance was worse than inadequate.

By this time, Warburg Pincus had fully funded its original $25 million commitment and had spent some $15 million more to finance both acquisitions and operating losses. Moreover, the investment banking firm of Alex. Brown had placed an additional $25 million of convertible preferred stock with institutional investors at a price pleasingly above our cost, in the sort of post-venture private placement that we had pioneered at Eberstadt. But the company was bleeding cash.

I recall sitting on the floor of the "telephone room" in the house my wife and I then rented on the downeast coast of Maine, participating in a board of directors' conference call in August 1994. The news was not quite as dire as what I had learned over the back fence about the state of play at Bethesda Research Laboratories some dozen years earlier. Most importantly, there was no question about where authority lay to act in response to the news. And, in opportune fashion, Mike Fields had already introduced me to an exceptional candidate to step in as war leader in the struggle for business and investment survival.

In parallel fashion to Mike, Geoff Squire had dropped out of high school in his native country of England when he was fifteen to program computers for the Gloucestershire County Council. Subsequently employed by the British subsidiary of CACI, a US consulting firm, he had discovered that his employer had acquired the UK license for the Oracle database software but had no interest in trying to learn how to sell a software product. So Geoff left CACI with the right to bring

Oracle to market in the United Kingdom. His success there led to his joining Oracle in order to build out its business across Europe, country by country, and then to Japan and the rest of Asia. In each geography he bootstrapped the business by selectively selling limited distribution rights to fund the recruitment of sales and service professionals. In less than a decade he had built a $1 billion, highly profitable business, drawing no capital from Oracle's headquarters in Silicon Valley.

Geoff had been liberated from Oracle early in 1994 when Larry Ellison, Oracle's founder and controlling shareholder, decided that Geoff's decentralized model, which endowed strong local managers with the resources and the mandate to meet local market needs, had to yield to a centrally directed, integrated organization designed to serve global customers. Geoff had agreed to advise Mike on OpenVision's European operations, but was understandably committed to an extended period of recuperation. I hung up on the conference call and reached Geoff in England. He agreed to get directly involved as soon as he returned from a long-planned cruise. He was on the job by Labor Day to conduct an exhaustive analysis of the company and soon laid out a turnaround plan for John Vogelstein and me. John asked him how much more cash he would need: the answer was about $10 million. John said we would reserve an incremental $15 million. In November, with Mike's enthusiastic support, Geoff signed on as CEO. It was the smoothest transition in which I have ever played a role. This time all three elements were in place to execute an effective hedge against the unanticipated: cash, control, and effective new leadership.

The remainder of the story has two parts: building a great business and reacting to the market's valuation of it. For the former, within twelve months, Geoff had reduced head count by one-third and doubled revenues. He did it by determining which products were actually being bought, closing down those that were not, and concentrating all resources behind those that were. The key technology, acquired from a second-tier computer company, Control Data, managed the efficient backup of data across computer networks whose scale and complexity were growing with the business significance of the exploding number of applications running on them. By the spring of 1996, OpenVision was solidly profitable and growing fast: an initial public offering at an attractive valuation followed. Six months later, the process that led to the most successful merger in the history of enterprise software began.

The OpenVision/VERITAS merger

Compared to the arduous path we pursued through OpenVision's birth and rebirth, Mark Leslie, a technical expert with sales and marketing experience, had created a significant business in utterly inverse fashion. He had been recruited to try to save a failed computer company, Tolerant Systems, whose lead venture capital investor was none other than Fred Adler. Mark's death-bed diagnosis identified two pieces of software for managing data efficiently and reliably within the confines of a discrete computer. They had been developed to give Tolerant's machines a competitive edge but potentially had wider application in the world of UNIX systems. Mark and his team, having renamed the company VERITAS, turned the proprietary code into stand-alone products. The commercial breakthrough came when Sun Microsystems contracted to embed the VERITAS File System and the VERITAS Volume Manager into its version of UNIX. Other vendors of workstations and servers followed. By 1996, VERITAS also was a publicly traded, highly profitable, fast-growing systems software company.

That autumn I received a phone call from Steve Brooks, a director of VERITAS whom I had known for years as a shrewd and knowledgeable technology investment banker. The purpose of the call was to introduce the idea of bringing VERITAS and OpenVision together. The complementarity appeared to be extraordinary. VERITAS's products managed data at the level of the computer operating system. Its channel to market was through original equipment manufacturers who incorporated the software into their own systems and paid royalties to VERITAS for the privilege. OpenVision's major product backed up and restored data across large-scale networks of computers. It appeared likely that the two technologies could be integrated to provide unique functionality for managing data. At least as valuable an asset was OpenVision's direct channel to enterprise customers through its own sales force.

Each company was on target to achieve somewhat more than $30 million in revenues, and both companies were generating cash, although VERITAS's business model was inherently more profitable. My response was to suggest that Geoff Squire and Mark Leslie meet. The outcome was expressed with characteristic crisp precision by Geoff when he called me immediately after the meeting: "We have to put these two companies together, and you should know that Mark will run it."

We agreed on the terms of trade by the end of 1996, and the merger was completed in the following April, with VERITAS as the surviving entity. One incident along the way illustrates yet again the inherent uncertainty of economic life and the relevance of that one conjoint hedge – Cash and Control – available to mitigate it. Just as the terms of the merger were being documented for shareholder approvals, the outstanding head of the OpenVision sales force advised Geoff that he had received an offer he could not refuse to become CEO of a start-up. The venture backers who were recruiting him had convinced him that the worst imaginable outcome would yield him $1 million.

Having lived through the ups and downs and ups of OpenVision, the head of sales was all but committed to the new opportunity, and his wife was supporting the move. So I flew to San Francisco to meet with the two of them in a private room next to the American Airlines Admirals Club, having had a brief conversation with John Vogelstein before I left New York. In the course of two hours, I managed to convince them that Warburg Pincus would reserve $1 million as a back-up insurance policy in case the merger with VERITAS did not pay off personally in equivalent or greater amount. The ability to seal that agreement with a handshake represented the outward and visible authority conferred by Warburg Pincus. I subsequently learned from Mark that he considered the head of sales crucial to the success of the merger: his loss would have killed the deal.

Which would have been expensive! The OpenVision/VERITAS merger closed as the great dotcom/telecom boom and bubble were beginning to gather force. The two companies, which had separately recorded sales of $36 million each in 1996, combined to generate $1.2 billion of sales in 2000, augmented by one additional acquisition. The market value of VERITAS peaked in 2001 at more than $40 billion. In response to the emergent bubble, and driven by the mutually reinforcing effect of John Vogelstein's study of the equity markets through the ages and my own direct education at Cambridge in the market history of 1929, we began to distribute our shares to our limited partners in the summer of 1998. By October 1999, we had fully distributed our investment position for a cumulative value of $750 million, measured as of the date of each distribution, versus a total cost of $55 million. Those shares, priced in aggregate at the peak of the bubble, were worth

$4 billion. Bernard Baruch, the legendary stock market speculator and presidential advisor, is said to have remarked that he had made all his money by "selling too soon."

Building OpenVision and merging it with VERITAS completed an accelerated education in the magnitude of the opportunity opened up by IBM's loss of environmental control of commercial computing. That education extended back from the dynamics of the marketplace to define an investment strategy and to prove a business model jointly crafted to exploit the opportunity at high speed and at large scale. Along all of these dimensions, OpenVision proved to be the dress rehearsal for the launch of BEA Systems.

6   Apotheosis

From ECsoft to OpenVision, the foundation was constructed for the creation of BEA Systems: as a business, one of the most crucial engines of transformation at the core of the digital economy, and as an investment, one of the all-time great successes in the history of venture capital. The story of BEA dramatizes the complex dynamics of the Innovation Economy. The engine of its initial growth was research funded by a state-sanctioned monopoly that, when liberated to compete commercially, had no idea how to do so. Its phenomenal growth was also a function of the maturation of the internet, offspring of the Defense Advanced Research Projects Agency, as an environment for commerce. Its competitive success was conditioned on the inability of IBM, the dominant force in computing, to cannibalize its own proprietary products and the profits they generated. And the extraordinary investment returns that it delivered were due in good measure to the speculative excess of equity investors who had recognized the emergence of a new, digital economy. BEA, that is to say, represented the apotheosis of the Three-Player Game's fostering of the Innovation Economy.

At the more mundane level where the practitioner labors, BEA's success both as a venture investment and as an operating business did not emerge in a vacuum. On the contrary, to identify and realize the opportunity it represented was the combined and contingent consequence of multiple strands of education: in the alternative architectures of the computer industry, in the evolving technologies of computer systems, in the different business models available to start-up companies, and in the recurrent inefficiency of the stock market's manner of valuing enterprises under the recurrent pressures of speculation. From my perspective, BEA emerged from a context thirty years in the making.

In yet more narrow terms, the story began with a dinner with Bill Coleman in San Francisco in the early autumn of 1994, when OpenVision teetered on the brink. Bill and I had been introduced by a specialist executive recruiter, Nancy Albertini. Not long before, Bill had left Sun Microsystems, where, as head of its integration services business, he and his team had pushed client–server computing to its limits in the effort to support the application requirements of Sun's major corporate customers. As Bill described the software necessary to enable client–server computer systems to handle the transaction volumes required by business-critical applications, my experience with IMI and SHL resonated.

Bill and I had had a close encounter some years earlier, but without actually meeting. He had been the visionary director of engineering of VisiCorp in the early 1980s. While the company's spreadsheet franchise was being subjected to devastating attack, Bill's focus had been on a far horizon. Sharing Xerox PARC's imaginative sense of how the human–machine interface had to evolve, Bill had been working on VisiOn, the first-ever implementation of a graphical user interface on an industry-standard, general-purpose microprocessor. The Xerox STAR had delivered responsive performance, but the custom processor that was designed especially for it had rendered the machine prohibitively expensive. The sluggish responsiveness of VisiOn was the necessary consequence of the limited performance of the microprocessor technology of the time. I recall that when I encountered VisiOn at the COMDEX trade show in the summer of 1982, the latency was so bad that it made me want to start smoking again while waiting for the screen to refresh.

When I finally met Bill face to face a decade later, he had standing with me as a far-sighted entrepreneur who could anticipate the need for software that the world would discover it had to have, and who had also survived a failed start-up. And so the first step toward the apotheosis of my career as a venture capitalist – funding the creation of BEA Systems, where Bill was the initial B – began in the wreckage of the first generation of PC application software.

Bill recognized that the vast majority of the world's work that involved moving money between buyers and sellers was transacted and recorded by monolithic, centralized, inflexible IBM mainframe computers. The distributed client–server systems that constituted OpenVision's target market could not scale to handle that traffic and could not be trusted with the traffic they did handle. Bill had reflected on Sun's slogan: "The network is the computer." If that were the case, then the network needed an operating system: software to distribute the workload across all of the resources connected through the network, to control the utilization of each resource, and to ensure the fail-safe reliability of the distributed system. Moreover, he could hope with some confidence that IBM, still swimming in the monopoly profits from its vast population of proprietary mainframe and mid-range computers, would not address the emergent challenge of open, distributed computing given the radically lower profit margins that it offered.

By the time we finished dinner, Bill and I were finishing each other's sentences, and we had agreed to expand the conversation to include the two proto-partners whom Bill had recruited to his project. Ed Scott, then still executive vice president of Pyramid, a middling com-puter company that was in process of being sold, had cofounded Sun Microsystems Federal with Bill ten years earlier. Alfred Chuang, an incandescently intelligent young technologist, had been the architect of Sun's Microsystems' "Sun on Sun" project, which had attempted to move all of Sun's business applications from IBM mainframes to Sun's own machines; he knew firsthand the limits of client–server comput-ing. Together, the team had conceived an audacious plan to address the need for "an operating system for the network," a market hole of potentially staggering size.

Bill and Alfred had mapped the technology necessary to fill that hole. Alfred had designed a wall chart to illustrate the components of an "object transaction monitor" (OTM) and the ancillary functions necessary to the task. Alfred's OTM was a modernized generalization of the technology that IMI's engineers had invented to scale up the capacity of Oracle's database. Its purpose was to enable client–server networks to run the same sort of large-scale, transaction-intensive applications as mainframe computers, with the same degree of reli-ability. Under strict confidentiality, my Warburg Pincus colleagues and I were exposed to the design and the plan to implement it during a long day at the Saratoga Inn in the foothills that enclose the south-west corner of Silicon Valley. The discussion begun there continued through the autumn. We all agreed on the magnitude of the market need and the feasibility of the technical solution. But building a soft-ware platform from scratch would take years. Moreover, customers were unlikely to commit their most critical business processes to newly released, unproven technology delivered by a start-up.

The research project

Collectively we worked through my multidecade experience of the perennial excess supply of technology relative to currently perceived market needs and, as well, the imperative to create a cash-positive business as rapidly as possible. By the end of the year we had agreed on a project. Warburg Pincus would fund $750,000 to enable Bill, Ed and Alfred, supported by Stewart Gross and Cary Davis of our IT investment team and selected consultants, to conduct a six-month research program. In return, Warburg Pincus would have first call on financing the venture thereby defined.

The deliverables were an exhaustive set of market and technology assessments of existing distributed mission-critical computing solutions (collectively dubbed the "Red Book") and, second, a complementary synergy and business-model analysis (called the "Blue Book"). As I write, I have the two books in front of me, each an exercise in integrating strategic understanding with tactical detail to an extent unmatched in my professional career. The team demonstrated that there were indeed potentially available technologies, currently occupying marginal market niches, whose acquisition would accelerate the venture by years. In parallel, working back from its comprehensive survey of relevant business and financial applications, the team also constructed a prioritized map of the market.

The significance of this work transcends the founding of BEA. By simultaneously focusing on both the technology and its applications, the team was acting out the nonlinear way that innovation actually evolves. Novel technology stimulates the invention of new applications. But as the applications are defined and deployed, they feedback to put new demands on the enabling technology. That feedback can reach all the way upstream to induce innovative research and discovery in the underlying science: from the steam power of the first industrial revolution through electrification and on to information and communications technology, the historical record is replete with instances of such complex systemic behavior.[1]

In the more narrow terms of the BEA project, the dual research exercises did more than generate documents. The process itself was

---

[1] See T. Bresnehan, "General Purpose Technologies," in B. H. Hall and N. Rosenberg (eds.), *Handbook of the Economics of Innovation*, 2 vols. (Amsterdam: North-Holland, 2010), vol. 2, pp. 770–782.

a mutual and reciprocal education in how we all thought about the world and an opportunity for constructing hypotheses for exploring it and protocols for testing those hypotheses. Given our contemporaneous experience with OpenVision, it was comforting that both Bill and Ed had extensive experience with start-ups and understood the critical need for operational discipline no matter how grand the mission. Moreover, all of the founders had been through the near death of Sun Microsystems, which had itself faced an enormously challenging transition from workstations to compute servers some years before.

The research project was completed in June 1995. In parallel, following the OpenVision model, we worked through the terms of line-of-equity financing, this time scaled to $50 million. If the company came to be fully funded, Warburg Pincus would own a substantial majority of it.

With studied lack of imagination, we had referred to the research effort as Project BEA, a title based on the cofounders' first initials. The name stuck when we officially launched the company.

Acquisition of Tuxedo

The business plan that emerged from the research project was audacious in the extreme, for it proposed to attack the core of IBM's commercial computing citadel. It could not have been implemented – it would not even have been conceived – without a different sort of intervention by the American state in the market economy. This was action by the Anti-Trust Division of the Department of Justice affecting two of the primary sources of technological innovation: IBM and AT&T. IBM's monopoly of the punched cards used in its pre-computer data processing machines had been ended by a consent decree in 1936. In 1959, a second consent decree required that IBM agree to sell its products rather than make them available only on lease; leasing the machines had been a powerful competitive tool that both locked in customers and disadvantaged potential competitors who lacked IBM's financial resources. But the most important event occurred in 1969. When the Justice Department launched a third assault that would last for thirteen years until abandoned by the Reagan Administration in 1982, IBM preemptively responded by unbundling software from its computers. The creation of an independent software industry followed.

As for AT&T, its position as the monopoly provider of long distance telephone service had been established in 1913 by the Kingsbury Commitment, whereby the company agreed to allow independent phone companies to connect to its network and to deliver "universal service" across the country. In 1956, a consent decree with the Justice Department confirmed the Kingsbury Commitment, but the price was AT&T's agreement to restrict its activities to the regulated business of the national telephone system. The Anti-Trust Division's focus on AT&T eventually led, in 1982, to the break-up of AT&T. But, in the meantime, the result of the 1956 agreement was that AT&T broadly licensed a range of powerful innovations that were applicable to the emerging computer industry, to the benefit not only of BEA Systems and Warburg Pincus but of the Innovation Economy broadly defined.

The success of a technology start-up is contingent on countless variables. A path we did not take exemplifies just how contingent it can be. One of the technologies identified in the Red Book was UniKix, an emulation of IBM's mainframe transaction-processing platform, Customer Information Control System (CICS), which was implemented for computers running UNIX. It was owned by Bull, the French national champion of computing, which was a perennial competitive failure except when the customer was a direct or indirect arm of the French state.

Bull had been kept alive then and still is to this day by episodic injections of cash by the French state. The UniKix management team, based in the United States, yearned for liberation, and given our intense desire to launch BEA Systems with actual revenues and customers, we listened to their entreaties almost too well. To our exceptional good fortune, Bull rejected our offer to acquire UniKix. Retrospectively, our offer was far too generous, as Bull would have received no less than 37.5 percent ownership of the venture. Starting with the second-rate UniKix technology and encumbered by Bull as a major shareholder, BEA would likely have been far less successful operationally, and the stock market's valuation of the company would likely have been far lower. In any case, we were saved by the senior management of Bull, whose overvaluation of their asset allowed us to reconsider this mode of entry into the market and happily walk away.

That was the path not taken. The actual launch of BEA came with the acquisition of two independent value-added resellers of the market-leading relevant technology, Tuxedo, known technically as a distributed transaction processing monitor. This move brought our start-up some $15 million of annualized revenues, a set of major corporate customers, and a cadre of technologists skilled in the deployment and tuning of Tuxedo. They also delivered a very valuable option. Tuxedo had been developed in AT&T's Unix Systems Laboratory, a component of Bell Labs, and had been designed to enable AT&T's UNIX operating system (which was originally oriented toward scientific and engineering applications) to support large-scale, transaction-intensive applications. As with UNIX, under the predivestiture rules of the game, AT&T had been required to license Tuxedo widely. Both of our service-company acquisitions had legal right to the software code, and one of them had a license to the brand name. But the core development team of first-class software engineers still resided within Unix Systems Laboratory.

I had first encountered Tuxedo in circumstances that demonstrated AT&T's utter inability to comprehend competitive commercial markets. At one of Esther Dyson's PC Forum conferences in the early 1990s, Tuxedo was displayed as a desktop working environment on the client side of a client–server network. It was conspicuously out of place in this setting. It was true that Tuxedo could support the graphical user interface that was becoming mandatory for all enterprise as well as consumer software applications. But Tuxedo was deep infrastructure software whose deployment and maintenance required skilled and experienced systems engineers. It had no business showing up at PC Forum as a potential competitive alternative to Windows.

AT&T's inability to exploit UNIX or Tuxedo had been presaged a decade earlier. Then, a fundamental rationale for AT&T's agreement to divest the Regional Bell Operating Companies in settlement of the federal antitrust litigation had been to end the regulatory prohibition on AT&T's application of its enormous technical resources to computing. However, although the Bell System knew how to deliver reliable communication services to captive customers, investments by AT&T and its former subsidiaries in competitive commercial computing failed without exception.

This doom was evident at the internal launch of AT&T's strategy for competing with IBM, a multimedia extravaganza laid on for top management by the leaders of the newly chartered AT&T Information Systems. Someone who was present told me that while all in attendance waited in breathless silence for the reaction of CEO Charlie

Brown, who had negotiated the divestiture agreement with the Justice Department, Brown was heard to address his immediate subordinates: "Jesus Christ! We just gave away the wrong half of this goddamn company!"[2]

AT&T ultimately accepted the failure of its dream to compete with IBM. In June 1993, it sold the entire Unix Systems Laboratory to Novell, a vendor of software for networking personal computers that also had a daunting dream: to contend with Microsoft for ownership of the architecture of PC-level software. For this, both UNIX and Tuxedo were wildly unsuited. Like Microsoft's products, Novell's were either bundled with PCs or sold through hands-off distribution channels, including retail stores. As complex, enterprise-class infrastructure software, Tuxedo was typically purchased as a component of a multimillion-dollar project and required on-site engineers for installation. When I heard that Novell proposed to sell a shrink-wrapped version of Tuxedo, I wondered whether it would micro-miniaturize a couple of systems engineers to package in the box along with the software.

Through the autumn of 1995, Ed sought to convince Novell's management of these truths. BEA now controlled some 80 percent of Tuxedo's modest revenues and was planning to use its license position to attack the market aggressively. These factors contributed to his bargaining position, but BEA could still benefit both from bringing on board the Tuxedo technical team and controlling the future intellectual property they created. At our board meeting in January 1996, Ed reported a breakthrough. Novell's new CEO, Bob Frankenberg, had grown up to senior executive level at Hewlett-Packard and knew the world of enterprise computing well enough to agree with BEA's proposal. Characteristically, Ed had created a transaction that would enable BEA to bootstrap the purchase: Novell would grant BEA a comprehensive license to all the intellectual property on a basis that would yield royalties equal in projected amount to the profits that Novell forecast it would earn over the next several years, together with an option to acquire the intellectual property outright. As we

---

[2] Some years later I met an executive who had sold his software company to AT&T and seen it fail utterly. He asserted that such was the insight of AT&T's marketing team that, were the company to acquire Kentucky Fried Chicken, it would take the lead spot at half-time of the Super Bowl to advertise that "AT&T Sells Cold, Dead Chicken!"

collectively congratulated Ed, I assured all that before the deal was done, Novell would require Warburg Pincus to guaranty the minimal payments due under the proposed contract, some $40-plus million that would take our exposure well above the agreed $50 million commitment.

In anticipation, I invited Bill, Ed and Alfred back to New York to lay out the deal and its significance for John Vogelstein. This they did with compelling and comprehensive force. As he left the conference room, John signaled me to join him, "Of course, we have to do this," he said, "and you should get some warrants for doing it." That is, Warburg Pincus should be compensated with additional equity for providing the guaranty. As we already were entitled to some 75 percent of the ownership of BEA Systems, and as the founders had more than fulfilled our highest expectations during the year of study and execution in which we had collaborated, I decided not to argue with John. Instead, I emulated Admiral Nelson at the Battle of Copenhagen, although in this case it was a deaf ear rather than a blind eye that I turned to my commander.

Subsequently, I learned how critical to BEA's future success our ability to respond in real time had been. One of AT&T's licensees of Tuxedo was Tandem Computer, still a formidable presence in the computer industry with its fault-tolerant systems. Its CEO at the time was Roel Pieper, whose previous job had been running Unix Systems Laboratory when it was still owned by AT&T. Thus, Pieper was uniquely equipped to grasp Tuxedo's value. He told me that he had called Bob Frankenberg as soon as he learned that Tuxedo was for sale, only to be told it was already under contract.

By acquiring all of the commercial rights to Tuxedo and the supporting technical resources, BEA was transformed into a business with annualized revenues in excess of $100 million by January 31, 1997, the end of its first full fiscal year, and was reaching positive cash flow from operations. With Tuxedo as the engine of market penetration, BEA was attacking exactly the enterprise markets and applications where the default option for all customers was IBM's CICS, native to its proprietary mainframes. IBM was aware of the possibility that UNIX-based client–server systems would encroach on its turf. In 1994, it had acquired a small software company out of Carnegie Mellon University in Pittsburgh with a distributed transaction process monitor called Encina. BEA was doubly fortunate. Not only did Encina perform poorly on the key "-ilities" – reliability and scalability – relative to Tuxedo, IBM felt no incentive to make it competitive, given the enormous cash flows generated by CICS and the hardware and service revenues CICS dragged along.

For several months, one strategically minded senior executive in IBM's software business, John Swainson, pursued discussions with BEA. Swainson correctly foresaw that BEA and the alternative, innovative computing architecture that Tuxedo represented posed an existential threat to IBM's mainframe franchise. But he never was authorized to name a number and enter negotiations to acquire BEA, so we were saved from the possibility of selling too soon.

Instead, BEA went public. April 14, 1997, was the worst day on NASDAQ that year. BEA had filed with the SEC to sell 5 million shares at an expected price in the range of 10 to 12. The underwriters, led by Goldman Sachs, advised that financing could not be completed above 6. Jointly with BEA's founders, Warburg Pincus agreed to accept the terms, minimizing the dilution of equity ownership by refusing to increase the number of shares. Critically, we could afford to accept the reduction in proceeds because the company was already cash positive from operations. Only three months later, BEA's shares had tripled from the offering price, and the company had executed what effectively was the second half of its IPO, this time selling 6 million shares to the public at 17 and establishing both a liquid market and a meaningful war chest. The successful, though haphazard, IPO had been contingent on the acquisition of Tuxedo.

Acquisition of WebLogic

The second decisive acquisition that made BEA successful was contingent on that timely IPO. By 1998, the explosive growth of the internet as an environment for conducting commerce was visible to all interested parties. But none of the extant technologies had been designed to accommodate online electronic transactions with literally millions of simultaneous users. As BEA worked to augment Tuxedo to enable it to support ecommerce, a number of start-ups surfaced and almost as rapidly were acquired. One was snatched up by Sun, and another by Netscape, which was facing Microsoft's challenge for ownership of the web browser market. Alfred, who was running BEA's engineering operations, identified a third start-up whose technology met his exacting standards, and he convinced Bill of the strategic value of the proposed acquisition.

The venture and its product were called WebLogic. As of September 1998, it had cumulative revenues of $500,000. As the bubble began to inflate with the promise of the economic transformation being wrought by the internet, so did the valuation of start-ups. WebLogic's asking price was no less than $150 million, or some 15 percent of BEA's then $1 billion market valuation, which was itself inflated by speculative fever. Had BEA not been able to use its own stock as the currency for the acquisition, it could not have happened.

As it was, the discussion at BEA's board meeting was strenuous in the extreme. Carol Bartz – then CEO of Autodesk, former head of worldwide operations at Sun, and a powerfully supportive presence on the board since the launch – assured Alfred and Bill that they were insane to propose such a transaction. She added me to that assessment when I supported them. But Alfred's deep analysis of both the market and the technology prevailed, especially because Warburg Pincus, by far the largest stockholder, was committed to the deal.

The acquisition of WebLogic represented a conscious decision to refuse to accept the terms of the innovator's dilemma and instead to attack our own core business before anyone else could. Tuxedo, whose development reached back some fifteen years, was a massive software platform whose installation and tuning took months of work by teams of highly trained engineers. It was typically sold as the core technology of a major project, a sales process that itself typically took many months. WebLogic incorporated the most advanced software engineering techniques to achieve rapid deployment and high performance; it could be readily scaled from single-user to very large application environments. BEA was now a trusted source of mission-critical software for the enterprise market, and word spread across the technical communities that WebLogic was the way to transform the internet into an effective and secure platform for commerce.

The success of WebLogic was so great that it generated intense internal conflict. In return for convincing the board to bet 15 percent of the company on WebLogic, Alfred was tasked with turning it from a product into a business. This he accomplished by leveraging free downloads of single-user versions over the internet to proliferate the software inside enterprises large and small. The proliferation happened so rapidly that the Tuxedo sales force was sideswiped. Multimillion dollar deals that had been in the works for months were shelved as the alternative technology seized customers' attention.

The visceral ferocity of the war within BEA was brought home to me at a company-wide meeting in downtown San Francisco that I attended with Nancy Martin. I had recruited Nancy from SHL Systemhouse following the company's acquisition by MCI. At Warburg Pincus, she created an internal Information Technology Strategy and Assessment (ITSA) function in order to reduce our dependence on outside consultants. Nancy was a favorite of the WebLogic team because she understood the breakthrough innovation embodied in their code; I was well known to the Tuxedo team. Now we found ourselves literally back to back and under assault. Nancy was assailed by her WebLogic friends, who denounced the "dead-in-the-head dinosaurs" from AT&T, while the latter yelled at me about the "undisciplined cowboys" who were destroying Tuxedo's value. Bill responded creatively, by making Alfred head of sales. Alfred resolved the conflict by constructing a multitiered sales model across both products. At the same time, key elements of the Tuxedo technology were reimplemented in WebLogic to enhance the latter's performance over all the functional attributes important to customers – scalability, reliability, availability, security – further confirming WebLogic's and BEA's market leadership. The result was phenomenal growth: from $290 million in the fiscal year ended January 31, 1999, to almost $500 million the following year, and more than $800 million in the fiscal year ended January 31, 2001.

The conjuncture that linked BEA's growth as a business with the stock market's evaluation of the "new economy," at whose core BEA played a key role, made BEA one of the all-time great venture investments. BEA's stock, having been split 2:1 in December 1999 and again in April 2000, reached an all-time peak of 85 in December 2000, or 320 on the shares originally issued to the public in April 1997 at six. In August 1999, Warburg Pincus began to distribute its ownership: within sixteen months, the $54 million cash investment had been transformed into liquid, freely tradable shares with cumulative value at time of distribution of $6.5 billion. Our effort to declare victory was strenuous: in only sixteen months we made twelve distributions, the two largest of which each amounted to $1.3 billion and were made only two weeks apart in February 2000. Even so, we had disposed of only 85 percent of our holdings when the bubble specific to BEA's stock deflated in early 2001.

As a company, BEA did not escape the general retrenchment in technology markets that followed the bubble. In BEA's case, that retrenchment was reinforced by the fact that IBM finally responded to the technological revolution that had undermined its generation-long franchise in enterprise computing. But BEA continued to generate substantial cash flow while investing in new technology. In April 2008, even as it was establishing market leadership in the third wave of distributed computing, technically known as service-oriented architecture (SOA), BEA was acquired by Oracle for $8.5 billion, more than five times its then annual revenue.

BEA and the Innovation Economy

The BEA story yields multiple lessons in the dynamics of the Innovation Economy. First, Schumpeterian revolutions do not announce themselves in advance. Timely identification of the emergent force at the frontier of successful innovation is a function of hard work, immersive education and repeated – seemingly endless – exercises in trial and error. In retrospect, the concatenation of contingencies on which my hugely fruitful 1994 dinner with Bill Coleman turned seem so improbable as to define the operation of blind chance. The narrative that took me and my colleagues from ECsoft and IMI to SHL and OpenVision and on to BEA draws only on the experience directly relevant to reading the market for commercial computing at enterprise scale. And yet there were and are heuristics to guide the venture capitalist. The most important that I learned along the way revert back to the fundamentals set out by those students of capitalism: Braudel and Marx, Schumpeter and Keynes.

The super-profits available to any capitalist at any time are a function of necessarily transient and contingent opportunities for extreme arbitrage. For the founders of BEA and for Warburg Pincus, the arbitrage was defined by technology, mastery of which promised to move the world of commerce to an entirely new world of distributed transaction generation, capture and processing. To identify the practical potential for that arbitrage and its economic significance turned on deep engagement both with innovative computing technology and its capabilities and with the stressed structure of the overlapping markets that that technology could be directed to address. At a deep level, this double task is no different from what Braudel described: the evaluation in parallel of the capabilities of maritime navigation and the forecast conditions of demand for and supply of pepper 500 years ago.

Successful as BEA was as a venture, and conjoined as the founders and Warburg Pincus were as partners in that venture, the relevance of Marx at this level of analysis demands respect. From Marx I take the separability of financial capital from the assets – physical and digital – in which it transiently instantiates itself. That this separability is never absolute is, of course, what places an enormous burden on the concept of liquidity. Marx's assumption that the capitalist can always exchange commodities for more money is a hypothesis subject to the test of the market, and all too often it fails the test when it must most be relied on. But what Marx got entirely right is that success for the capitalist can be defined in theory and – at least sometimes – realized in practice regardless of the fate of the venture as an operating enterprise.

In the establishment of BEA, the entrepreneurial founders and the capitalist financiers at Warburg Pincus directly addressed Schumpeter's challenge with respect to the relationship between the entrepreneur and the financier. Bill and Ed had survived failed start-ups, and each had an earned respect for the value of access to capital. The research project had created the opportunity for all of us to calibrate our qualities as collaborators. Our joint decision to extend the OpenVision line-of-equity financing model reflected our several positive conclusions and was decisive in enabling Warburg Pincus to commit in timely fashion to the opportunity to take control of Tuxedo. In turn, that decisive move transformed a project into a business – one substantial enough to go public and therefore able to acquire WebLogic in time to ride the wave of ecommerce into the bubble. But the very success of this partnership between entrepreneurs and financiers, represented by a radically nonstandard financing model, should exemplify its rarity and emphasize, too, the potential for conflict that Schumpeter identified.

And so, as is only to be expected when considering the returns to financial capital, we come to Keynes's appreciation of stock market valuation driven by speculation rather than the calculation of "the prospective yield of assets over their whole life."[3] Thanks to the bubble

---

[3] J. M. Keynes, *The General Theory of Employment, Interest and Money*, in E. Johnson and D. Moggridge (eds.), *The Collected Writings of John Maynard Keynes*, vol. 7 (Cambridge University Press and Macmillan for the Royal Economic Society, 1976 [1936]), p. 158.

and, equally, to our recognition that it was a bubble, the return on Warburg Pincus's investment in BEA amounted to more than 120 times the cost, or an internal rate of return of 225 percent over an average life of just more than four years. At the time we commenced our distributions in August 1999, Warburg Pincus owned slightly more than 168 million shares. If we had held that position all the way to the company's acquisition by Oracle in April 2008 for $19.375, we would have received $3.26 billion in cash, approximately half the return actually realized; moreover, because the average life of the investment would have been three times as long, or more than twelve years, the internal rate of return would have been only 40 percent, less than one-fifth of that actually earned.

Along the way, the shares traded as low as $4.95. Had we been forced by circumstances (no doubt unanticipated!) to liquidate then and at that price, our position would have been valued at $833 million, and the investment would have generated a realized profit of less than one-eighth of that actually earned. As it turned out, the timely realization of our investment in BEA was largely responsible for generating a net internal rate of return to our limited partners from the fund in which it was held of almost precisely 50 percent, thereby contributing to the firm's ability to raise another fund during the post-bubble valley of disillusionment.

Doing capitalism successfully thus turns to an extraordinary extent on reading the market for financial assets, as much as it does on the seemingly more fundamental tasks of reading the markets for physical assets while assessing the technological innovations that will render new assets more productive and old assets obsolete. And here is found a pair of framing facts that are profoundly counterintuitive to anyone trained in the discipline of neoclassical economics, where efficiency is the prime virtue in theory and in practice. The success of BEA as a company and as an investment turned on capitalization of the results of two processes, each of which was decoupled from any calculus of economic return.

In the first instance, the foundational technology – Tuxedo – on which the company was built had been funded by the monopoly profits of AT&T, which had been diverted to support the scientists and engineers of Bell Laboratories rather than returned to AT&T's customers in lower prices or to its stockholders in higher dividends. Moreover, the world of digital computing and microelectronics, on which the technology was based, and of the internet, through which it transformed the economy, had been directly shaped and funded by the federal government, which was motivated by concern for national security, not return on investment. In the second instance, the climax of the investment was driven by a frenzy of short-term speculation entirely focused on riding the psychology of the market and no longer interested in the prospective cash flows from the business represented by the common stock. In other words, as investors in this triumphant example of the Innovation Economy, Warburg Pincus was a beneficiary of what to a narrowly focused economist would appear to be the generation of waste.

The historical context in which BEA was built and valued was, of course, unique: the intersection of the technological revolution in distributed computing with the realization that the internet is an environment for conducting commerce in a new way. But the elements of the Three-Player Game of innovation were the same as they have been since the first industrial revolution. As before, the Innovation Economy depended on sources of funding that tolerated apparently wasteful investment both in advancing the frontier of scientific discovery and in exploring the new economic space created when derived technology was deployed. Upstream in the process through which the market economy was again transformed, the state indirectly sanctioned the monopolies whose profits funded discovery and invention, and then took on direct responsibility for investment in research when those monopolies were legislated or competed away. And downstream, at critical historical moments, a bubble in the financial markets provided funding to construct and explore new economic space before any rational calculus could be applied to quantify the returns available from its exploitation. In all their wasteful excess, bubbles have been necessary drivers of economic progress.

PART III

Understanding the game: the role of bubbles

7   The banality of bubbles

The bubble into which Warburg Pincus liquidated the bulk of its investment in BEA Systems was extreme, but it was not unique. My awareness of the prelude to the Crash of 1929 had persisted some thirty years after my scholarly engagement with economic policy in response to the financial crisis and economic contraction of 1929–1931. At that time the Radio Corporation of America (RCA) had been an emblem of the "new economy": broadcasting represented the revolutionary application of scientific innovation to a commercial medium of boundless potential. An image of the RCA stock price from the mid-1920s through its apogee and beyond served me as a *momento mori* for speculative excess, especially as VERITAS Software and BEA Systems were swept up by the 1998–2000 version.

Figure 7.1 sets out the development of the stock price for RCA, VERITAS and BEA over the six years, denominated in months, beginning with January 1926 in the case of RCA and with January 1997 in the case of VERITAS and BEA. Because I had once studied the trajectory of RCA's stock after it rose by a factor of ten in less than two years, it was easy to foresee what awaited the shares of VERITAS and BEA when they rose by broadly comparable multiples over an even shorter period of time.

The persistent recurrence of speculative excess is a defining feature of financial capitalism wherever and whenever bankers are flush with cash to invest in liquid secondary markets in financial assets. Three canonical personifications of financial capitalism can be abstracted from the historical record. In Fernand Braudel's version, financial capitalism is heroic. It is as if "the characteristic advantage of standing at the commanding heights of the economy ... consisted precisely of not having to confine oneself to a single choice, of being able, as today's businessman would put it, to keep one's options open."[1]

---

[1] F. Braudel, *The Wheels of Commerce*, trans. Sian Reynolds, vol. 2 of *Civilization and Capitalism, 15th–18th Century*, 3 vols. (New York: Harper & Row, 1982), p. 381.

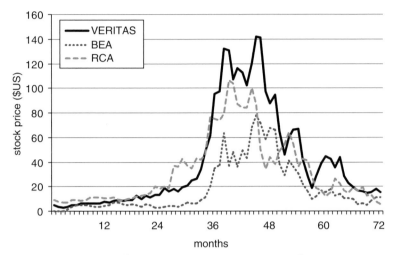

Figure 7.1 Stock prices for RCA, 1926–1932, VERITAS Software, 1997–2003 and BEA Systems, 1997–2003
Source: Graph constructed for the author by D'Maris Coffman of the Centre for Financial History, Newnham College, University of Cambridge.

From within the Clinton White House, beaten into putting a balanced budget before all other policy priorities, James Carville called out financial capitalism as the ultimate bully: "I used to think that if there was reincarnation, I wanted to come back as the president or the pope or a .400 baseball hitter. But now I want to come back as the bond market. You can intimidate everybody."[2]

A less flattering portrait of financial capitalism captures the recurrent waves of speculative boom and bust that express the essential behavior of financial institutions and markets, whose participants are compelled to make commitments today in the face of inescapable uncertainty about the world in which the consequences of those commitments will be realized. Nicholas Sibley, once the public face of the leading investment firm in Hong Kong, characterizes financial capitalism as a lush: "Giving capital to a bank … is like giving a gallon of beer to a drunk: you know what will come of it, but you can't know which wall he will choose."[3]

It is Sibley's version that concerns us now.

[2] Available at en.wikiquote.org/wiki/James_Carville.
[3] D. C. Fildes, "City and Suburban," *The Spectator* (October 3, 1998).

Early bubbles in France and England

Historically, the appearance of bubbles transcends both political regimes and market structures. Comprehending this is the first and critical step to grasping how capitalism works. The second step is to understand that the phenomenon of bubbles challenges received doctrines of neoclassical economics: the dual hypotheses of efficient markets and rational expectations. The third step cuts against the bulk of the literature on the wastefulness of bubbles and the inevitable crashes that follow; it is to recognize the role that financial speculation has played in funding the episodic deployment of revolutionary technology at systemic scale. Thus, I am concerned to illustrate how boringly repetitive – how banal – the emergence of speculative excess is, precisely because it has played a historic role as the engine of transformation, driving growth in economic productivity and living standards for the 250 years of the modern era.

This rhyming of financial history reaches back far beyond the 1920s. In modern memory the phenomenon dates back to the Dutch tulip mania of 1636–1637.[4] Sixty years later, as London emerged to rival Amsterdam, the mid-1690s witnessed the launch of some 100 new joint stock companies, enterprises whose ownership was represented by more or less freely transferable equity securities. Their shares offered outlets for speculative investment to those who could not gain access to the shares of the few established monopolies, first among which was the East India Company, dating from the reign of England's James I. The purposes of the stock promotions ranged from the recovery of shipwrecks in search of treasure to the seemingly more mundane manufacture of linen. In the former instance, a "projector" absconded with the funds provided by Daniel Defoe and others; in the latter, the incompetence of its founders forced the Linen Company to purchase for resale at a loss goods it did not itself know how to produce.[5]

The London stock market boom of the mid-1690s was accompanied by a proliferation of equity derivatives, notably put and call options, which respectively carried the right – but not the obligation – to sell or buy shares at an agreed price for an agreed period of time. This was not the first and would not be the last time that a speculative wave was accompanied by financial innovations: tulip bulb futures had been traded in Amsterdam in the 1630s. As at other times, the derivatives could equally be employed to leverage opportunity for gain as to manage risk of loss.[6]

"The close association between gambling and investment was constantly reinforced at this time" due in good part to the proliferation of lotteries, sponsored both by private promoters and by the state, which gradually evolved a structure of public finance to fund Britain's participation in Europe's perennial dynastic wars of the period.[7] Most of the new joint stock companies disappeared without a trace, with the notable exception of the Bank of England, but the lotteries left a rich legacy in the form of probability theory. Samuel Pepys wrote to Isaac Newton that the lotteries had

almost extinguished for some time at all places of publick conversation in this towne, especially among men of numbers, every other talk but what relates to the doctrine of determining between the true proportions of the hazards incident to this or that given chance or lot.[8]

Cultural memory of that first English stock market boom has been overshadowed by the canonical South Sea Bubble, which swept London in 1720. At the time and since, the South Sea Bubble was linked to the contemporaneous Mississippi Bubble in Paris: John Blunt in London and John Law in Paris both saw the potential for harnessing the speculative spirit of the nascent stock exchange to meet the endless need for finance by states perpetually at war, most often with each other. An incentive to speculation in each case was the prospect of monopoly profits on trade with the New World.[9] In each case, the offer of private gain was meant to serve a public purpose: an extraordinarily imaginative, bold exercise in state finance.[10] Here was a creative, collaborative game to be played between financial capitalism and the state. And, given the inherent instability of the former, it was

---

[6] *Ibid*. 24–30.   [7] *Ibid*. 48–51, 157.   [8] Quoted *ibid*. 52.
[9] R. G. P. Frehen, W. N. Goetzmann and K. G. Rouwenhorst, "New Evidence on the First Financial Bubble," Yale International Center of Finance Working Paper 09–04 (2009).
[10] P. M. Garber, "Famous First Bubbles," *Journal of Economic Perspectives*, 4 (1990), pp. 35–54.

a game that was doomed at birth in both locales. This is a fact worth recalling whenever a politician, driven by opportunism or ideology, proposes the privatization of the social safety net.

A private company would fund the haphazardly accumulated debt of the state by issuing its shares to the public, this at a time when organized markets in long-term government debt were hardly known. For those charged with managing the public debt, the offer was administratively appealing: they could eliminate the high transaction costs of dealing with individual creditors by transferring responsibility to a single entity that would function like a giant investment trust, a sort of Berkshire Hathaway whose asset would be government debt.[11] The Bank of England had been established fifteen years earlier for a similar purpose.

In Paris, manic buying was limited to Law's Mississippi Company, which merged with the Banque Royale and in parallel secured a monopoly on all of France's international trade. The shares in Law's new vehicle, the Compagnie des Indes, rose by a factor of twenty during the second half of 1719, fueled by Law's issuance of paper currency far in excess of the Bank's holdings of specie. In London, the shares of Blunt's South Sea Company rose from less than £100 to £1,000 during the first six months of 1720. Realized gains spilled over into the markets for other assets, financial and real. London's far more mature machinery for manufacturing products to meet the speculative appetites of investors went into high gear.[12] In each case, the inevitable collapse generated an orgy of political recriminations, legal proceedings and personal tragedies.

The long-term consequences of the twin bubbles were radically different in the two countries. In France, Law's catastrophic failure was followed by deepening disarray in the state's finances and ever more corrupt and oppressive efforts to raise needed funds. In Britain, the South Sea scheme counterintuitively served to continue the extended process of consolidating government debt and stabilizing public finances.[13] Various attempts to regulate the stock exchange and to

---

[11] I am indebted to D'Maris Coffman of Newnham College, Cambridge, for this insight.

[12] As inaccurately recorded long after the fact in C. Mackay, *Extraordinary Popular Delusions and the Madness of Crowds* (Petersfield: Harriman House, 2009 [1841]).

[13] Murphy, *Origins of English Financial Markets*, p. 221.

limit the potential for speculation did not preclude the gradually accelerating deployment of liquid capital into agricultural improvements. Even the notorious Bubble Act of 1720, which prohibited the creation of new joint stock companies, is now read as special-interest legislation intended to bar competitors from bidding for investors against the South Sea Company; it was barely enforced in the years that followed.[14] It certainly did not prevent the emergence of speculative investment in new transportation networks – turnpikes and canals – in the early 1770s or the full-blown Canal Mania of the 1790s.[15]

For my immediate purpose, the most significant attribute of the South Sea Bubble was the extraordinarily wide range of projects that served as the objects of speculation, amplifying the phenomenon of the 1690s. Writing from hearsay some 120 years later, Charles Mackay compiled a list of eighty-six "bubble companies" that were declared illegal in 1720, ranging from straightforward proposals for "the importation of Swedish iron" and for "making glass bottles" to more grand, even grandiose, schemes for "paving the streets of London" and "furnishing funerals to any part of Great Britain." Of course, Mackay includes the iconic – and now generally deemed apocryphal – project: "For carrying on an undertaking of great advantage, but nobody to know what it is."[16] To my mind, this enormous range of speculative projects carries the most important historical lesson and analytical challenge: anything, it appears, can be the object of speculation, whether that speculation is expressed through the lending of capital for projects with minimal likelihood of generating cash sufficient for repayment or through the purchase of shares at valuations impossible to relate to the cash flow fundamentals of the economic assets they represent.

Following the end of the Napoleonic Wars, London was clearly established as the leading international financial center. As such, it was the locus for repeated outbreaks of speculative fever. David Kynaston's history *The City of London* documents the phenomenon. The first two (of four) volumes cover the century from 1815 to 1914: across this span, Kynaston identifies no fewer than ten waves of speculative fever on the floor of the London Stock Exchange. The first speculative boom

[14] R. Harris, "The Bubble Act: Its Passage and its Effects on Business Organization," *Journal of Economic History*, 54(3) (1994), pp. 610–627.
[15] Kindleberger and Aliber, *Manias, Panics and Crashes*, p. 62.
[16] Mackay, *Extraordinary Popular Delusions*, pp. 50–58.

of the nineteenth century became visible at the start of 1825. The Duke of Wellington himself anticipated the inevitable outcome, as reported by a close friend: "He thinks the greatest national calamities will be the consequence of this speculative mania, that all the companies are bubbles invented for stockjobbing purposes & that there will be a *general crash*."[17]

The boom was compounded of investments in foreign loans, especially those issued by the newly liberated Latin American republics; foreign mines, particularly the silver mines (real and fanciful) of Latin America; and domestic promotion of canals and less tangible projects initiated by the unregulated provincial banks. Deposits that had been placed with these "country banks" and typically devoted to financing local commerce were diverted to pursue the far higher nominal returns offered by issuers about whom the country banks knew nothing.[18]

The Bubble of 1825 was significant not only because it was the first of the new century, as Europe – with America in tow – emerged from a generation-long world war, with its accompanying restrictions on trade and payments, into an epoch of commercial expansion, industrial investment and, at least aspirationally, political liberalization. As was the case 100 years earlier, speculation spread from a plausible core narrative – some canal companies had proven themselves commercially, and the final collapse of the decrepit Spanish empire in America did open new markets to Britain – to the far-fetched and outright outlandish. Moreover, it was the occasion for the first forced intervention of a central bank as lender of last resort to the money market and the banking system, as documented and dramatized by Walter Bagehot two generations later in *Lombard Street*.

The necessity and the effectiveness of the Bank's initiative were both hard won. Bagehot summarized the experience in language that has

---

[17] D. Kynaston, *A World of its Own: 1815–1890*, vol. 1 of *The City of London*, 4 vols. (London: Pimlico, 1995), p. 65; emphasis in original.

[18] Larry Neal emphasizes such asymmetric information as the prime source of the bubble and subsequent crash in L. Neal, "The Financial Crisis of 1825 and the Restructuring of the British Financial System," *Federal Reserve Bank of St. Louis Review* (May/June 1998), pp. 53–76. The same sort of behavior was demonstrated 180 years later by the German *Landesbanken*, which made large-scale purchases of complex asset-backed derivatives in the run-up to the Crisis of 2008.

become foundational for evaluating all the many subsequent such episodes, those that failed as well as those that succeeded:

The success of the Bank on this occasion was owing to its complete adoption of right principles. The Bank adopted these principles very late; but when it adopted them, it adopted them completely. According to the official statement, "we," that is, the Bank directors, "lent money by every possible means and in modes which we had never adopted before; we took in stock on security, we purchased Exchequer Bills, we made advances on Exchequer Bills, we not only discounted outright, but we made advances on deposit of Bills of Exchange to an immense amount in short, by every possible means consistent with the safety of the Bank." And for the complete and courageous adoption of this policy at the last moment the directors of the Bank of England at that time deserve great praise, for the subject was then less well understood than it is now; but the directors of the Bank deserve also severe censure for previously choosing a contrary policy, for being reluctant to adopt the new one; and for at last adopting it only at the request, and upon a joint responsibility with the Executive Government.[19]

The Bank had been compelled to learn the most basic law of crises: when each player attempts to self-insure retrospectively – that is, when each player seeks Cash and Control in response to the unanticipated – only the open offer of collective insurance by a credible counterparty can prevent catastrophe. From the seminal events of 1825, the fine balance is evident between the leave-it-alone liquidationism that dominated policy during the slide into the Great Depression in 1931–1933 and the intervention *à outrance* that marked central bank policies during the autumn and winter of 2008–2009. In 1825, the Bank's initial delay and manifest reluctance exhibits the inevitable tension generated, on the one hand, by the need for the authorities of the state to protect both financial capitalists and the market economy that depends upon them and, on the other hand, by the certainty that any extension of such protection will only encourage them to provoke such a crisis again – propagating what has come to be called moral hazard.[20]

---

[19] W. Bagehot, *Lombard Street: A Description of the Money Market* (New York: Charles Scribner's Sons, 1999 [1873]), pp. 202–203.

[20] No doubt the Bank's reluctance to run the risk of loss by intervening reflected its own status as a private, profit-making institution. Neal records how action was forced by the government's threat to charter new competition, a threat that was fulfilled anyway. Neal, "Financial Crisis of 1825," pp. 71–72.

In his analysis of the role of the central bank, in *Stabilizing an Unstable Economy*, Hyman Minsky summarizes the core challenge that the dynamics of financial capitalism create for the authorities:

In as much as the successful execution of lender-of-last-resort functions extends the domain of [central bank] guaranties to new markets and new instruments, there is an inherent inflationary bias to these operations; by validating the past use of an instrument, an implicit guaranty of its future value is extended. Unless the regulatory apparatus is extended to control, constrain and perhaps even forbid the financing practices that caused the need for lender-of-last-resort activity, the success enjoyed by this intervention in preventing a deep depression will be transitory; with a lag, another situation requiring intervention will occur.[21]

Decennial dramas before 1914

The pattern of a financial bubble that funds investment in all sorts of speculative projects followed predictably by panic and crash and then, often, by more or less effective appeal for state relief has repeated itself throughout the history of commercial and industrial capitalism. During the long century preceding 1914, there was not a decade without such a drama. Just focusing on London, in 1835 the first, "little" Railway Mania – one in which realizations actually managed to match expectations – was followed the next decade by the "great" Railway Mania of 1845, which culminated in the Crisis of 1847 and the suspension of the Bank of England's spanking new charter, enacted only three years earlier.[22]

In the mid-1850s, London contributed financially to the enormous railway boom in the United States and suffered accordingly in the Crash of 1857.[23] In 1863, even as the American Civil War was forcing contraction on Britain's textile industry, a financial innovation from France – the joint stock investment bank, modeled on the Crédit Mobilier to direct liquid capital into physical investments – became a signal object of "a major bull market, in which almost 700 new

---

[21] H. P. Minsky, *Stabilizing an Unstable Economy* (New Haven, CT: Yale University Press, 1986), p. 52.
[22] Kynaston, *A World of its Own*, pp. 102–103, 151–154.
[23] A. D. Chandler, *Scale and Scope: The Dynamics of Industrial Capitalism* (Cambridge, MA: Harvard University Press; Belknap Press, 1977), pp. 90–91.

companies were registered and the City was awash with speculative froth."[24] Kynaston proceeds:

The new finance houses were not helped by the fact that during the year after their launch there took place ... a wave of company promotions so relentlessly opportunistic as to darken the name of *any* new financial concern. "Most unblushing have been the appropriations made for services in the establishment of banks," declared Morier Evans in his aptly named *Speculative Notes* (1864), asserting that "the amount of transparent jobbery almost recognized in the light of day, has exceeded that known to have existed in the great bubble period of 1824–25, or the later railway mania of 1845."[25]

Only seven years later, one of the financial entrepreneurs of 1863–1864 led another feverish bull market. Albert Grant (formerly Albert Gottheimer), whom Kynaston identifies as "the real-life Melmotte" of Trollope's *The Way We Live Now* – that definitive rendering of the culture of speculative excess – himself summarized the spectacle. The year 1871, he wrote,

was a year and an era when everyone was seeking what he could make on the Stock Exchange. There is a peculiar fascination to some people in making money on the Stock Exchange. I know hundreds who would rather make £50 on the Stock Exchange than £250 by the exercise of their profession; there is a nameless fascination, and in the year 1871 the favorite form of making money on the Stock Exchange was by applying for shares, selling them at whatever premium they were at, and the money was considered made – I say considered honourably made.[26]

Note, above all, the obvious irrelevance of the real assets nominally represented by the shares. More than a century later, at the peak of the IPO mini-bubble of 1983, Eberstadt participated in underwriting the first venture-backed company ever to go public with a market valuation of $1 billion. I well recall the dialogue between two traders, quoted in the *Wall Street Journal* on the day following the offer: "What's a Diasonics?" "I don't know, but we have to buy some!"

Domestic company promotions were not the only objects of speculation in the early 1870s. London saw yet another "craze for foreign

---

[24] Kynaston, *A World of its Own*, p. 220.
[25] *Ibid.* 223.   [26] Quoted *ibid.* 266.

loans" at the time. Paraguay, Costa Rica, San Domingo and Honduras became notorious for borrowing, according to *The Economist,*

immense sums which they could never have paid, and which they never meant to pay ... and what is more extraordinary than all that, in several cases, they, the borrowing states, obtained scarcely any of the money because it was intercepted by the persons who framed the devices. Those who cheated the English public cheated also – and that upon the largest scale – those in whose names they borrowed.[27]

The third Honduras loan in 1872 stretched the willing disbelief of the greedy herd beyond the breaking point. Its purpose was to fund "A 'ship railway,' by which ocean-going ships would be raised from the sea by hydraulic lifts, transported across the Isthmus on fifteen parallel tracks that would carry a giant cradle, and slid onto the water on the other side."[28]

A decade later, the "Brush Boom" ignited the London Stock Exchange with "a wave of popular enthusiasm for anything to do with the pioneering world of electricity, electric lighting and the manufacture of electrical equipment."[29] It is worth lingering on this event, because of its significance – entirely negative – for long-term, strategic interaction between the financial capitalism of London and Britain's version of the Innovation Economy. Certainly, it began with a bang. The Brush Electric Light Company was the target:

There was such a rush for the shares as had never been seen before in Lombard Street, the whole street being blocked by the crowd pressing to get to the bank to pay in their applications ... The capital was enormously oversubscribed, all the well known City names amongst the list of subscribers, and the shares, which on allotment were to be £3 paid, were on the day of the prospectus dealt on the London Stock Exchange at £7 per share, or £4 premium.[30]

The 133 percent pop would have been worthy of a dotcom IPO in 1999.

Brush proceeded to franchise its patents to subsidiary companies under the Electric Lighting Act of 1882. But its fundamental technological and legal position was challenged by "a handful of powerful bears" on the Stock Exchange even as its subsidiaries failed to develop their concessions. Thomas P. Hughes, author of the magisterial *Networks*

---

[27] *Ibid.* 269.   [28] *Ibid.* 269–270.   [29] *Ibid.* 341.   [30] *Ibid.*

of Power: Electrification in Western Society, 1880–1930, reports the denouement:

A year after the bright promise of the spring of '82, the Anglo-American Brush Company stood revealed as a patent-holding and manufacturing company which had been founded on an arc-lighting system that was no longer outstanding in its field and on an incandescent-lamp patent of doubtful value.[31]

A dozen years later, Alexander Siemens pronounced the epitaph on the Brush Boom, offering a homily on the problematic relationship between financial speculation and innovative enterprise:

However much other causes may have contributed to delay the development of electrical engineering, it is clear that the principal one must be looked for in the exaggerated expectations that were raised, either by ignorance or by design, when the general public first seriously thought of regarding electricity as a commodity for everyday use.

At that time the promoters of electric companies preached to the public that electricity was in its infancy, that the laws of science were totally unknown, and that wonders could be confidently expected from it. There was a short time of excitement to the public and of profit to the promoters; then the confidence of the public in electricity was almost destroyed and could only be regained by years of patient work.[32]

Kynaston suggests that the consequences of the Brush Boom had even more general significance, setting London firmly against financing those new industries – "above all electrical engineering, chemicals and in due course motor cars ... high tech and capital intensive" – where America and Germany were establishing leadership.[33] The Brush Boom is a signal example of how financial speculation can discredit innovative technology. As we shall see, it stands out against the decisive moments, before and since, when it was precisely speculative bubbles in financial assets that enabled fundamental innovation to be funded before it was possible to assess the economic returns therefrom in any rigorous way. Again and again, it has been the opportunity for financial investors to sell shares into a rising market that has motivated investment by entrepreneurs in real assets that embody frontier technology.

---

[31] T. P. Hughes, *Networks of Power: Electrification in Western Society, 1880–1930* (Baltimore, MD: Johns Hopkins University Press, 1993), p. 62.
[32] Kynaston, *A World of its Own*, p. 342.   [33] *Ibid.* 342.

If Schumpeter's entrepreneur in principle loses other people's money, historically financiers have been able to win from speculation even when the projects they fund ultimately fail, and it is the entrepreneur and the purchasers of the original investors' shares who lose.

In 1882, the City of London and its clients took a figurative bath in the most economically significant technological innovation of the time – and fled. Four years later, they collectively plunged into the most traditional of speculative assets in pursuit of *auri sacra fames*. The discovery of gold on the Witwatersrand in South Africa generated the first wave of the "Kaffir Circus" on the floor of the London Stock Exchange, as brokers fought with each other for access. Kynaston takes note of "an adage, beloved of the Stock Exchange [that] dates from about this time: 'a mine is a hole in the ground owned by a liar.'"[34] In reality, the great South African gold boom had legs, although it had to wait for convincing evidence that innovative mining technology could open up the deep mines and that cyanide could be used to extract gold from pyretic ore. When the market did become convinced in late 1894, the boom that followed "became one of those phases of City history that almost ranked with the South Sea Bubble in terms of mythological status."[35] The value of annual production on the Rand rose 50 percent, from £5.18 million to £7.84 million, and the net British purchase of shares to fund the increase is estimated at some £40 million. So great was the volume of trading that it spilled out from the floor of the Stock Exchange and continued after hours. When in March 1895 the police attempted to clear the area, the Battle of Throgmorton Street erupted as the brokers refused to suspend their dealing and move on.

Anticipation of the Boer War, which was to break out in 1898, finally closed down the Kaffir Circus, although Westralian promotions continued haphazardly to attract speculative interest. Under their shadow, a notorious promoter named Harry Lawson attempted to incite his own bubble in the prospective investment returns from the nascent automobile industry. Following the spectacular success of the IPO of the Dunlop Rubber Company, whose pneumatic tires enabled the cycling craze of the mid-1890s, Lawson acquired British rights from Daimler and established the British Motor Syndicate (BMS), with the

---

[34] *Ibid.* 396.
[35] D. Kynaston, *Golden Years: 1890–1914*, vol. 2 of *The City of London*, 4 vols. (London: Pimlico, 1995), p. 109.

customary array of peers of the realm as directors. Its initial offering of
£100,000 was followed by the launch of the Great Horseless Carriage
Company by way of a £750,000 flotation. Less than a year from its
IPO, the BMS was back with a proposed £3 million offering, no less
than £2.7 million of which was to go to the selling shareholders, led, of
course, by Lawson. This finally was too much. Kynaston muses:

> Did it matter that by far the most important financial intermediary in the
> early history of the British motor-car industry was a crook? The answer
> is surely yes, for quite apart from the specific matter of the shortages of
> working capital adversely affecting pioneer producers such as Daimler, the
> Lawson saga marked the beginning of what would be an uneasy, mutually
> mistrustful relationship between that industry and the City. The industry,
> not unnaturally, feared being ripped off again; the City, just as naturally,
> perceived the industry was full of unprofitable "lemons" and was reluctant
> to subscribe or encourage the subscription of further capital. The analogy
> with the electrical industry, following the catastrophic "Brush Boom" of the
> early 1880s, is painfully obvious.[36]

In May 1910, London saw the last explosion of speculation before the
First World War. "Rubber Fever" was the occasion, as the prospects of
cheap rubber from the plantations of the east seized the city's imagination. On the floor of the Stock Exchange "the scenes were even more
frantic than those experienced during the Kaffir Boom fifteen years
earlier," but in a matter of months it was over.[37]

The great American trust bubble

As the London Stock Exchange was immunizing itself against the funding of innovative technology, New York demonstrated an even more
extreme reaction to the economic consequences of that great wave of
transformational technology, the railroads. Throughout the industrializing world, the radical reduction in manufacturing and transportation
costs occasioned by the railroad construction boom unleashed forces
that reflected parallel revolutions in the scale of production and the
extent of markets. While real incomes rose as never before, everywhere
the response of "the dealers … in any branch of trade and manufactures" was exactly as Smith had reported more than 100 years before:

---

[36] *Ibid.* 148.   [37] *Ibid.* 520.

"to widen the market and to narrow the competition."[38] In Europe, cartels predominated. In the United States,

the Sherman Act, which passed as a protest against the massive number of combinations that occurred during the 1870s and 1880s, clearly discouraged the construction of loose horizontal federations of small manufacturing enterprises formed to control price and production.[39]

In place of cartels, the trust movement was born, dramatizing a classic crux in The Three-Player Game: the state moves to enable competition in the market economy, and financial capital counters to freeze it in place. In order to pursue its goal, the trust movement required active, liquid markets in the securities of the industrial companies and franchised utilities that were its stock in trade. In this it was served by the regulatory reforms that the New York Stock Exchange (NYSE) had enacted in response to the long deflation of the same "first Great Depression," from 1873 to 1893, that had motivated the architects of the trusts. Reduced returns from the railroad securities that had utterly dominated trading induced a search for new instruments. The reforms in New York, which tightened listing requirements and fostered collaboration with the less regulated New York Curb Exchange, enabled the NYSE to establish itself as "the blue chip market, creating an imprimatur of quality ... [that] greatly advanced the education of unsophisticated American investors of the late nineteenth century."[40]

In my hands is a remarkable document from that time, a thick volume whose pages have begun to crumble: John Moody's *The Truth about the Trusts: A Description and Analysis of the American Trust Movement*, a first edition of which I found in my father's library some twenty years ago. On his way to establishing his firm as an authority on the financial status of American business, Moody provided detailed analyses of the formation of the seven "Great Industrial Trusts"

---

[38] A. Smith, *The Wealth of Nations* (New York: Random House, 1937 [1776]), p. 250.

[39] A. D. Chandler, *The Visible Hand: The Managerial Revolution in American Business* (Cambridge, MA: Belknap, 1977), p. 375.

[40] L. Neal and L. E. Davis, "Why Did Finance Capital and the Second Industrial Revolution Arise in the 1890s?" in N. R. Lamoreaux and K. Sokoloff (eds.), *Financing Innovation in the United States: 1870 to the Present* (Cambridge, MA: MIT Press, 2007), pp. 140–141.

and summary information on no fewer than 298 "Lesser Industrial Trusts," plus thirteen "Important Industrial Trusts in process of Reorganization or Readjustment," eight "Telephone and Telegraph Consolidations," the 103 "Leading Gas, Electric Light and Street Railway Consolidations," the six "Great Steam Railroad Groups," and ten "Allied Independent Steam Railroad Systems."[41] From this exhaustive and exhausting exercise emerges a robust, meta-economic defense of "the modern Trust" as "the natural outcome or evolution of the societal conditions and ethical standards which are recognized and established among men to-day as being necessary elements in the development of civilization."[42]

To those schooled in the doctrine of free and efficient markets, Moody's rhetoric must seem alien, even pernicious. But writing at the intersection of the market economy and financial capitalism as each reached its first full maturity on the back of 100 years of globalizing industrialization, Moody correctly read the trust movement as a natural, even necessary response to the competitive forces that were being unleashed at a scale and with a ferocity never before experienced. The trust movement represented no more and no less than an effort to control the market economy in order to ensure sufficient cash flows to validate the financial obligations of market participants.[43] In doing so, it leveraged a genuine innovation in financial engineering that linked the combinations of industrial assets with the value of the financial assets that represented them. For the value of the newly created trusts was to be based not on the *historic* rate of dividends paid by their constituents but on the *prospective* dividend-paying capacity of the combination. Of course, in all previous bubbles – whether or not they proved to have funded productive assets – prices had decoupled from backward-looking measures of value by definition. But in the case of the trusts, forward-looking benchmarks of value were explicitly defined at the outset.

---

[41] J. Moody, *The Truth about the Trusts: A Description and Analysis of the American Trust Movement* (New York: Moody Publishing Company, 1904).

[42] *Ibid.* 494.

[43] For an insightful discussion of the multidimensional economic and political stresses caused by the episodic waves of globalization beginning in the later nineteenth century, see H. James, *The End of Globalization: Lessons from the Great Depression* (Cambridge, MA: Harvard University Press, 2001).

Moody rationalized the much-criticized phenomenon of "watered" capital: shares issued in excess of the book value of an enterprise's hard assets:

In forming combinations of all kinds, a certain amount of the securities are usually issued for good-will, patent rights, franchises and so forth. Very often stock is issued without its specific purpose being explained beyond the statement that *the amount issued is based upon the earning power of the property* ... The "good-will" or "watered" stock usually anticipates the value of the monopoly element, and, of course, if this feature does not turn out to be as important as expected, there frequently is no other asset back of the "good-will" or watered stock, and a general collapse follows.[44]

Chandler notes that access to the liquid (whether watered or not) shares of the trusts proved powerfully attractive:

The manufacturers who organized trusts were surprised by Wall Street's interest in obtaining their trust certificates ... Manufacturers soon realized that they could use the growing market as a source of funds for working and investment capital. They were also quick to appreciate that the demand for industrial securities enhanced the values of their own companies. Expanded demand for industrial securities permitted manufacturers to obtain a handsome rate of exchange when they completed a merger by turning over the stock of their little known small enterprises for that of a nationally known holding company.[45]

A sure indication that the speculation would end in tears was the fact that "financiers began to take sizable blocks of stock as payment for arranging and carrying out a merger."[46] The same signal was evident at the peak of the credit bubble of 2004–2007, when the banks that originated complex derivatives chose to hold their products as if the AAA credit ratings they had participated in fabricating had substantive meaning.

Chandler cites sources that count 212 combinations in the years 1898–1902 and the contemporaneous disappearance of 2,634 firms through merger. But by 1903 the trust bubble had burst. The *Wall Street Journal* compiled a table, reproduced in Moody's work, to show that from peak to trough the aggregate market value of the leading

[44] Moody, *The Truth about the Trusts*, pp. xix–xx; emphasis added.
[45] Chandler, *The Visible Hand*, p. 332.   [46] *Ibid.*

100 industrial stocks had declined by 43.4 percent.[47] "No sympathy," Moody asserted, "needs to be wasted on the many noisy speculators who are now loudly condemning all Trusts because they themselves happened to be caught in a speculative crash."[48]

In a broader sense, no sympathy need be expended regarding the trust bubble itself, as investors had sought to capitalize on prospective monopoly profits that were apparently accessible at one moment of time, as if the dynamics of competition – driven ultimately by techno-logical innovation – could be captured and frozen. And yet, even as it failed, this doomed effort to invoke Cash and Control in the face of the economic and financial uncertainty occasioned by technological innovation demonstrates the historical relevance of the strategy I dis-covered eighty years later.

The spirit of speculation

Ten unsustainable bull market runs on the London Stock Exchange in ten decades and the trust bubble in New York: such a review must dis-pel any notion that speculative excess is a distinctive feature of more recent times. On the contrary, the spirit of speculation is ever present. One of the pleasures of the journey of writing this book has been the discovery of previously unknown fellow travelers. One such is the once prominent now forgotten Wall Street legend Philip Carret, who published a how-to book provocatively titled _The Art of Speculation_ in 1927, just when his generation's maximum opportunity was at hand. Much of Carret's book is a sensible tutorial on the typology of financial instruments, on the structure of balance sheets and income statements, and on the more or less treacherous strategies for attempt-ing to win easy money from the market. But he goes deeper, as when he identifies the stock market speculator's economic role as a provider of liquidity – "increased marketability" is Carret's term – for "long-pull" investors.[49] Carret specifies that "the road to success in speculation is the study of values" but goes on to observe, after paying due heed to management's discretionary authority to run a business in disre-gard of the interests of the stockholders, that there is "no logical basis

[47] Moody, _The Truth about the Trusts_, p. 479.   [48] _Ibid._ xxi.

[49] P. L. Carret, _The Art of Speculation_ (Columbia, MD: Marketplace Books, 2007 [1927]), p. 8.

for any assumption regarding the relation between book and market values."[50]

In line with the theme of this chapter, Carret offers a splendid prospect to his novice reader: "Limitless horizons stretch before the would-be speculator. All the commodities of commerce are possible subjects for his trafficking."[51] Carret is most compelling when he describes the challenge to the studious speculator represented by the "ripples and waves" of price movements driven by mere gamblers:

To attempt to trade on such movements is mere gambling with the odds against the trader by a considerable margin. It is astounding that thousands of otherwise intelligent persons persist in trying to make money in this way. Commonly accepted figures of somewhat dubious origin are frequently cited to show that 90% to 95% of all margin players lose money in the stock market. The deep-seated gambling instinct, the well-founded belief that in widely fluctuating markets there must be opportunities for profit nevertheless bring fresh recruits to the brokerage offices in constant streams.[52]

Carret's gamblers were rediscovered two generations later by theorists who have attributed the emergence of bubbles to the activity of mindless "noise traders." Writing as the bull market that would peak in October 1929 gathered force, Carret had truly seen nothing yet.

The super-bubble

For almost all of the two generations that followed the Crash of 1929, the financial markets were "repressed," as Carmen Reinhart and Kenneth Rogoff put it.[53] Banking regulation, foreign exchange controls and generalized risk aversion constrained systemic speculation for almost half of the twentieth century. In the United States, the first stirrings of postwar exuberance could be discerned in the "-onics" boom beginning in the early 1960s, so named for the electronics companies sponsored by the Defense Department and NASA, and in the "Money Game" – the go-go stock market of the late 1960s. The stagflation years of the 1970s deferred the recovery of exuberance, a recovery that I observed first hand in the reawakening of the market for IPOs in

---

[50] *Ibid.* 10, 41.   [51] *Ibid.* 47.   [52] *Ibid.* 57.
[53] C. M. Reinhart and K. S. Rogoff, *This Time is Different: Eight Centuries of Financial Folly* (Princeton University Press, 2009), pp. 205–207.

1983. To us, those few months seemed like a peak of frenzy, but they amounted to mere foothills relative to the spectacular excess of the dotcom/telecom bubble.

The mini-bubble in the IPO market of 1983 marked the onset of an unprecedented global phenomenon, a generation-long "super-bubble," to use George Soros's term. During the course of twenty-five years, contemporary financial institutions and markets proved themselves as prone to speculative excess as those of the *laissez-faire* nineteenth-century regime of small-state capitalism, when, across the industrializing world, public sectors were on the order of 10 percent of national economies or less. In the modern case, however, the breaking of each wave of speculation generated only modest recession in the real economy. As reflected in the reduced volatility of the time series that registered economic fluctuations, this came to be known as the Great Moderation. But behind the seeming stabilization the world economy entered a leverage cycle that reached historically unprecedented levels.[54] It was punctuated by a sequence of bubbles in relatively discrete categories of financial assets: the junk bonds in the late 1980s that fueled a takeover boom in the United States; emerging market debt in the mid-1990s; the dotcom/telecom bubble in the stock market in 1998–2000. After that bubble burst at the turn of the millennium, the focus became residential property, not only in the United States but also across Europe and in key emerging markets, from central Europe to China. Over the whole period, from 1981, the debt of the US private sector rose from 123 percent of GDP to 290 percent, household debt doubled to 100 percent of GDP, and the ratio of household debt to disposable income increased from 65 percent to the unsustainable level of 135 percent.[55]

The parallel transformation of Wall Street in the course of a generation can also be quantified. In 1970, the aggregate financial assets of the nation's security brokers and dealers were $16 billion. During the first half of the 1980s, as the new business model took hold, total financial assets surged from $33 billion in 1979 to $185 billion in 1986. Following a brief pause, growth exploded in the 1990s as

[54] See J. Geanakoplos, "The Leverage Cycle," in D. Acemoglu, K. Rogoff and M. Woodward (eds.), *NBER Macroeconomic Annual 2009*, vol. 24 (University of Chicago Press, 2010), pp. 1–65.

[55] N. Roubini and S. Mihm, *Crisis Economics: A Crash Course in the Future of Finance* (New York: Penguin, 2010), pp. 82–83.

balance sheets increased by more than 5 times to almost $1.5 trillion in the eleven years from 1990 to 2001. From there they doubled in the next five years, reaching $3 trillion in 2007.[56]

Taking an even longer view, Hyun Shin shows that the growth in the assets of the financial sector – commercial banks and securities broker-dealers – moved in step with the assets of the nonfinancial corporate and household sectors from the early 1950s to 1980, each rising by a factor of ten. Then came an enormous divergence. The balance sheets of the commercial banks remained aligned with those of nonfinancial corporates and households, all rising to the 2007 peak by slightly less than ten times. But as the investment banks – the broker-dealers – transformed themselves from agents into principals they grew their increasingly leveraged assets by no less than a factor of 100.[57]

The succession of bubbles in different classes of financial assets that collectively constituted the super-bubble confirmed the banality of the phenomenon in general terms. But, cumulatively, as their consequences were repeatedly contained by the effective interventions of governments and regulators, they transcended the banal and set the stage for a phenomenon that truly was different: the first global crisis of big-state capitalism.

---

[56] Federal Reserve, Flow of Funds Accounts, L. 129, 1965–2009. www.federalreserve.gov/releases/z1/Current/data.htm.
[57] H. S. Shin, *Risk and Liquidity* (Oxford University Press, 2010), pp. 168–170.

8   Explaining bubbles

The financial Crisis of 2008 and its economic consequences have spawned an enormous academic literature across the spectrum of empirical and theoretical scholarship. Yet the number of rigorous works of historical analysis that take financial discontinuities as their focus is limited. The two that stand out are Charles Kindleberger's *Manias, Panics and Crashes: A History of Financial Crises*, originally published in 1978 and updated in 2011 by Robert Aliber, and Carmen Reinhart and Kenneth Rogoff's recent contribution, *This Time is Different: Eight Centuries of Financial Folly*. The former indicates by means of its subtitle that its authors evaluate "manias" largely in terms of the panics and crashes that follow. The latter is the definitive chronicle of currency debasement, debt default and banking failures. Bubbles, recent and long ago, have attracted less attention.[1]

Manias and the credit system

A first step toward comprehending the dynamics of bubbles is to distinguish the consequences of speculative excess in the credit markets from the effects of speculative excess in the equity markets. Manias that infect the credit system generate the great financial crises and subsequent contractions in real economies. Such contractions are inevitable when – as is necessarily the case in the real world – markets are incomplete and effective hedges are unavailable. As Franklin Allen and Douglas Gale conclude in *Understanding Financial Crises*:

When markets are incomplete, financial institutions are forced to sell assets in order to obtain liquidity. Because the supply of and the demand for

---

[1] C. P. Kindleberger and R. Z. Aliber, *Manias, Panics and Crashes: A History of Financial Crises*, 6th edn. (New York: Palgrave Macmillan, 2011) and C. M. Reinhart and K. S. Rogoff, *This Time is Different: Eight Centuries of Financial Folly* (Princeton University Press, 2009).

liquidity are likely to be inelastic in the short run, a small degree of aggregate uncertainty can cause large fluctuations in asset prices. Holding liquidity involves an opportunity cost and the suppliers of liquidity can only recoup this cost by buying assets at firesale prices in some states of the world; so, the private provision of liquidity by arbitrageurs will always be inadequate to insure complete asset-price stability. As a result small shocks can cause significant asset-price volatility. If the asset-price volatility is severe enough, banks may find it impossible to meet their fixed commitments and a full-blown crisis will occur.[2]

A compromised banking system that is counting its losses from funding speculative projects necessarily reduces the supply of credit, on which all economic activity depends. Equity bubbles, by contrast, tend to leave relatively little wreckage behind. The run up to the Great Crash of 1929 was financed only to a limited extent by credit, even before margin requirements were imposed by the authorities to limit borrowing to fund the purchase of stocks. Lester Chandler calculates that at their pre-Crash peak total loans to Wall Street brokers and dealers amounted to less than 10 percent of the value of shares listed on the New York Stock Exchange.[3] A recession did follow the crash in equity prices in October 1929. But it took the successive wave of banking crises in 1931–1933 to freeze the market economies of the world into the Great Depression.

Kindleberger and Aliber and Reinhart and Rogoff agree that "private debt surges," often fueled by an influx of capital from abroad – a "capital flow bonanza"[4] – are the critical conditions that precede financial crises. Kindleberger and Aliber expand on this theme:

The cycle of manias and panics results from the pro-cyclical changes in the supply of credit; the credit supply increases relatively rapidly in good times and then when economic growth slackens, the rate of growth of credit has often declined sharply ... During the economic expansion investors become increasingly optimistic and more eager to pursue profit opportunities that will pay off in the distant future while the lenders become less risk-averse. Rational exuberance morphs into irrational exuberance, economic euphoria develops and investment spending and consumption spending increase.

[2] F. Allen and D. Gale, *Understanding Financial Crises* (Oxford University Press, 2007), pp. 127–128.
[3] L. V. Chandler, *American Monetary Policy, 1929–1941* (New York: Harper & Row, 1971), pp. 31–32.
[4] Reinhart and Rogoff, *This Time is Different*, p. 157.

There is a pervasive sense that it is "time to get on the train before it leaves the station" and the exceptionally profitable opportunities disappear. Asset prices increase further. An increasingly large share of the purchases of these assets is undertaken in anticipation of short-term capital gains and an exceptionally large share of the purchases is financed with credit.[5]

Kindleberger and Aliber here invoke the qualitative model developed by Hyman Minsky, his Financial Instability Hypothesis, which has two theorems. First, "the economy has financing regimes under which it is stable, and financing regimes in which it is unstable." And, second, "over periods of prolonged prosperity, the economy transits from financial relations that make for a stable system to financial relations that make for an unstable system."[6] The credit system and the economy at large progress (or degenerate) through successive stages of confidence and risk-taking. The initial, conservative stage is that of hedge finance: the operating cash flows of borrowers are sufficient both to service outstanding debts and to repay them as they mature. As expectations of borrowers and lenders are validated by experience, they jointly move into the phase of speculative finance: operating cash flow is sufficient to make timely payment of interest, but the principal must be rolled over and refinanced to prevent default. Finally, the system moves into the stage of Ponzi finance, where debtors must borrow the interest they owe in order for the fiction of solvency to be maintained.[7]

I knew Minsky well during the last decade of his active career, before he retired from Washington University in St. Louis to join the Levy Economics Institute at Bard College. We were introduced, appropriately enough, by a fellow board member of the Mark Twain Banks. Thus, at a time when he and his work lay beyond the scope of mainstream economics and finance, I had the opportunity to grasp his prescient analysis of the historically unprecedented emergence of big-state capitalism. As the super-bubble of 1982–2007 unfolded stage by stage, this proved to be an extraordinarily valuable advantage.

---

[5] Kindleberger and Aliber, *Manias, Panics and Crashes*, p. 13.
[6] H. P. Minsky, "The Financial Instability Hypothesis," The Levy Economics Institute of Bard College Working Paper 74 (1992), pp. 7–8.
[7] H. P. Minsky, *Stabilizing an Unstable Economy* (New Haven, CT: Yale University Press, 1986), p. 70.

Big-state capitalism

It took interacting transformations in the institutional, intellectual and technological environments to produce the super-bubble. The first was the emergence of big-state capitalism from the aftermath of the Depression and the Second World War. Whether the change was principally driven by political commitments to public welfare, as in Europe, or by commitments to national security, as in the United States, the weight of the state in the national economy increased from less than 10 percent *circa* 1929 to more than 30 percent in the United States and as much as 50 percent in parts of Europe. As Minsky understood, here was the critical institutional bulwark against "it" – a Great Depression – happening again.[8]

To explain the stabilizing role the big state plays, Minsky identified the three complementary contributions that substantial fiscal deficits make to a financially stressed economy: they generate income and employment; they generate cash flow that protects the corporate sector from the reduction in revenues generated by household decisions to save rather than spend; and they supply low-risk investment instruments for investors when the state issues securities to finance its own negative cash flow. Minsky continues:

> The effect of Big Government on the economy is much more powerful and pervasive than is allowed by the standard view which neglects the financial-flow and portfolio implications of a government deficit. The standard view focuses solely on the direct and secondary effects of government spending ... on aggregate demand. The expanded view allows both for the cash flows that other sectors need in order to fulfill commitments and for the need for secure assets in portfolios in the aftermath of a financial disturbance.[9]

Throughout the super-bubble, government deficits were complemented by aggressive central bank interventions whenever needed. In the United States, these came to be personified as the "Greenspan Put." First successfully deployed in response to the stock market crash of 1987, then offered in support of the extended resolution of the savings and loan crisis from 1989 to 1994, it was repeated in 1998, when the blow-up of Long-Term Capital Management capped the Russian and

[8] H. P. Minsky, *Can "It" Happen Again?: Essays on Instability and Finance* (New York: M. E. Sharpe, 1982).
[9] Minsky, *Stabilizing an Unstable Economy*, p. 21.

Asian debt crises, and again invoked when the dotcom/telecom bubble definitively burst in 2001. On each occasion, the Fed reduced its policy interest rate and aggressively supplied reserves to the banking system.

George Soros has echoed Minsky in attributing the super-bubble to the increasing credibility of government commitments to underwrite the health of the private sector:

> What made the super-bubble so peculiar was the role that financial crises played in making it grow. Since the belief that markets could be safely left to their own devices was false, the super-bubble gave rise to a series of financial crises ... Each time a financial crisis occurred, the authorities intervened, merged away or otherwise took care of the failing financial institutions, and applied monetary and fiscal stimuli to protect the economy. These measures reinforced the prevailing trend of ever increasing credit and leverage, but as long as they worked, they also reinforced the prevailing misconception that markets can be safely left to their own devices. It was the intervention of the authorities that saved the system; nonetheless these crises served as successful tests of a false belief, and, as such, they inflated the super-bubble even further.[10]

Recently, Moritz Schularick and Alan Taylor quantified Soros's observation, taking a long view from 1870 to the present. In the earlier epoch of small-state capitalism, until 1939, the ratio of bank loans to the broadly defined money supply grew at an annual rate of just 0.11 percent compared with an annual growth of 2.19 percent – twenty times greater – in the postwar era. And this is before account is taken of the emergence of the nonbanking sources of finance, the "shadow banking" system of securitized vehicles and hedge funds that proliferated from the 1980s. Schularick and Taylor's conclusion echoes that of Soros:

> The stable relationship between money and credit broke down after the Great Depression and World War 2, as a new secular trend took hold that carried on until today's crisis. We conjecture that these changes conditioned, and were conditioned by the broader environment of macroeconomic and financial policies: after the 1930s the ascent of fiat money plus Lenders of Last Resort – and a slow shift back towards financial *laissez-faire* – encouraged the expansion of credit ... Aiming to cushion the real economic effects of financial crises, policy-makers have prevented a periodic deleveraging of

---

[10] G. Soros, *The Soros Lectures at the Central European University* (New York: Public Affairs, 2010), p. 39.

the financial sector resulting in the virtually uninterrupted growth of leverage we have seen up until 2008.[11]

Thus, the maturation of the Three-Player Game reflexively contributed to the game's systemic instability.

Modern finance theory

The second enabling factor in the generation of the super-bubble took place in the realm of theory. Modern finance theory equipped the players both with tools for defining and deploying novel securities and with strategies for trading and hedging them. Theory also rationalized the retreat of the regulatory state. As Minsky correctly predicted, only action by the authorities "to control, constrain and perhaps even forbid the financing practices that caused the need for lender-of-last-resort activity" could prevent its recurrence. Instead, in the political domain the super-bubble was signally accompanied by the repeal of Glass–Steagall in 1999 and the legislated exemption of derivatives from regulatory oversight in 2000. The consequence was the financialization of the economic system to a degree never before known.

The foundations of the theoretical revolution in finance were laid in the 1950s, when Kenneth Arrow and Gerard Debreu created the mathematical model of general equilibrium on the basis of the posited existence of an infinite array of contingent contracts specifying what goods and services are to be delivered where and when and under what conditions.[12] I have always thought of the Arrow–Debreu model of what is necessary for the notion of general equilibrium to be theoretically imaginable as a sort of existence *dis*proof: the world it defines is utterly contrary to the world we live in and know. But its mathematics was seized on as a road map toward the Utopia of complete and efficient markets, whose realization would eliminate any legitimate role for the state in the market economy beyond that of watch keeper.

[11] M. Schularick and A. M. Taylor, "Credit Booms Gone Bust: Monetary Policy, Leverage Cycles and Financial Crises, 1870–2008," *American Economic Review*, 102(2) (2012), p. 1058.

[12] K. J. Arrow and G. Debreu, "Existence of an Equilibrium for a Competitive Economy," *Econometrica*, 22 (1954), pp. 265–290.

At roughly the same time, Harry Markowitz established the basis of the capital asset pricing model (CAPM) by defining risk as the statistical variance of a time series of stock prices.[13] Ten years later, Fischer Black, Myron Scholes and Robert Merton jointly and severally developed a method for pricing options that radically extended the range of financial instruments and the scale on which they were traded.[14] To hopeful theorists and practitioners alike, it seemed that the imaginary perfectly and perpetually hedged world of Arrow–Debreu was within their grasp. And so the theorists of academic finance weighed into this most contested front in the Three-Player Game.

Donald MacKenzie, in his comprehensive work *An Engine Not a Camera*, exhaustively explores the manner in which modern finance theory served not as a camera for representing the behavior of the financial markets, but as an engine for transforming them:

Finance Theory has become incorporated into the infrastructure of financial markets in at least three ways: technical, linguistic and legitimatory. All three are most evident in the case of financial derivatives, the emergence and development of which have been perhaps the most dramatic change in global finance since the start of the 1970s.[15]

At the technical level,

Derivatives-pricing models implemented in software give large players in the derivatives market, notably investment banks, the ability mathematically to analyze and decompose the risks involved in their portfolios, and this is vital for their capacity to operate on a large scale in this market.

Linguistically, "The theory offers a way of talking about markets, especially about markets whose complexity might otherwise be baffling." And, finally, decisively, in a way that legitimized a revolution:

To say of a financial market that it is "efficient" – that its prices incorporate, nearly instantaneously, all available price-relevant information – is

---

[13] H. M. Markowitz, "Portfolio Selection," *Journal of Finance*, 7(1) (1952), pp. 77–91.

[14] F. Black and M. Scholes, "The Pricing of Options and Corporate Liabilities," *Journal of Political Economy*, 81(3) (1973), pp. 637–654 and R. C. Merton, "Theory of Rational Option Pricing," *Bell Journal of Economics and Management Science*, 4(1) (1973), pp. 141–183.

[15] D. MacKenzie, *An Engine Not a Camera: How Financial Models Shape Markets* (Cambridge, MA: MIT Press, 2008), p. 250.

to say something commendatory about it, and that has been what orthodox financial economics has said about the central capital markets of the
advanced industrial world ... Derivatives were haunted by the impression,
held not only by lay-people but by many market-regulators, that they were
simply wagers on the movement of prices ... Economists helped make the
financial derivatives markets possible by providing initial legitimacy.[16]

The triumph was confirmed when the accountants and regulators
bought into the doctrine of market efficiency by requiring that assets
and liabilities be marked to market on the balance sheets of banks and
of their customers, providing a potent accelerant to the systemic movement into the regime of Ponzi finance.[17]

It is an error to blame the theorists of finance exclusively for the
catastrophe that ensued. The practitioners were all too inclined to
short circuit the mathematics in the name of computational con-
venience. Thus, what came to be established as the standard methodology for assessing potential loss – Value at Risk (VaR) – was the
invention of practitioners who constructed a tool that excluded the
most extreme possible outcomes, since it is defined to quantify what
is likely to occur some specified 95 percent or 99 percent of the time.
All too often the VaR methodology was implemented through models
that assumed a "normal" distribution of returns, even though observation readily showed that the distribution of positive and negative
returns on investment were exhibiting "fat tails," the statistical signals
of bubbles and busts. Again, in the name of efficiency, the historical
record that was examined to establish the distribution of returns was
often no more than two or three years. And since the entire purpose
of risk management is to limit possible gains in order to limit possible
losses, managers incentivized by one-way compensation plans typically turned a blind eye while the traders in the front office, where the
money was made – equipped with better computers and more testos-
terone – gamed the risk officers in the midoffice.

The capstone to the translation of modern finance theory into
market-transforming instruments came with the invention of credit
derivatives in 1997 and their subsequent hijacking. The original purpose of the young innovators at J. P. Morgan was to distribute and
diversify the bank's book of corporate loans. Unlike corporate bonds,

---

[16] *Ibid.* 251–252.
[17] H. S. Shin, *Risk and Liquidity* (Oxford University Press, 2010), pp. 9–10.

whose standardized contracts had enabled trading in more or less liquid markets for hundreds of years, loans were too customized to be liquid. The credit default swap enabled the bank to transfer the risk of default on a diversified portfolio of corporate loans, and thus reduce its required reserves, while still retaining ownership of the obligation and the relationship with the customer that the obligation represented. It was an unequivocal contribution to increasing the efficiency of the bank's management of its balance sheet.

Critically, however, the term *swap* in this context was and is misleading. The instruments that had emerged in the foreign exchange and fixed income markets involved the unconditional swap of two financial assets – a stream of fixed versus floating interest rate payments for a specified period, for example, or a defined amount of dollars for pounds. But a credit default swap contract is an entirely contingent arrangement whereby one party buys protection by paying a periodic fee to its counterparty, who in turn will pay an agreed sum only if and when an event, typically a default, occurs to a third, "reference" entity. If this sounds like an insurance policy, in economic substance it is. But the entirely unregulated credit default swap contract differs from legally defined insurance in two critical respects. First, the protection seller is under no obligation to establish reserves against the contingent obligations established by the contract. Second, the protection buyer need have no "insurable interest" in the referenced entity, so the instrument was as available to those who wished to bet on the health of an issuer of debt as to those seeking to hedge an already exposed position.

The attraction of this innovation was demonstrated by the explosive growth in the gross nominal amount of credit default swap contracts outstanding, from zero to $60 trillion in a decade. Credit default swaps provided the illusion of effective risk transfer and therefore entitled their purchasers to earn incremental returns from taking on more risk. But the effectiveness of the risk transfer was only as good as the access to cash of the weakest counterparty in the daisy chain. The regulators and the ratings agencies all bought into the fantasy of risk reduction because exposure to the underlying pool of debts was more broadly distributed.

As would not have surprised Minsky, with the proliferation of credit default swaps came a radical shift in the nature of the underlying portfolios of securities whose risk of default was being distributed.

From the relatively conservative, low-risk loans on the books of J. P. Morgan where it all began, credit default swaps were applied to any and all structured financial products, most notoriously to the collateralized debt obligations whose underlying assets were high-risk, subprime mortgages. Should the risk of default of the underlying liabilities ever become correlated in the real world beyond the financial sector, the daisy chain of risk transfer would turn into a chain reaction of liquidations.[18]

The IT revolution and the bursting of the super-bubble

Finally, the impact of modern finance theory on modern finance practice would never have been realized except for the IT revolution. In no sector of the world economy did advances in computing have a more revolutionary effect than in finance. Here was a world peopled by smart, rich and intensely competitive players who were swimming in oceans of data. The trading desks rapidly moved beyond deploying computers merely to transact and record the growing volume of trades on the stock exchange. Traders mobilized computers to analyze data in order both to identify opportunities for profitable arbitrage and to create new instruments for trading, from swaps of currency and interest payments, to instantaneously updated stock indices, to asset-backed securities of all sorts, beginning with mortgages and extending to credit card receivables and student loans.

None of this profusion would have been imaginable, let alone possible to implement, without computers. Wall Street was the first commercial market that seized on the new, post-IBM architecture of distributed computing, arming its traders with high-performance workstations and networking them to databases that could both capture trades and provide the data to inform trading strategies. As I learned directly through OpenVision/VERITAS and then through BEA, Wall Street was *the* market for innovative IT. By making it possible to transform credit instruments that had traditionally been bought and held by lenders into tradable securities, computerization enabled the extension of the originate-and-distribute model from the equity

---

[18] G. Tett, *Fool's Gold: How the Bold Dream of a Small Tribe at J. P. Morgan was Corrupted by Wall Street Greed and Unleashed a Catastrophe* (New York: Free Press, 2009), chapters 3 and 4.

and bond markets across the entire spectrum of credit, even as it also offered the false promise of constructing insurance against loss.

Hyun Shin has provided a rigorous analysis of the construction of the financial catastrophe of 2008 that pulls together its contributing elements. Underwritten by the Greenspan Put and the offsetting contributions of the big state at each stage of cumulating stress, the banks could maintain their target levels of leverage through the bursting of each bubble and out the other side. When the market value of their equity again rose, it was reflected in their balance sheets and reduced the ratio of assets to capital below the targeted level. The resultant excess capital could be deployed in more lending to the nonfinancial sector, and indeed it was, as standards on residential mortgages fell to derisory levels. But, critically, when the supply of assets from the nonfinancial sector proved inadequate, the banks could lend to each other: taking in each other's washing, as it were, to push the assets of each back to the desired level. And the supply of assets from the financial sector – defined and rationalized by modern finance theory and produced through the application of IT – was literally limitless.[19] However, no possible increase in the cash flows of the market economy could validate the excessive structure of finance. A modest uptick in late payments on mortgages was all it took to trigger the end of the game.

The bursting of the super-bubble in 2008 has had grave consequences for economic performance and for political agendas across the developed world. Nowhere have the consequences been more extreme, however, than in the disciplines of economics and finance, separated from each other's interdependent embrace a long generation ago and now in process of recombining. For the financial crisis and its economic consequences have shattered the assumption that financial markets are necessarily efficient and that they will reliably generate prices for financial assets that are locked onto the fundamental value of the physical assets embedded in the nonfinancial, so-called real economy. If that assumption were correct, economics and finance could go their separate ways, confident that each could take the efficiency of the other for granted. Now that it has most dramatically been proven *not* to be correct, understanding the contingent interaction of financial capitalism and the market economy has become the central issue.

---

[19] Shin, *Risk and Liquidity*, pp. 111–125, 153–160.

Theoretical explanations

As we have seen, bubbles in the prices of financial assets are found everywhere, and the more those bubbles are leveraged by the extension of credit, the greater "the grand piano smash" (my mother's term) that must follow. But it is the emergence of the asset price bubble itself – the divergence of the market price of an asset from the discounted present value of the cash flows that accrue to the owner – that has challenged theorists. Until lately, it was necessary for the most part to rely on higher journalism and popular history to explore this subject: from Daniel Defoe's *Anatomy of Exchange Alley*, replete with tales and denunciations drawn from the South Sea Bubble, to Charles Mackay's *Extraordinary Popular Delusions and the Madness of Crowds*, and on to John Kenneth Galbraith's *The Great Crash* and John Brooks's *The Go-Go Years*.[20] The most comprehensive and insightful volume is Edward Chancellor's *Devil Take the Hindmost*, published in 1999 just as the dotcom/telecom bubble was adding another chapter to his history of financial speculation.[21]

All attempts to model equity bubbles in rigorous fashion must begin by standing up to the founding dogma of complete and efficient markets. To repeat, this asserts the prices of financial assets incorporate all relevant information and correspond to the fundamental economic value of the real assets they represent. Given the obvious lack of realism in its assumptions, the Efficient Market Hypothesis (EMH) came under early assault, notably by Sanford Grossman and Joseph Stiglitz's demonstration of "the impossibility of informationally efficient markets."[22] Just how vulnerable the EMH has become in its successively weaker forms is demonstrated by Hashem Pesaran, who rigorously explores the emergence of bubbles and crashes when the beliefs of heterogeneous investors converge at times of greater-than-normal

[20] D. Defoe, *The Anatomy of Exchange Alley; Or, a System of Stock-Jobbing* (Stamford, CT: Gale ECCO, 2010 [1719]); C. Mackay, *Extraordinary Popular Delusions and the Madness of Crowds* (Petersfield: Harriman House, 2009 [1841]); J. K. Galbraith, *The Great Crash, 1929* (New York: Houghton Mifflin, 1988 [1954]); J. Brooks, *The Go-Go Years: When Prices Went Topless* (New York: Ballantine, 1974).

[21] E. Chancellor, *Devil Take the Hindmost: A History of Financial Speculation* (New York: Penguin, 1999).

[22] S. J. Grossman and J. Stiglitz, "On the Impossibility of Informationally Efficient Markets," *American Economic Review*, 70(3) (1980), pp. 393–408.

occasion for hope of profit or fear of loss.[23] Perversely, however, the most unrealistic response to the undermining of EMH proved for a generation to be the most influential within the discipline. Through the Rational Expectations Hypothesis (REH), the assumptions necessary to conclude that financial markets behave as if they were complete and efficient are displaced from the world out there to the mind of the "rational representative agent." This agent is supposed not only to have access to all relevant information and the capacity to process it, but also to have a model of what that information means – what economic processes generate the information and what their future realizations will be – that happens to be true.[24]

The overriding justification for the mind games of EMH and REH are that – if we suspend our disbelief and accept their premises – the markets of the financial system will efficiently allocate capital across the competing alternative projects available in the real economy. So advocates of EMH and REH begin by denying the reality that only imperfect information is available to economic and financial actors in the world in which we are doomed to live.[25]

At an even deeper level, the pursuit of allocative efficiency as the core economic virtue blinds its acolytes to the dynamics of the Innovation Economy, where the waste generated by experimentation is essential to progress and tolerance of that waste is a prime condition for leadership at the frontier. For when economic growth over time is driven by unpredictable bursts of technological innovation that is speculatively financed, the allocation of resources to research and development at any moment in time is bound to appear inefficient in static economic terms. Conversely, any attempt to express the Innovation Economy's dynamics as an exercise in "intertemporal optimization" by rational agents operating in efficient markets will sacrifice relevance in pursuit

[23] H. Pesaran, "Predictability of Asset Returns and the Efficient Market Hypothesis," in A. Ullah and D. E. Giles (eds.), *Handbook of Empirical Economics and Finance* (Boca Raton, FL: Chapman and Hall/CRC, 2010), pp. 281–312.

[24] Robert E. Lucas Jr., the founding theorist of the doctrine, summarized the path to REH in his Nobel Prize lecture: "Nobel Lecture: Monetary Neutrality," *Journal of Political Economy*, 104(4) (1996), pp. 661–682. Available at www.nobelprize.org/nobel_prizes/economics/laureates/1995/lucas-lecture.pdf.

[25] R. Frydman and M. Goldberg, *Beyond Mechanical Markets: Asset Price Swings, Risk, and the Role of the State* (Princeton University Press, 2011), pp. 55–102.

of rigor. So Giovanni Dosi characterizes the New Growth Theory developed by Paul Romer, Philippe Aghion and others:

Innovation is endogenized into economic dynamics as either a learning externality or the outcome of purposeful expensive efforts by profit-maximizing agents. However, in the latter case the endogenization comes at ... a major price ... of reducing innovative activities to an *equilibrium* outcome of optimal intertemporal allocation of resources. Hence by doing that, one loses also the genuine Schumpeterian notion of innovation as a disequilibrium phenomenon – *at least as a transient.*[26]

The core vulnerability of both EMH and REH is the assertion that price as set in the equity markets equals fundamental value, defined as the net present value of expected cash flows to be generated by the physical asset that underlies the financial asset. Explaining swings in asset prices not associated with any evident change in the fundamentals has challenged theorists for a long generation. In 1982, Olivier Blanchard (now chief economist of the IMF) and Mark Watson circulated a paper that took the aberration seriously, "Bubbles, Rational Expectations and Financial Markets."[27] While they maintain the standard neoclassical assumption that the data-generating process somewhere out there in the "real economy" is stationary and that the fundamental value of the traded securities is known, they could not statistically disprove the deviation of observed share prices from the present value of expected cash flows to be distributed to investors throughout the life of the issuing firm.

Three years later, Jean Tirole published a neoclassical model in which bubbles serve to transfer goods from the young to the old and are well

---

[26] G. Dosi, *Further Essays on Economic Organization, Industrial Dynamics and Development* (Cheltenham: Edward Elgar, forthcoming), p. 7. Emphases in original. In their comprehensive survey of neoclassical growth theory, Aghion and his collaborator Peter Howitt explicitly consider the fundamental critique offered in A. Bannerjee and E. Duflo, "Growth Theory Through the Lens of Development Economics," in P. Aghion and S. N. Durlauf (eds.), *Handbook of Economic Growth* (Amsterdam: Elsevier North-Holland, 2005) before themselves noting the existence of "other important issues that either have been barely touched on or simply not addressed at all," such as "the impact of financial bubbles" and "the contribution of basic science and open research to growth." P. Aghion and P. Howitt, *The Economics of Growth* (Cambridge, MA: MIT Press, 2009), pp. 429–430 and 439–440.

[27] O. Blanchard and M. Watson, "Bubbles, Rational Expectations and Financial Markets," National Bureau of Economic Research Working Paper 945 (1982).

behaved: that is, the bubbles grow at the real rate of interest in his toy economy.[28] In the informal notes appended to his formal model, however, Tirole observes both that the "financial market fundamental" of an asset, as defined above, may differ from its "real market fundamental," its value in actual consumption, and that there may exist "ambiguity about the definition of the real market fundamental."[29] His conclusion – that bubbles are "not inconsistent with optimizing behavior and general equilibrium" – served as a sort of blessing on the ability of mainstream neoclassical theory to accommodate apparently deviant market behavior, masking a deep tension that persists below and behind the formal models.

Though neither Blanchard and Watson nor Tirole attempted to identify the sources of the discrepancy, over the past twenty years an increasingly rich literature has emerged with exactly that object in view.[30] In 1990, Brad DeLong, Andrei Shleifer, Lawrence Summers and Robert Waldmann published their challenge to efficient market orthodoxy – known ever since as DSSW – in the University of Chicago's *Journal of Political Economy.* "Noise Trader Risk in Financial Markets" demonstrated how random trading by ignorant "noise traders" (Philip Carret's "stock market gamblers") could so increase the risks facing definitionally rational "arbitrageurs" that the latter could not afford to bet against the former.[31]

Seven years later, Shleifer and Robert Vishny carried the argument a major step forward in their paper "The Limits of Arbitrage."[32] Not only do the rational arbitrageurs face noise traders who can move prices randomly, but they are dependent on investors who evaluate the quality of their investment managers – the arbitrageurs – by observing short-term performance. As prices deviate farther and farther from what the arbitrageur (somehow) "knows" is fundamental value, motivating the arbitrageur to increase her bets against the market, the more likely it is that investors will pull their funds out and force

[28] J. Tirole, "Asset Bubbles and Overlapping Generations," *Econometrica*, 53(5) (1985), pp. 1071–1100.
[29] *Ibid.* 1091–1092.
[30] See F. Allen, A. Babus and E. Carletti, "Financial Crises: Theory and Evidence," *Annual Review of Financial Economics*, 1 (2009), pp. 109–110.
[31] J. B. DeLong, A. Shleifer, L. Summers and R. Waldmann, "Noise Trader Risk in Financial Markets," *Journal of Political Economy*, 98(4) (1990), pp. 703–738.
[32] A. Shleifer and R. Vishny, "The Limits of Arbitrage," *Journal of Finance*, 52(1) (1997), pp. 32–55.

liquidation – just when the "rationally" expected returns are at their most attractive.

Shleifer and Vishny model the instance when the noise traders are inappropriately pessimistic and drive prices down. In such a case, the use of leverage by the arbitrageurs can only exacerbate the decline, since the fixed burden of debt must be liquidated as the value of the collateral held against it declines. The power of this mechanism is now being documented in a huge and growing body of work explicating the dynamics of the Crisis of 2008. But the limits of arbitrage apply equally on the upside. The crucial factor is how conditions on the right-hand side of the investor's balance sheet – the terms on which she has access to funding – dominate management of the left-hand side of her balance sheet. These are what determine how long she can fight the tape and afford to be wrong.

A dramatic demonstration in the real world of the inverse Shleifer–Vishny model is provided by the disparity in outcome for two great investors, Warren Buffett and Julian Robertson, when they declined to participate in the dotcom/telecom bubble. Buffett's funding base – the insurance premiums of Berkshire Hathaway – was and is self-renewing and thus effectively perpetual: he manages a closed-end fund. The only recourse for a dissatisfied investor is to sell or short the stock, and, indeed, Berkshire Hathaway radically underperformed the NASDAQ and actually declined during the final two years of the bubble. But, while the dogs barked, Warren Buffett's caravan passed by. In devastating contrast, investors in Julian Robertson's Tiger Group of hedge funds were subject only to the conventional three-month lock-up. The Tiger Group peaked in assets and performance in 1998. In recognition of his long record of superior performance, his investors gave Robertson the benefit of the doubt, waiting until the first quarter of 2000 before they forced him to close down and return their remaining capital, precisely at the moment when the Bubble passed through its apogee and burst.

Andy Haldane of the Bank of England has looked at the volatility of stock prices relative to retrospective measures of the relevant "discounted expected profit streams" and found that

on average over the past century, U.S. stock prices have been three times more volatile than fundamentals … But the trend in the degree of excess volatility is also telling. Up until the 1960s, prices were around twice as volatile as fundamentals. Since 1990, they have been anywhere from six to ten times more volatile. Excess volatility in equity prices has risen as financial innovation has taken off.[33]

A research program worth pursuing would address the relationship between the institutional transformation of the equity markets over the past two generations and their behavior. Josh Lerner and Peter Tufano have laid foundations for this research as they consider the significance of the development of the mutual fund industry. Between 1950, when the postwar boom in such funds had not yet begun, and 2008, mutual funds – marked to market daily in an intensely competitive and transparent marketplace – went from accounting for less than 1 percent of household assets in the United States to 10 percent, while direct holdings of stocks and bonds declined from slightly more than 50 percent to less than 30 percent.[34] Managers of mutual fund assets can afford to be wrong for only a limited time. Moreover, as a portion of all equity fund assets, index funds have risen from 4 percent in 1995 to almost 14 percent in 2009.[35] And index funds are contractually committed on a daily basis to tracking the movement of share prices, however volatile and extreme, thereby reducing the weight of countervailing, mean-reverting pressure in the market.

Once again, an innovation intended to extend the asserted efficiency of the equity market likely has contributed to the increased divergence between prices and values, however the latter are defined. Most recently, in a *reductio ad absurdum* of the privileging of transactional efficiency, computer-driven "high frequency trading" has come to dominate the volume of transactions on the equity markets. In pursuit of transient mis-pricing of securities relative to short-term trends and correlations with other security prices, computer algorithms are tuned to execute massive volumes of small orders to exploit apparent arbitrage opportunities while minimizing impact on price. What matters here is that

---

[33] A. Haldane, "Patience and Finance," paper presented to Oxford China Business Forum, Beijing, September 9, 2010, p. 15. www.bis.org/review/r100909e.pdf.

[34] J. Lerner and P. Tufano, "The Consequences of Financial Innovation: A Counterfactual Research Agenda," paper presented to a meeting of the Commission on Finance and Growth, Watson Institute for International Studies, Brown University, December 10, 2010, p. 30.

[35] Investment Company Institute, *2010 Investment Company Fact Book* (Washington, DC: Investment Company Institute), p. 33.

more than half of equity trading volume has come to reflect strategies that by definition and design include no reference whatsoever to the elusive fundamental value of the underlying economic asset.

Separate from the rational-bubble literature, a second major strand of theory has focused on the psychological traits of individuals to explain deviations from rational behavior as defined by the requirements of neoclassical theory. Daniel Kahneman and Amos Tversky received their Nobel Prize for the development of Prospect Theory, a tool for understanding how people evaluate – and typically favor – outcomes that are certain versus gambles that have an equal expected probabilistic value. Typically, subjects offered the choice between the certainty of receiving $1.00 and having a 50:50 probability of receiving $2.00 or nothing will opt for certainty. The quantity of expected value that a person will surrender in order to secure an outcome with certainty is precisely the measure of the person's risk aversion.[36] Perversely, neoclassical economists have seized on Prospect Theory to attribute the failure of the financial markets to behave as the models say they should to the stubborn determination of human beings to refuse to behave as theory would have them do.

More recently, a growing number of scholars have developed "models of speculative trading, driven by heterogeneous beliefs," as Princeton's José Scheinkman and Wei Xiong characterize this work.[37] Following the collapse of the dotcom/telecom bubble, I discovered the research program of Mordecai Kurz of Stanford, which he characterizes as "Rational Beliefs." Kurz rigorously demonstrates that many models of how the world works are consistent with the statistical track record: thus, conflicting views of price relative to value may be equally "rational," and the risk that one's model is wrong adds "endogenous uncertainty" to the volatility inherent in future realizations of the economic fundamentals.[38]

In complementary fashion, Scheinkman and Xiong demonstrate how "overconfidence creates disagreement among agents regarding asset fundamentals." Critically, in purchasing shares, each investor

[36] D. Kahneman and A. Tversky, "Prospect Theory: An Analysis of Decision under Risk," *Econometrica*, 47 (1979), pp. 263–291.

[37] J. Scheinkman and W. Xiong, "Advisors and Asset Prices: A Model of the Origins of Bubbles," *Journal of Financial Economics*, 89 (2008), pp. 268–287.

[38] See M. Kurz, "Rational Beliefs and Endogenous Uncertainty," *Economic Theory*, 8(3) (1996), pp. 383–397.

also acquires an implicit option to sell those shares to another, more confident investor: "Agents pay prices that exceed their own valuation of future dividends because they believe that in the future they will find an investor willing to pay even more."[39] In so doing they stimulate price increases and trading volume independent of any signal that the fundamentals have improved. Blanchard and Watson observed back in 1982 that this essentially Ponzi aspect of the bubble makes its demise inevitable, given that the supply of greater fools is finite.[40]

In 2007, Harrison Hong of Princeton and Jeremy Stein, who later served as president of the American Finance Association, explicitly advocated the use of disagreement models from within the mainstream of financial economics. Hong and Stein reached back through Kindleberger and Aliber to recapture the notion of overtrading, which classical economists from Adam Smith to John Stuart Mill had deployed to identify episodes when speculation provoked increased trading volume as buyers purchase commodities to realize capital gains from their resale, rather than for actual use in consumption or production.[41]

In my view, this behavioral-finance literature complements rather than contradicts the rational-bubble literature. The rational-bubble approach is useful because it shows that even adherence to the radical assumptions of REH cannot protect investors from the uncertainties of the real world: what is specified to be rational behavior by each individual itself generates the systemic phenomena of bubbles and crashes. On the other hand, the behavioral-finance approach needs to be extended into the world beyond the financial markets. I return to my first lesson in practical finance, about the process by which an objective analyst values a private company. The fundamental value of any company emerges from parallel exercises to mobilize necessarily incomplete information from the company's own historical financial results, from the market's valuation of problematically comparable companies, and from completed merger and acquisition transactions involving such companies. The degree of confidence with which one asserts the fundamental value will range along a spectrum that reaches

[39] J. Scheinkman and W. Xiong, "Overconfidence and Speculative Bubbles," *Journal of Political Economy*, 111(6) (2003), p. 1183.

[40] Blanchard and Watson, "Bubbles, Rational Expectations and Financial Markets," p. 8.

[41] Kindleberger and Aliber, *Manias, Panics and Crashes*, p. 30.

virtual ignorance when a start-up proposal to commercialize a novel technology is under consideration.

To the extent that embedded within both literatures is a residual faith in the touchstone of a knowable fundamental, it is missing the first reality of the equity markets. William Goldman, novelist and screenwriter, legendarily defined the law of Hollywood to be: "No one knows anything." The law of the equity markets is both softer and more complex: "No one knows enough, and everyone at some level knows that about herself and everyone else." Models of equity bubbles that privilege some set of investors as knowing more than any investor can know must be flawed.

Even more deeply irrelevant, however, are market models that begin by supposing the existence of a rational, representative agent. The capital markets are populated by a diversity of human beings with widely varying beliefs and degrees of confidence in their beliefs about possible future outcomes. The markets, after all, were invented to enable a range of participants to trade titles to assets with each other. And so the notion of a representative agent is incoherent, justifiable only by the fanciful belief that trading activity will costlessly converge to the fundamental value that, by hypothesis, the representative agent already knows.

The phenomenon that terminated the dotcom/telecom bubble in 2000 stands witness. From the third quarter of 1999, the value of total distributions by venture capital funds to their limited partners rose sharply, from $3.9 billion in the third quarter of 1999 to $10.7 billion in the fourth quarter of that year, then almost doubled again in the first quarter of 2000 to $21.1 billion. This was by far the largest realization by venture capital firms ever. At the same time, the ratio of stock distributions to cash distributions increased from 1.27 in the third quarter of 1999 to 2.91 in the fourth quarter of that year, then peaked at 3.93 in the first quarter of 2000. By distributing shares rather than selling them and distributing cash, the venture funds could mark the value of their realizations at the market price before the impact of incremental sales from the previously illiquid supply was felt.[42] Having been locked up, typically for six months, by the terms of their contracts

[42] M. D. McKenzie and W. H. Janeway, "Venture Capital Fund Performance and the IPO Market," Centre for Financial Analysis and Policy, University of Cambridge Working Paper 30 (2008), p. 39.

with the underwriters of the IPOs, venture capitalists were finally free to allow their limited partners to sell to the greater fools, and sell they did. But note: both generation and observation of this signal requires the existence of multiple traders in the market disagreeing with each other as to the relationship of price to value.

Shortly after the bubble burst, Eli Ofek and Matthew Richardson analyzed the "steep rise in the number of insider transactions" and drew the appropriate conclusion:

Towards the latter part of 1999 and particularly in spring 2000, there were a large number of investors – insiders, venture capitalists, institutions and sophisticated investors – who were free to sell their Internet shares (through the unwinding of their lockup agreements). To the extent that these investors did not have the same optimism about payoffs the existing investors had, their beliefs would get incorporated in stock prices. As the amount of potential selling increased, this new class of investors (whether pessimistic or agnostic) began to overwhelm the optimistic ones.[43]

The increase in trading volume at the peak of the bubble directly contradicts rational-bubble models that would see volume decline as prices deviate progressively farther from the supposedly known fundamental.

The shifting balance of diverse opinions and degrees of confidence, as revealed through price and volume data observable by all market participants, in turn feeds back to condition the opinion and confidence of each. This is the information externality that pervades the market, inducing successively more sophisticated applications of game theory to elucidate market behavior. Shin has captured the dual role played by the prices of financial assets. On the one hand, they represent imperfect reflections of expectations of fundamental values. But, on the other, they are signals to action for investors:

When the decision horizons of market participants are shortened due to short-term incentives, binding constraints, or other market imperfections, then short-term price fluctuations affect the interests of these market participants, and hence will influence their actions. There is then the possibility of a feedback loop, where anticipation of short-term price movements will

---

[43] E. Ofek and M. Richardson, "DotCom Mania: The Rise and Fall of Internet Stock Prices," *Journal of Finance*, 58(3) (2003), p. 1131.

induce market participants to act in such a way as to amplify these price movements.[44]

This is the phenomenon that George Soros, drawing on a lifetime of engagement with financial markets, has termed "reflexivity." And this is why, even when the fundamental is known, bubbles and crashes in asset prices are observed. Note the volatility of bond prices, where future cash flows are defined by explicit contract: prices of investment-grade bonds fluctuate, and term spreads and credit spreads move in and out, responding to different investors' expectations of the uncertain future, even while the payoffs remain known this side of default.[45]

All exercises in modeling the endogenous uncertainty native to financial markets and the decoupling of prices from any attempt to define value reprise the famous "beauty contest" that Keynes deployed in the *General Theory*:

Professional investment may be likened to those newspaper competitions in which the competitors have to pick out the six prettiest faces from a hundred photographs, the prize being awarded to the competitor whose choice most nearly corresponds to the average preferences of the competitors as a whole; so that each competitor has to pick, not those faces which he himself finds prettiest, but those which he thinks likeliest to catch the fancy of the other competitors, all of whom are looking at the problem from the same point of view. It is not a case of choosing those which, to the best of one's judgment, are really the prettiest, nor even those which average opinion genuinely thinks the prettiest. We have reached the third degree where we devote our intelligences to anticipating what average opinion expects the average opinion to be.[46]

In the same spirit, Andreas Park and Hamid Sabourian have shown how informed investors may be led by their observation of market action to abandon their own beliefs and choose to follow the herd or act against the crowd. As they do, they alternatively add to momentum or help market prices revert to the mean. In either case, their behavior is "rational" in that it is based on a calculus of expected value in

---

[44] Shin, *Risk and Liquidity*, p. 10.
[45] I owe this insight to José Scheinkman.
[46] J. M. Keynes, *The General Theory of Employment, Interest and Money*, in E. Johnson and D. Moggridge (eds.), *The Collected Writings of John Maynard Keynes*, vol. 7 (Cambridge University Press and Macmillan for the Royal Economic Society, 1976 [1936]), p. 156.

the relevant short run, as they weigh their own "private information" against the evidence generated by the market.[47]

Finally and fundamentally, in this term *rational* and in its antithesis there is a nexus of confusion that infects both academic and popular discussion of how economic and financial agents think and act. Much of this originated with the hijacking of the term by the theorists of REH. For, as Roman Frydman and Michael Goldberg have written:

> A rational, profit-seeking individual understands that the world around her will change in non-routine ways. She simply cannot afford to believe that, contrary to her experience, she has found a "true" over-arching forecasting strategy, let alone that everyone else has found it as well.[48]

But confusion is also created when the deployment of heuristics – rules of thumb that help investors make decisions under uncertainty – is branded as irrational. In the most basic terms, it seems inappropriate to call risk aversion irrational when over millions of years evolutionary pressures expressed Thomas Hobbes's vision of the human state: "worst of all, continual fear, and danger of violent death; and the life of man, solitary, poor, nasty, brutish, and short."[49]

Forty years of experience at the frontier where innovation meets the financial markets lead me to commend Frydman and Goldberg's effort to define a middle ground between the mechanical models of REH, on the one hand, and an anything-goes approach, on the other. Identification of qualitative signals for "guardedly moderate revisions" of forecasting strategies in light of new information is how prudent investors behave.[50] It corresponds to the "procedural rationality" that, a generation ago, Herbert Simon defined as the alternative to the utility-maximizing "substantive rationality" that had already come to render the neoclassical model "essentially tautological and irrefutable."[51]

[47] A. Park and H. Sabourian, "Herding and Contrarian Behavior in Financial Markets," *Econometrica*, 79(4) (2011), pp. 973–1026.

[48] R. Frydman and M. Goldberg, "The Imperfect Knowledge Imperative in Modern Macroeconomics and Finance Theory," in R. Frydman and E. Phelps (eds.), *Micro-Macro: Back to the Foundations* (Princeton University Press, forthcoming), p. 27.

[49] T. Hobbes, *Leviathan*, ed. R. Tuck (Cambridge University Press, 1993 [1664]), chapter 13.

[50] Frydman and Goldberg, "The Imperfect Knowledge Imperative," pp. 36–37.

[51] H. A. Simon, "Rationality in Psychology and Economics, Part 2: The Behavioral Foundations of Economic Theory," *Journal of Business*, 59(4)

Prudent, procedurally rational investors are forever trying to recognize whether the current regime in which stocks are trading is dominated by mean reversion or by momentum up or down, knowing that the longer one regime persists, the more surely it will shift to the alternative. The most creative theorists of finance and its most strategically oriented practitioners both recognize the pressing need for advancing a research program that begins with such facts of financial life instead of the misleading formalisms of EMH and REH.

As a contribution to the prospective exploration of these market environments, I find myself reverting to the original source of my interest in computing, conceived almost forty years ago. Imagine a virtual market populated, first, by a set of share-issuing companies, the predictability of whose operating results range from high (AT&T, 1970) to nil (early-stage IPO, anytime). Then add a set of investors who vary across two dimensions. The first is the degree to which each is able to evaluate the predictability of the various issuers' performance. The second is the degree of liquidity of the funding base, that is, the investor's relative ability to hold a position against the crowd. Then let the game begin.

In sum, Cassius was wrong. The fault is, indeed, in our stars. Born into a universe in which the Second Law of Thermodynamics holds and time's arrow moves in one direction only, we cannot run the equations backward. We spend half our time arguing about the meaning of a past that we have actually experienced, and the other half speculating about an infinite array of alternative futures. In this context, attributing market inefficiency to the irrationality of investors is fundamentally misfocused. Rather, let us say that by and large they – we – do the best we can. We deploy the heuristics that evolved from our survival in such a universe to evaluate the more or less misleading patterns discernible in history's unfolding tapestry as more or less inadequate guides to our behavior.

There is a certain heroic quality to the struggle of the new finance theorists to model the behavior of market participants who know that they cannot know enough and that they have only a limited time during which they will be allowed to be wrong, to stand out against the crowd. I am convinced that Keynes would honor their efforts, even

(1986), p. 222. Also see H. A. Simon, "Rationality as a Process and Product of Thought," *American Economic Review*, 68(2) (1978), pp. 1–16.

while pushing them to go further in accepting the ontological uncertainty inherent in the universe:

We should not conclude ... that everything depends on waves of irrational psychology. On the contrary, the state of long-term expectation is often steady, and, even when it is not, the other factors exert their compensating effects. We are merely reminding ourselves that human decisions affecting the future, whether personal or political or economic, cannot depend on strict mathematical expectation, since the basis for making such calculations do not exist; and that it is our innate urge to activity which makes the wheels go round, our rational selves choosing between the alternatives as best we are able, calculating where we can, but often falling back for our motive on whim or sentiment or chance.[52]

[52] Keynes, *General Theory*, pp. 162–163.

9   The necessity of bubbles

Why do bubbles matter, aside from the crashes that their excesses engender? They matter because they not only transfer wealth from greater to less-great fools, and to the knaves who prey on the former. Occasionally – critically – they transfer wealth to fortunate opportunists and insightful entrepreneurs in the market economy who are granted access to cash on favorable terms and put it to work with astounding consequences. Bubbles matter because, as Keynes put it so characteristically well,

The daily revaluations of the Stock Exchange … inevitably exert a decisive influence on the rate of current investment. For there is no sense in building a new enterprise at a cost greater than that at which a similar existing enterprise can be purchased; while there is an inducement to spend on a new project what may seem an extravagant sum, if it can be floated off on the Stock Exchange at an immediate profit. Thus certain classes of investment are governed by the average expectation of those who deal on the Stock Exchange as revealed in the price of shares, rather than by the genuine expectation of the professional entrepreneur.[1]

A generation later, James Tobin and William Brainard explicitly extended and operationalized Keynes's insight by defining the ratio q:

the ratio between two valuations of the same physical asset. One, the numerator, is the market valuation: the going price in the market for exchanging existing assets. The other, the denominator, is the replacement or reproduction cost: the price in the market for newly produced commodities.[2]

---

[1] J. M. Keynes, *The General Theory of Employment, Interest and Money*, in E. Johnson and D. Moggridge (eds.), *The Collected Writings of John Maynard Keynes*, vol. 7 (Cambridge University Press and Macmillan for the Royal Economic Society, 1976 [1936]), p. 151.

[2] J. Tobin and W. C. Brainard, "Asset Markets and the Cost of Capital," in R. Nelson and B. Balassa (eds.), *Economic Progress: Private Values and Public Policy, Essays in Honor of William Fellner* (Amsterdam: North-Holland, 1977), p. 235.

Tobin's q, as it has come to be known, quantifies the apparent arbitrage opportunity created by a disparity between the valuation of corporate assets in the financial markets and the cost of investing in new ones. In yet another instance of the informational inefficiency inherent in the financial markets, the continuous flux of such arbitrage opportunities offers the ability to beat the market with persistence to those who are tuned in, as Edward Chancellor has documented with respect to one London-based asset manager.[3]

Tobin's q may be greater than 1, if monopoly rents of a dominant firm are capitalized, or less than 1, when new technology renders existing assets obsolete. Either way, it quantifies in rough order the most crucial relation in the dynamics of the Innovation Economy: Keynes's bridge between speculation and enterprise. Thus it expresses the dimension of the Three-Player Game along which I have lived my life as a practitioner: the dimension played between financial capitalists and the market economy.[4]

Keynes's meditation on speculation versus enterprise stops short before he considers precisely those "classes of investment" for which no "genuine expectation" about the return can be well established, by the professional investor or by anyone else. Indeed, although it is true that "the energies and skill of the professional investor and speculator are mainly occupied ... not with making superior long-term forecasts of the probable yield of an investment over its whole life,"[5] from time to time they have been focused on investments with enormous economic significance, for they embody innovative, transformational technology. And it is these investments that are the most uncertain.

---

[3] E. Chancellor (ed.), *Capital Account: A Money Manager's Reports from a Turbulent Decade, 1993–2002* (New York: Thomson Texere, 2004), especially pp. 7–41.

[4] A demonstration of how far from reality neoclassical financial economics has evolved is that a working paper for the National Bureau of Economic Research published in January 2012 begins by asking: "How can one explain the attention devoted to secondary financial markets? Why does the press so frequently report the developments in the stock market? Can this be rationalized in a world where secondary market prices are passive ... in that they merely reflect expectations and do not affect them, as in many economic models, *including most of those used in the asset-pricing literature*?" P. Bond, A. Edmans and I. Goldstein, "The Real Effects of Financial Markets," National Bureau of Economic Research Working Paper 17719 (2012), p. 3; emphasis added.

[5] Keynes, *General Theory*, p. 154.

That is precisely why their deployment depends so often on the forces of speculation, not those of enterprise. Roman Frydman and Michael Goldberg put it nicely:

> In the vast majority of cases, the prospects of investment projects – the stream of future returns – cannot be understood in standard probabilistic terms ... This is obviously true for investments in innovative products and processes for which estimates of returns cannot be based solely on the profit history of existing products and processes.[6]

Academic rediscovery of Keynes's bridge

Following on the most recent world-class bubble in the financing of transformational technology, academic economists have finally awakened to the significance of Keynes's insight as applied to innovation. Three recent papers are indicative. The first, by George-Marios Angeletos and Guido Lorenzoni of MIT and Alessandro Pavan of Northwestern University, builds a theoretical link between the dynamics of the financial markets and the economics of technological innovation. The authors extend the mainstream paradigm to demonstrate how rational entrepreneurs and traders – all of whom know that they do not know enough – observe each other's behavior and construct "higher-order beliefs" to rationalize respectively their own overinvestment in physical assets and overpricing of the corresponding financial assets.[7] Angeletos, Lorenzoni and Pavan summarize their formal analysis of "the interaction between the real and the financial sectors of a[n] ... economy with dispersed information about the profitability of a new investment opportunity" thus:

> By conveying a positive signal about profitability, higher aggregate investment ... increases asset prices, which in turn raises the incentives to invest. This two-way feedback between real and financial activity makes economic decisions sensitive to higher-order expectations and amplifies the impact of noise on equilibrium outcomes. As a result, economic agents may behave *as if* they were engaged in a Keynesian "beauty contest" and the economy may

---

[6] R. Frydman and M. Goldberg, *Beyond Mechanical Markets: Asset Price Swings, Risk, and the Role of the State* (Princeton University Press, 2011), pp. 41–42.

[7] G.-M. Angeletos, G. Lorenzoni and A. Pavan, "Beauty Contests and Irrational Exuberances: A Neoclassical Approach," National Bureau of Economic Research Working Paper 15883 (2010).

exhibit fluctuations that may appear in the eyes of an external observer *as if* they were the product of "irrational exuberance." Importantly, these effects are symptoms of inefficiency, are driven purely by the dispersion of information, and obtain in an otherwise conventional neoclassical setting.[8]

One may suppose that the authors' repeated resort to the italicized *"as if"* and their insistence on the "conventional neoclassical setting" in which their "rational" agents operate are necessary acts of obeisance to the still dominant neoclassical gods. But their use of the phrase "dispersion of information" cannot conceal that they are, in fact, exploring the consequences of decisions made in the face of ontological uncertainty, the unavoidable circumstance at the core of Keynes's economics. The authors are all but transparent when they recognize explicitly that "the effects analyzed in this paper are likely to be stronger during periods of intense technological change, when the information about the profitability of new investment opportunities is likely to be highly dispersed."[9] Of course, the missing information is not "dispersed"; its bits and pieces are not scattered out there, available to be assembled and thereby render the market efficient. That information can be discovered only in retrospect, as a consequence of the decisions made in its absence by entrepreneurs and traders doing the best they can.

The two other papers are mirror images of each other. James R. Brown, Steven Fazzari and Bruce Petersen provide an empirical analysis of the dependence of young high-tech firms on access to external equity capital to fund research and development. Analyzing data from the decade 1994–2004, they tracked the correlation between the extraordinary increase in new equity issues for young firms and the growth in research and development (R&D) spending far above trend. They found that "the financial cycles for young high-tech firms alone can explain about 75 percent of the *aggregate* R&D boom and subsequent decline" associated with the tech bubble.[10] Here is a well-defined signal of the necessity of bubbles to finance extension of the frontier of innovation. These empirical findings confirm the characteristically insightful theoretical intuition of Joseph Stiglitz. Some fifteen years earlier, Stiglitz extended his exploration of the effects of information asymmetries to

---

[8] *Ibid.* 31–32; emphasis in original.   [9] *Ibid.* 32.
[10] J. R. Brown, S. M. Fazzari and B. C. Petersen, "Financing Innovation and Growth: Cash Flow, External Equity, and the 1990s R&D Boom," *Journal of Finance*, 64(1) (2009), p. 152; emphasis in original.

include "capital market imperfections," noting in particular how the riskiest corporate expenditures (those devoted to funding research and development) by the most vulnerable firms ("young" ones) are likely to be the most volatile: reduced disproportionately in economic downturns and increased disproportionately in booms.[11]

In counterpoint, Ramana Nanda and Matthew Rhodes-Kropf construct a theoretical model to explore the consequences of what they call "financing risk," the probability that innovative ventures will not be funded even in the absence of any adverse change in the "fundamental" estimated net present value of the project. In an appropriate (although implicit) invocation of Keynes's beauty contest, the authors model how early-stage venture capitalists evaluate the likelihood that others will fund later-stage rounds and carry the start-up to an IPO or acquisition by a strategic buyer. Despite the neoclassical baggage that requires that all forecasts must be correct in order to establish the necessary "rational equilibrium," they provide theoretical validation for the line-of-equity financing strategy that we at Warburg Pincus pragmatically invented. Only an investor with resources sufficient to fund an indefinite number of rounds can be certain to "break the No-Invest equilibrium" and enable a worthy venture to reach positive cash-flow or successful exit regardless of the capital market environment.[12] More generally,

very radically new technologies, such as railways, motor cars, internet or clean energy technologies ... may in fact need "hot" financial markets, where financing risk is extremely low and many investors are in the market, to help with the initial diffusion of such technologies.[13]

John Eatwell has neatly summarized the useful role bubbles can play in the equity markets. Considering how rational investors may be inhibited from funding major innovations by the challenge of scale, by their inability to capture positive externalities and by the very long-term nature of the potential returns, Eatwell writes:

[11] J. Stiglitz, "Endogenous Growth and Cycles," in Y. Shionnoya and M. Perlman (eds.), *Innovation in Technology, Industries and Institutions: Studies in Schumpeterian Perspectives* (Ann Arbor, MI: University of Michigan Press, 1994).

[12] R. Nanda and M. Rhodes-Kropf, "Financing Risk and Innovation," Harvard Business School Working Paper 11–013 (2011), p. 25.

[13] *Ibid.* 36.

The usefulness of bubbles derives from their effect in alleviating social inefficiencies that derive from rational individual actions. In other words, I suggest that, in the absence of bubbles, rational individual actions result in a socially irrational outcome, and that the bubble, by inducing irrational acts in individuals, may (and only, may) shift the economy toward a more socially rational position.[14]

That Eatwell plays with the loaded term *rational* should not obscure the positive, if messy, conclusion: bubbles can overcome a potential coordination failure to generate a new and more productive economy. The seemingly perverse opportunity to make money by speculating in risky financial assets regardless of the fate of the real investments so funded is – precisely – the vehicle of economic progress.

All of this work, theoretical and empirical, has been motivated by the great bubble of the late 1990s. But its significance transcends ad hoc explanation and rationalization of that singular event. These scholars are reconstructing the reciprocal interdependence of investment in financial and real assets, of financiers and entrepreneurs, of the financial system and the real economy. In their rediscovery of Keynes's economics at this fundamental level, whether acknowledged or not, they have demonstrated as much insight as those who have rediscovered the relevance of Keynes's macroeconomic policy response to the failure of private sector demand, and they will, I expect, have at least as much impact in the long run.

Financing new networks

A decade ago, at the turn of the millennium, I was living and working in the middle of the dotcom/telecom bubble, which was composed of two overlapping but quite distinct ingredients. First, like the nineteenth-century railroad booms and the electrification boom of the 1920s, the bubble funded the build-out of physical infrastructure to support the global deployment of the internet and the World Wide Web riding on top of it. Second, it funded an accelerated exploration – a quasi-Darwinian exercise in trial and error – to discover what to do with this new economic environment that, for the first time

---

[14] J. Eatwell, "Useful Bubbles," in J. Eatwell and M. Milgate (eds.), *The Fall and Rise of Keynesian Economics* (Oxford University Press, 2011), p. 88.

ever, integrated reciprocal flows of information and transactions over arbitrarily long distances and complex networks.

In the first of these aspects, there was a clear echo of previous waves of financial mania whose economic consequences had been the pioneering deployment of new networks: physical infrastructure to revolutionize transportation, communication and the distribution of electric power. The economic value of such networks is notoriously difficult to evaluate. One line of argument derives from Metcalfe's Law, which asserts that the value of a network grows proportionately with the square of the number of connected devices or users.[15] But a network's value is not only a function of the number of nodes. It is also a function of the uses to which the network is devoted, the applications that ride on it.

The transformational transportation networks – the turnpikes, canals and railroads of the eighteenth and nineteenth centuries – served as more efficient channels for the physical movement of goods and people between established centers of production and consumption. As links between densely populated nodes were completed, however, railways became engines of economic development, opening up new territories to settlement and simultaneously forcing the re-architecting of production and consumption across the entire domain served. With respect to the communications networks, the application of the telegraph may have been obvious, as a near-instantaneous means of transmitting abstracts of messages that were alternatively delivered slowly by post. Even so, the reduction it caused in the latency of communications revolutionized financial trading as the lag in reporting prices between geographically distant markets – first Chicago and New York, then New York and London – disappeared.

An informative uncertainty attended the initial deployment of telephony and wireless. In the case of the telephone, in an inversion of what would become its standard use for direct communication between individuals, the broadcast of entertainment to the home was an early application: by the first years of the 1890s, the Electrophone Company in London was offering concerts, opera, music hall variety and even church services by subscription; the entertainments were delivered

---

[15] See S. Simeonov, "Metcalfe's Law: More Misunderstood than Wrong?" *HighContrast* (blog) (July 26, 2006). http://blog.simeonov.com/2006/07/26.

to homes, hospitals and other venues via telephone.[16] Conversely, point-to-point communication by wireless telegraphy served as the principal application of radio communications until the introduction of public broadcasting after the First World War.

Electrification offers an even more relevant historical analogy to the past generation's revolution in information and communications technology. Joseph Nye explores at length the search over forty years for commercially rewarding applications of electric power: from municipal lighting and streetcars through the electrification of manufacturing to the proliferation of domestic appliances.[17] To an extent even greater than was the case with the growth of electrical grids, the deployment of the internet created a space of possible applications of a dimensionality that transcended simplistic analogies such as the information superhighway. It took the wastage of a bubble to fund the exploration that would yield Amazon and eBay and Google.

The commercial development of electricity presages that of information and communications technology. Each of these is a general-purpose technology (GPT) whose development and deployment demonstrates the nonlinear nature of the innovation process. Timothy Bresnehan offers a basic definition:

A GPT (1) is widely used, (2) is capable of ongoing technical improvement, and (3) enables innovation in application sectors (AS). The combination of assumptions (2) and (3) is called "innovation complementarities" (IC).

More precisely, IC means that innovations in the GPT raise the returns to innovation in each AS and *vice versa*.[18]

The key factor is the positive feedback between innovations in the core body of the GPT and the various domains of application – from residential lighting to manufacturing in the case of electricity, from supply-chain management to social media in the case of the internet. The consequence can be sustained innovation over an extended period of time as the GPT improves along multiple dimensions in response

---

[16] BBC News, "The 19th Century iPhone," May 17, 2010. http://news.bbc.co.uk/1/hi/technology/8668311.stm.

[17] J. Nye, *Electrifying America: Social Meanings of a New Technology* (Cambridge, MA: MIT Press, 1992), pp. 85–97, 111–132, 185–206, 238–277.

[18] T. Bresnehan, "General Purpose Technologies," in B. H. Hall and N. Rosenberg (eds.), *Handbook of the Economics of Innovation*, 2 vols. (Amsterdam: North-Holland, 2010), vol. 2, p. 764.

to demands from those engaged in discovering what it is good for. If the scope of the GPT is broad enough, "the relevant increasing returns also matter at the aggregate level."[19]

Given the radical uncertainty about future economic returns, two modes of financing have prevailed to fund the initial, pioneering construction of networks. Each of them is decoupled from the rational calculation of gain from the project over its economic life. One has been state investment in pursuit of national development or national security; the other, financial speculation. Bonds guaranteed by the State of New York funded DeWitt Clinton's Erie Canal in the 1820s, and the National Interstate and Defense Highways Act of 1956 launched the interstate highway system. Of course, the US Defense Department's ARPAnet was the precursor of the internet, whose extraordinarily robust packet-switching architecture was designed to survive thermonuclear war.

The manner in which France's railroad system was engineered had demonstrated long before that agents of the state can plan and implement the construction of a novel, transformational network infrastructure. The French system was from the beginning far more economically efficient in its layout of routes and in their construction than were the systems in Britain and the United States, where the alternative mode was dominant: recurrent bubbles of financial speculation financed uncoordinated projects that were haphazardly proposed and built by competing promoters.[20] But no matter how networks are deployed, discovering what they are economically good for requires the sort of trial-and-error experimentation that both feeds on and feeds speculation.

Within the dotcom/telecom bubble

In the midst of the whirlwind of the late 1990s, there was little time to reflect on the economic significance of the bubble in the long sweep of history. From that time, however, I can extract an illustrative example of the link between frenzy in the financial markets and real investment in physical assets, yet another narrative of contingency and chance at the interface of financial speculation and technological innovation.

---

[19] *Ibid.* 765.
[20] F. Dobbin, *Forging Industrial Policy: The United States, Britain and France in the Railway Age* (Cambridge University Press, 1994), pp. 25, 95–157.

Covad was a child of the Telecommunications Act of 1996, which required that the incumbent local telephone monopolies – the "Baby Bells" – open their central switching offices to accommodate new Competitive Local Exchange Carriers (CLECs). A year before, Netscape's IPO in August 1995 had heralded the promise of the internet as a new medium, potentially accessible to all. But physical access for more than the most constrained uses would be a function of the availability of high-speed, broadband data channels with capacity that would be multiples of that of the minimal and expensive dial-up connections allowed by "POTS," the plain old telephone service delivered by the Bells. While other start-ups, such as Level 3 and Global Crossing, set about laying fiber optic cables for broadband backbone networks in competition with AT&T and the other long-distance carriers, Covad was the first of a number of CLECs launched to deliver broadband access over the copper wires of the local loop.

Two members of our tech team at Warburg Pincus discovered Covad in the summer of 1997. Henry Kressel is among the most distinguished venture capitalists of his or any generation.[21] His role with respect to Covad was strikingly appropriate. By the early 1980s, Henry had already completed a successful career as a physicist, having risen to lead solid state research at RCA's Sarnoff Laboratories. There, he had been responsible for developing the reliable semiconductor lasers that, complemented by Corning's development of glass fiber technology, enabled fiber optic communications. Henry had uprooted himself professionally as he saw RCA lose its way in the early 1980s, had earned an MBA at Wharton and had joined Warburg Pincus. There he established an extraordinarily productive partnership with another Wharton alumnus a generation younger. Joe Landy carried the venture capitalist's equivalent of a field marshal's baton in his knapsack. Covad was among a succession of rewarding steps on Joe's path to becoming co-CEO of Warburg Pincus.

Before they met Covad, Henry and Joe had already collaborated on a relevant and successful start-up called Level One, yet another of those successful investments that needed to be restarted along the way. Level One's initial launch had taken place before I joined Warburg

---

[21] Henry documents his experience of the three investments discussed below in H. Kressel and T. V. Lento, *Investing in Dynamic Markets: Venture Capital in the Digital Age* (Cambridge University Press, 2010), pp. 113–121, 143–148.

Pincus, when Henry and Joe led the firm to follow some marginal venture capitalists in backing a former Sarnoff colleague of Henry's named Bob Pepper. The first effort to design specialized semiconductor devices for digital data communications had failed when IBM acquired and effectively smothered Level One's initial customer. Unusually for Warburg Pincus, but in a way all too familiar to me, we were in the back seat of the car as it headed over the cliff and into bankruptcy and liquidation.

Pepper and Henry were convinced that the company's core technology could be repurposed into a nascent but promising application known as Digital Subscriber Line (DSL), which could deliver broadband access for the "last mile" over the copper wires that connected the phone company's central office to the home. Exploiting that opportunity, as usual, required new money to buy the necessary time to reposition the venture: Cash, that is, could be effectively deployed only if it purchased Control. And that, in turn, required that the other investors get out of the way. With some encouragement from me, Henry and Joe supported Pepper in a successful game of chicken with his original investors, and Level One was relaunched. By the summer of 1997, the company had both achieved a position of leadership in its new market and had uniquely equipped Henry and Joe to appreciate the technical feasibility of what Covad proposed to do.

The only cash investment Warburg Pincus ever made in Covad was $6 million to lead its first round. The goal was to prove the technology and the market demand in the San Francisco Bay Area and then, stepwise, to expand geographically, securing funding at progressively lower cost as the model was proved out in emulation of the successful deployment of cable television and wireless telephony. The initial application was supposed to be telecommuting so employees in the new knowledge economy could work from home.

But any such mundane consideration of what economic activity the new technology would support swiftly became irrelevant. Less than nine months after our investment, Bear Stearns approached us with a proposal to sell $300 million of junk bonds to enable full-bore acceleration of the plan – this for a company that in 1997 recorded just $26,000 (that is correct: twenty-six thousand dollars) of revenue. All that was required was a promise by Warburg Pincus to inject additional equity in twelve months if the company had not raised it away from us. Together with the common stock warrants that we received as payment for the promise, Warburg Pincus owned about 20 percent of Covad when it went public in January 1999. In a year and half, this raw start-up raised half a billion dollars of financial capital and had a market value of some $5 billion. Of course, this was one small component of the estimated $4 trillion of equity and debt raised and invested in broadband networks – backbone and local access – by start-ups and incumbents before the bubble burst.

Covad did indeed burst with the bubble, passing through Chapter 11 bankruptcy on its way to a renewed, post-bubble life. By then, however, Warburg Pincus had been the contingent beneficiary of Henry and Joe's discovery of another, even more compelling investment opportunity generated by the Telecommunications Act of 1996. Lockheed Martin was the source. One of its systems development units had won the contract to deliver the local-number portability mandated by the Act. This was a critical condition of competition in communications services, as it would allow customers to switch local carriers without having to change their telephone numbers. But the technical requirements were fearsome: specifically, the system would have to be able to change the relevant database in every single central office in North America in order to complete each transaction, or roll back all the changes made if any were not completed. The provider of such a system would own an exclusive franchise and would be responsible for managing the North American Numbering Plan, the foundation of telephone service in the United States and Canada.

Having demonstrated its ability to execute the demanding specifications, Lockheed Martin proceeded to compromise its ownership of the contract. Strict neutrality among the growing horde of competing carriers, legacy and new, was an absolute requirement. But Lockheed Martin had separately decided to buy the communications satellite company ComSat, a common carrier, and therefore had to divest itself of its no-longer-neutral business unit.

Joe and Henry engaged in a yearlong process, the first half of which involved negotiations of the terms and conditions of our purchase from Lockheed Martin and the latter half negotiations with the Federal Communications Commission to confirm *our* neutrality as an owner of what was to be called – cutely – "Neustar." It was necessary to establish a firewall of independent trustee-directors to ensure Neustar's autonomy. In a consequence both fortuitous and fortunate, our new investment required and rationalized acceleration of the liquidation of our investment in Covad, a process that had begun in the summer of 1999. Since Henry and Joe had been required to leave Covad's board, a rapid series of distributions and public sales of shares was not inhibited by any taint of insider information. Altogether, thanks to Neustar, our thirty-month engagement with Covad was completed in December 1999, with more than a year to spare before the bubble burst. And so a $6 million investment resulted in proceeds of just over $1 billion. In its turn, our $77 million investment in Neustar's much more robust and defensible business carried beyond the bubble and generated its own $1 billion return some five years later.

Waves of innovation

Covad exemplified the most obvious economic consequence of the bubble of 1999–2000: the deployment of network infrastructure on a scale not rationally imaginable by any investor other than the state, which had turned the internet over to private enterprise precisely to shift responsibility for its financing and for exploration of its potential uses. It thus carried forward a line of comparable exercises that began with the double wave of Britain's Canal Mania, first in the 1770s and again in the 1790s.

By the late eighteenth century, England's economy was generating a sufficient financial surplus and its capital markets were sufficiently mature to enable the private financing of the canals and the turnpikes that constituted the new transportation network literally underlying the First Industrial Revolution. The only legislation required was to endow the "projectors" with needed powers of eminent domain. Financing was so forthcoming that by 1824 more than sixty canal companies had been created, disposing of more than £12 million of capital.[22] By contrast, in the United States, as with DeWitt Clinton's pioneering Erie Canal,

the new canal systems of Pennsylvania, Maryland, Virginia and Ohio were financed almost wholly by the states and the port cities ... Only a government had the credit rating needed to raise the required funds; for their ability to pay interest on their bonds was based on the power to tax, as opposed

[22] C. Haacke, *Frenzy: Bubbles, Busts and How to Come Out Ahead* (New York: Palgrave Macmillan, 2004), p. 18

to private companies, which depended merely on anticipated profits from providing rights-of-way.[23]

But to finance the second network of innovative transportation infrastructure, the United States emulated Great Britain to the extent that it could, while supplementing speculative private finance with state subsidies.

The installation of the railways in Britain also came in two principal waves. The first, the "little" Railway Mania of the 1830s, is distinctive not only because it demonstrated the technical feasibility of the technology that, more than any other, would enable the new economy of the latter nineteenth century. Also, for once, a financial bubble was validated by the economic returns from the projects it financed. As Andrew Odlyzko has shown, speculative commitments in 1835–1836 led to real investments in railway construction that approximated 2 percent of gross domestic product in each of 1838 and 1839.[24] The part-paid structure of share subscriptions deferred the flow of financing to match expenditure on construction: typically, a £2 deposit on a £50 share underwrote application for parliamentary approval. If such sanction were received, investors would receive repeated calls, to be met on pain of sacrifice of the shares (not unlike the case with commitments to a venture capital fund today). It was not at all unusual for cost overruns to exceed the initial nominal amount of committed capital, requiring follow-on rights issues.

In the case of the first Railway Mania, construction and capital calls proceeded through the economic depression at the end of the 1830s, with the market price of shares often falling well below book value. However, Odlyzko provides examples of projects whose investors came out ahead, notably four of the most prominent lines: the London and South Western, the Liverpool and Manchester, the Grand Junction, and the London and Birmingham. Beyond the financial rewards, of the

---

[23] A. D. Chandler, *The Visible Hand: The Managerial Revolution in American Business* (Cambridge, MA: Harvard University Press; Belknap Press, 1977), p. 34.

[24] A. Odlyzko, "This Time is Different: An Example of a Giant, Wildly Speculative, and Successful Investment Mania" (2010). Available at www.dtc. umn.edu/~odlyzko/doc/mania01.pdf.

2,200 miles of railways approved by Parliament during the mania, no fewer than 2,000 were in service by 1843.[25]

This success was the basis for the second wave of Railway Mania. As *The Economist* recorded in 1848:

Prior to the commencement of the recent railway mania in 1844 this species of property had acquired a reputation for security and profit greater than any other similar speculations which had preceded them: while nearly every other class of joint stock speculations from 1824 downward, in which the accumulating capital of the country had been invested, had ended in ruin to the parties engaged, railways, as they then existed, appeared to promise a permanent security for very large dividends.[26]

Compared with the mere 2,000 miles of railways in service in 1843, some 12,000 additional miles were approved by Parliament in 1844–1848, entailing planned investment of some £100 million per year in an economy whose aggregate annual income has been estimated at perhaps £600 million. Actual investments averaged only £33 million in the late 1840s, and returns fell far short of expectations: construction costs were typically 50 percent above plan, operating expenses ran at 50 percent of revenues rather than the forecast 40 percent, and revenues themselves were 30–40 percent below projections.[27] An index of railway shares that peaked at 168 in July 1845 collapsed to 60 in October 1849.[28]

In the United States, the railroad boom that began in the late 1840s likewise consumed capital on an unprecedented scale. Compared with the $188 million invested in canals from 1815 to 1860, 73 percent of which was supplied by state and local governments, by 1859, Chandler reports, "The investment in the securities of private railroad corporations had passed the $1,100 million mark; and of this amount $700 million had been raised in the previous ten years."[29] Capital on this scale "could no longer be raised … from farmers, merchants and manufacturers living along the line of the road." By the start of the Civil War, New York had emerged as the centralizing financial node through

---

[25] A. Odlyzko, "Collective Hallucinations and Inefficient Markets: The British Railway Mania of the 1840s" (2010). Available at www.dtc.umn.edu/~odlyzko/doc/hallucinations.pdf.

[26] Quoted *ibid*. 73.   [27] *Ibid*. 76–78, 94–95.

[28] *Ibid*. table 3 (pp. 7 and 77).   [29] Chandler, *The Visible Hand*, p. 90.

which capital from Europe flowed to the burgeoning array of railroad projects. The explosion in railway securities during the 1850s

brought trading and speculation on the New York Stock Exchange in its modern form ... The new volume of business brought modern speculative techniques to the buying and selling of securities. Traders sold "long" and "short" for future delivery. The use of puts and calls was perfected. Trading came to be done on margin. Indeed, the modern call loan market began in the 1850s, as New York banks began to loan [*sic*] to speculators ... In the 1850s skillful securities manipulators were becoming nationally known figures. Jacob Barker, Daniel Drew, Jim Fiske, and Jay Gould all made their dubious reputations by dealing in railroad securities.[30]

The Crash of 1857 ended the speculation, but by the start of the Civil War, the United States had more than 30,000 miles of track in service, compared to 9,000 miles a decade earlier.[31]

Chandler explores in detail the interaction of speculators, investors and managers that determined the course of the American railroad industry. As in all industries characterized by high fixed costs – represented by the interest and repayments required to service the debt that financed construction – and marginal costs approaching zero, competition among railroads was inherently unstable this side of monopoly or cartel. Exactly the same dynamics would dominate the commercial airline industry before and after the fare-setting authority of the Civil Aeronautics Board was first established and then abolished, and the telecommunications industry, before and after the three generations of stabilization delivered by AT&T's legislated monopoly.

While the managers and investors sought good-faith agreements to limit competition, "it was ... the speculators who shattered the old strategies ... were the first to disrupt the existing alliances ... [and] precipitated system-building in American transportation." The second great wave of American railway construction, driven by the search for scale by the competing systems and funded by enormous speculation, came in the 1880s: "75,000 miles of track [were] laid down, ... by far the greatest amount of railway mileage ever built in any decade in any part of the world." No fewer than five trunk lines ran between Chicago and New York, ensuring that none could make money. And between 1894 and 1898 foreclosure sales alone aggregated over

[30] *Ibid.* 92.   [31] See www.answers.com/railroads.

40,000 miles of track, with a capitalization of over \$2.5 billion, "the most massive set of receiverships in American history."[32]

As the investment bankers led by J. P. Morgan set about cleaning up the financial mess and rationalizing the economics of the industry, in the country at large a new economy had definitively arrived. Brad DeLong, economist at Berkeley, captured the essence of the case and linked it to the most recent equivalent experience in a casual note published in *Wired* magazine (a bible of the NASDAQ bubble that has managed to survive) in April 2003, just three years after the bubble's peak. "Let us now praise famous men, the wild-eyed enthusiasts who begat the bubble-boom," DeLong begins.

Today's party line is that the gold rush brought both pain and gain. Fortunes were poured into over-flowing snake pits of fiber-optic cables which, like Web-ordered groceries, proved to be profit-free zones ... On the flip side, public markets paid for a build-out of the network infrastructure, and burn rates pushed the envelope of the culture.

In fact, history will look back and see gain and gain ... British investors in the U.S. railroads during the late 19th century got their pockets picked twice: first as waves of over-enthusiasm led to over-building, ruinous competition and unbelievable (for that time) burn rates, and second as sharp financial operators stripped investors of control and ownership during bankruptcy workouts. Yet Americans and the American economy benefited enormously from the resulting network of railroad tracks ... For a curious thing happened as railroad bankruptcies and price wars put steady downward pressure on shipping prices and slashed rail freight and passenger rates ... New industries sprang up.[33]

DeLong identifies the iconic example of the transformational business innovation – the "killer app" that exemplified the economic significance of the railroads – in the mail order businesses of Montgomery Ward and Sears Roebuck:

Mail a catalog to every household in the country. Offer them big-city goods at near big-city discounts. Rake in the money from satisfied customers. For two generations this business model – call it the "railroad services" business model – was a license to print money, made possible only by the gross over-building of railroads, the resulting collapse of freight rates, and the fact that railroad investors had to kiss nearly all their money good-bye.

---

[32] Chandler, *The Visible Hand*, p. 171.
[33] J. B. DeLong, "Profits of Doom," *Wired*, 11(4) (April 2003).

Even as Amazon and eBay were demonstrating their post-bubble momentum and even before Google's IPO, DeLong correctly anticipated the rhyming of history: "The same thing will happen with the froth that the bubble put on our 1990s boom. Investors lost their money. We will now get to use their stuff."[34]

Despite the evident transformation they wrought, the economic significance of the great railroad booms has been a subject of controversy among economic historians for more than forty years, ever since Robert Fogel's pioneering exercise in cliometrics, the application of econometrics to historical data.[35] Fogel's purpose was to extract the US railroad network from the statistical economy of 1890 in order to calculate the "social saving," or incremental reduction in transportation costs, that the railroads provided versus the hypothetical alternative of extended canals and improved roads. His debunking conclusion was that the benefit of lower costs attributable to the interregional railroads amounted only to some 0.6 percent of 1890 national income: "The absence of the interregional railroads would have retarded the development of the economy by about three months."[36] The intraregional social saving was modestly more significant, 1.8 percent to 2.5 percent of national income.[37] To take account of the impact of railroad construction on the nation's manufacturing industries, Fogel calculates the "value added in manufacturing attributable to railroad consumption of manufactured goods" at no more than 4 percent in 1859, the end of the first wave of construction, and notes that "in the absence of the railroads there would have been a considerable increase in the consumption of wagon and water services."[38]

Fogel gives the game away stealthily in an extended footnote:

The treatment of the differential in transportation costs as a differential in levels of national income is based on the assumption that there would have been no obstacle to a non-rail situation. More specifically, it is based on the assumption that national income would have fallen *only* because more productive resources were required to provide a given amount of transportation services and *that all productive resources not used in transportation would have remained fully employed.*[39]

[34] *Ibid.*
[35] R. Fogel, *Railroads and American Economic Growth: Essays in Econometric History* (Baltimore, MD: Johns Hopkins Press, 1964).
[36] *Ibid.* 46–47.   [37] *Ibid.* 84–85.
[38] *Ibid.* table 14.2 (p. 145).   [39] *Ibid.* 21 n. 10; emphasis added.

This bedrock, neoclassical presumption both underlies and undermines Fogel's entire approach. It is what mandates him, in another footnote, to dismiss "Keynesian issues of insufficient demand" from consideration.[40] Yet in the peak years of the first US railroad boom, during the mid-1850s, expenditures on the construction of railroads amounted to approximately $100 million per year, or some 20 percent of all capital formation in the United States, on the order of 3 percent of estimated gross national product.[41] In contemporary terms, this is greater than the annual expenditures under the American Recovery and Reinvestment Act of 2009, the stimulus program enacted in the first year of the Obama Administration that put a floor under the Great Recession. A grace note to the inappropriateness of Fogel's abstraction from the macroeconomic consequences of the railroad boom and bust is this: the economic aftermath of the Crash of 1857 is what induced Stephen Foster to write his classic dirge, "Hard Times Come Again No More."

DeLong caricatures and Chandler documents in detail the economic transformation that the railroads engendered in the United States, transcending their direct macroeconomic effect. They drove the westward movement of population and property development, the re-architecting of industrial organization, the evolution of accounting practice and principles, the emergence of nationally branded goods, and the creation of liquid exchanges for securities – in short, they transformed the core commercial and industrial and financial structures of the nation. To focus only on the marginal cost of transporting commodities as the measure of the railroad's economic significance does not trivialize Fogel's heroic efforts at data collection and analysis. Rather, it exposes the irrelevance of the framing neoclassical economic theory that specifies the problem Fogel addresses.

Of the new and expanded industries that accompanied the build-out and consolidation of the railroads, none required capital on the scale of the railroads or was as dependent on financial speculation. The telegraph system largely followed and was partly funded by the railroads, and local capital did the rest, as it did for the host of local telephone

---

[40] *Ibid.* 47 n. 58.

[41] Historical Statistics of the United States Millennium Edition Online, tables Df865–873, "Railroad Investment by Region: 1828–1860" and Ca219–232, "Gross National Product: 1834–1859 (Gallman)." Available at http://hsus.cambridge.org/HSUSWeb/index.do.

companies that sprang up in the last two decades of the nineteenth century. The Boston railroad financiers who funded the organization of the American Bell Company in 1880 eventually did have to turn to J. P. Morgan and Wall Street for capital, obtaining $100 million even as the financial crisis of 1907 pushed the banking system almost to collapse, hardly a time of speculative excess.[42] The iconic manufacturing and distribution companies of the new economy that emerged from the Second Industrial Revolution, in turn, relied on local businesspeople and commercial banks for both short-term and long-term loans. None, however, needed to go to the capital markets to finance the expansion that so quickly placed them among the largest business enterprises in the world.[43]

Nonetheless, the evolution of the US capital market that made it a welcome venue for the industrial and utility issues of the trust bubble at the start of the twentieth century proved its value to the Innovation Economy in the gathering boom of the 1920s. In this, Wall Street represents the mirror image of the City of London, the latter immunized against investing in technological innovation by the Brush Boom and the automobile financing frauds of the previous generation. Even before US entry into the First World War, nineteen new auto companies went public in 1915–1917 during a stock boom that raised $100 million in some fifty new issues. Thirteen of them had died by 1924, but one of the survivors was Chevrolet. In the two years that followed the motor stock boom, the market for securities in the United States was vastly expanded by the Wilson administration's mobilization of Wall Street and Hollywood to market war bonds to the mass public.[44]

The stock market's continued interest in funding the iconic industry of the age of mass production was illustrated by the repeated efforts in 1924 by the then leading brokerage firm of Hornblower & Weeks to convince Henry Ford to sell out in exchange for $1 billion in cash, to be financed by public market issues. Even without what would have been the largest industrial financing deal of the age, Mary O'Sullivan calculates, corporate stock issues in the late 1920s represented by far the greatest amount, proportionate to national income, ever: they reached

---

[42] Chandler, *The Visible Hand*, pp. 199–201.   [43] Ibid. 298.

[44] M. O'Sullivan, "Funding New Industries: A Historical Perspective on the Financing Role of the US Stock Market in the Twentieth Century," in N. R. Lamoreaux and K. L. Sokoloff (eds.), *Financing Innovation in the United States: 1870 to Present* (Cambridge, MA: MIT Press, 2007), pp. 198–199.

about 7 percent of national income in 1929, whereas even at the peak of the NASDAQ bubble, they amounted to barely 1.5 percent, slightly above the mean for the entire period from 1897.

During the 1920s, the public equity and debt markets played the critical role in funding the build-out of the systems that delivered electricity to industry and to households, regionally and at length nationally. The public utility holding companies, initially created to transfer technical expertise to local generating and distribution companies, evolved into vehicles for providing the necessary finance for an industry whose capital intensity rivaled that of the railroads.[45]

The dominant *economic* fact of the electric utility industry, determined by technology, was extreme capital intensity. This had two major implications. First, the industry had high fixed costs that had to be met in order for a utility to be profitable, and relatively low operating or variable costs ... A substantial amount of capital had to be raised before any electricity could be produced.

A second economic effect ... was that production was subject to significant economies of scale ... This meant that for most relevant output levels, marginal costs were below average costs ... If firms set a price equal to marginal cost (the point to which competition would drive prices under "normal" circumstances), they would be making economic losses.[46]

So electrification evolved through a dynamic feedback process that delivered both speculative capital and governmental regulation, generally at the state and local levels, the latter invoked to protect the prospective returns on the former. Once again, a collaborative game between the state and the market economy created an opportunity for financial capitalism. As the level of electrification for manufacturing industry and (nonrural) residential uses passed 50 percent in the early 1920s, consolidation of the industry into regional and even national holding companies was enabled by a frenzy on Wall Street terminated only by the Crash of 1929.[47] Before the frenzy ended, installed generating capacity in the United States had risen from 13 million to 33 million kilowatts.[48]

---

[45] Chandler, *The Visible Hand*, p. 393.
[46] W. J. Hausman, *The Historical Antecedents of Restructuring: Mergers and Concentration in the US Electric Utility Industry, 1879–1935*, report prepared for the American Power Association (1937), pp. 2–3.
[47] *Ibid*. 7.   [48] *Ibid*. fig. 8 (p. 42).

Two additional new industries were midwived by the stock market in the 1920s. Charles Lindbergh's flight in May 1927 ignited a speculative frenzy for aviation-related shares. Wright Aeronautical was the only publicly traded aviation company at the time. Its shares traded from 25 in April 1927 to 94¾ by the end of 1927. From mid-1928 through mid-1930, no fewer than 124 public issues raised $300 million, of which more than half had been raised prior to the Crash of 1929.[49]

Finally, to return to the source of my abiding sensitivity to the emergence of a bubble: radio is a classic example of the Three-Player Game in action. The pioneers of wireless technology on both sides of the Atlantic had found sufficient funding from angel investors. It was the discovery in 1920 of the "killer app" for wireless communications – broadcast entertainment – that triggered speculative interest, a development that was accompanied by the creation of RCA, under the direct sponsorship of the US Navy and War Departments, to pool ownership of the patents held by American Marconi, General Electric, AT&T and Westinghouse. Through early 1925, new companies and new offerings proliferated, some 258 in 1925 alone, the most prominent of which traded on the Curb Exchange. The inevitable collapse took radio stocks, excluding RCA, down by 92 percent from December 1924 to May 1926. Thereafter, RCA's successful enforcement of its patents limited new entry, but its own soaring stock price, from (split-adjusted) 7 at the bottom of the correction to 103 just before the Crash, induced a second wave of entrants beginning in March 1928.[50]

Notwithstanding the long hiatus of financial capitalism through the Depression, the Second World War and the immediate postwar period, by 1929 the American public equity markets had already evolved into the engine for

turning long-term financing into assets that could be realized through sale on the market at short notice ... Thus, through the magic of financial intermediation by investment banks, the productive sector received permanent equity financing while investors believed they had liquid assets.[51]

[49] O'Sullivan, "Funding New Industries," pp. 186–187.
[50] *Ibid*. 173–174.
[51] J. Kregel, "Financial Experimentation, Technological Paradigm Revolutions and Financial Crises," in W. Drechsler, R. Kattel and E. S. Reinert, *Techno-Economic Paradigms: Essays in Honour of Carlota Perez* (London: Anthem, 2009), p. 208.

When the post-Second World War golden age of broad-based economic growth unfolded under the new regime of big-state capitalism, the equity markets responded. They would be there to finance commercialization of the digital technologies spawned by the American military in its role as investor in research and lead consumer of digital products.

Speculation and innovation: an explanatory schema

This chronicle of the interdependence between epochal waves of financial speculation and the deployment of innovative technological infrastructure whose economic significance reveals itself only over decades invites construction of a systematic, explanatory narrative. I began my own search for such a narrative in 2000, as my generation's bubble was reaching its apotheosis. I had recognized that the literature on technology and technology-driven industrial development was much farther along than the literature on how that evolution had been financed. In response, I initiated a research project sponsored by the Social Science Research Council and led by two distinguished economic historians, Naomi Lamoreaux and the late Ken Sokoloff, whose output was a range of case studies, published in 2007 as *Financing Innovation in the United States, 1870 to the Present.*[52] In parallel, in 2003 I discovered the work of Carlota Perez and her book *Technological Revolutions and Financial Capital: The Dynamics of Bubbles and Golden Ages.*[53] In an appropriately recursive movement, that discovery was a function of Amazon's ability to work out that I would be interested in a book with such a title.

Perez applies her schema to five successive technological revolutions, as laid out in Table 9.1. In each case, the technological revolution begins with an "installation" period that climaxes in a frenzy of speculation, which is followed by a crash and an extended turning point, as that which was once innovative – even revolutionary – and not amenable to rational calculus becomes recognized as routine. Finally, the technology's deployment constitutes the construction of a previously unimaginable new economy. Figure 9.1 illustrates the process.

[52] N. R. Lamoreaux and K. L. Sokoloff (eds.), *Financing Innovation in the United States, 1870 to the Present* (Cambridge, MA: MIT Press, 2007).
[53] C. Perez, *Technological Revolutions and Financial Capital: The Dynamics of Bubbles and Golden Ages* (Cheltenham: Edward Elgar, 2002).

Table 9.1. *Five successive technological revolutions, 1770s–2000s*

Technological revolution	Popular name for the period	Core country or countries	Big bang initiating the revolution	Year
First	Industrial Revolution	Britain	Arkwright's mill opens in Cromford	1771
Second	Age of Steam and Railways	Britain, then spreading to Europe and the United States	Test of the "Rocket" steam engine for the Liverpool and Manchester Railway	1829
Third	Age of Steel, Electricity and Heavy Engineering	United States and Germany forging ahead and overtaking Britain	The Carnegie Bessemer steel plant opens in Pittsburgh, Pennsylvania	1875
Fourth	Age of Oil, the Automobile and Mass Production	United States at first vying with Germany for world leadership, later spreading to Europe	First Model T comes out of the Ford plant in Detroit, Michigan	1908
Fifth	Age of Information and Telecommunications	United States, then spreading to Europe and Asia	The Intel microprocessor is announced in Santa Clara, California	1971

Source: C. Perez, *Technological Revolutions and Financial Capital: The Dynamics of Bubbles and Golden Ages* (Cheltenham: Edward Elgar, 2002), table 2.1 (p. 11).

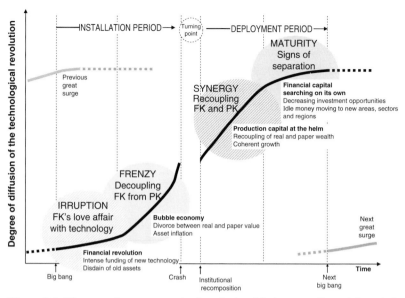

Figure 9.1 The recurring sequence in the relationship between financial capital (FK) and production capital (PK)

Source: Adapted from C. Perez, *Technological Revolutions and Financial Capital: The Dynamics of Bubbles and Golden Ages* (Cheltenham: Edward Elgar, 2002), fig. 4.1 (p. 37).

Throughout her analysis, Perez distinguishes financial capital, the agent of speculation in Keynes's formulation, from production capital, which is embedded in Keynes's "enterprise." Thus, in her explicitly neo-Schumpeterian characterization of the recurrent waves of creative destruction, Perez too has revitalized the approach to reading the world that I had inherited from my Cambridge mentors, Keynes's own students. In doing so she has constructed a framework for understanding the necessity of bubbles and the prospective cost of eliminating them from our economic life.

The process of moving from technical invention to funded innovation is messy and wasteful; the extreme skew in the returns of venture capital, within individual portfolios and across the multitude of funds and firms, testifies to this. So, too, do the bubbles of speculation in the financial markets that fund the deployment of innovations significant enough to make a broad economic difference, along with the detritus of scams and no-hopers that get swept along with them. Efficiency in the allocation of resources to satisfy current demands at a given moment of time – the hallmark of well-behaved markets in neoclassical theory – hardly captures the process through which conditions of life have been transformed by Perez's five great waves over more than 200 years. But can the ability to tolerate such waste be enhanced? Can the costs incurred when the speculative bubble bursts be limited in advance?

Certainly, there is no a priori set of economic principles that will yield an efficient outcome. Frank Dobbin observes that Britain, France and the United States all "produced rapid, dependable and cost-effective transport systems in relatively short order," although in each country the process of planning, funding and regulating the railways was radically different.[54] The one common element shared by British speculators, French state planners and the entrepreneurial American sources and seekers of subsidies is that rational calculation of economic returns was not a primary motivator. France from the 1820s with respect to the railways and the United States since the Second World War with respect to digital electronic technology demonstrate that the state can play a decisively catalytic, and not merely a constructive, role. But to explore the new space for innovative applications thereby created remains the realm of entrepreneurial finance, the world of bubbles and crashes.

Productive bubbles, destructive bubbles

The history of financial capitalism demonstrates the need to distinguish between bubbles along two different dimensions. One dimension is defined by the object of speculation. Only occasionally have speculators focused on fundamental technology instead of such assets as gold mines or houses that do not contribute to system-wide increases in productivity. The second dimension concerns the locus of speculative activity, distinguishing between bubbles that remain confined to the capital markets versus those that transcend the capital markets to suck in the institutions that accept deposits and provide the credit that fuels the ordinary workings of the market economy.

In the immediate past, the contrast is instructive between the respective consequences, positive and negative, of the dotcom/telecom bubble of 1999–2000 and the credit bubble of 2004–2007. When the

[54] Dobbin, *Forging Industrial Policy*, p. 223.

$6 trillion of nominal financial wealth created in the former and concentrated in equity securities was liquidated, the economic consequences were within the bounds of postwar experience, leaving the technological foundations and business models in place for the newest new economy. The great credit bubble will be remembered precisely for its destructive economic consequences and not for any physical legacy, least of all the abandoned tract houses scattered along the coastal regions of the United States and from Ireland and Spain to the emerging lands of Central and Eastern Europe. The dichotomy echoes that between the limited economic consequences of the stock market Crash of 1929 and the overwhelming impact of the international banking crises of 1931–1933.

Over the course of the past generation, rationalized and enabled by theory, the practice of finance was both deregulated and transformed. Credit was securitized both directly and through the superstructure of derivatives, and it was decoupled from the cash flows of the underlying economic assets. To the extent that the banks that constructed and distributed those claims held on to a portion of them, they imagined that, like their customers, they could lean on the insurance supposedly provided by credit default swaps: the ultimate instrument of self-deception constructed by modern finance.

The process of reregulating the financial system in response has barely begun, and if it is seriously undertaken it will be the work of years. Whatever the specific measures adopted in Washington and London, Brussels and Basel, the "fortress balance sheet" that enabled J. P. Morgan to survive the Crisis represents the relevant model. Sustained regulatory scrutiny will be as important as, and more problematic to maintain than, increased capital requirements. Only the combination of the two can limit the propensity of bankers to follow Hyman Minsky's movement from the prudence of hedged finance to the promised land of Ponzi.

What is to be done to limit the range of objects to which the speculative appetites of equity investors are recurrently drawn? Should anything be done at all? The negative reason for caution in enacting regulations in this sphere is the limited damage done to the market economy when money games on the stock exchange end in tears. The positive reason is the challenge of preemptively adjudicating which apparent folly will morph into the foundation of the next new economy.

The most powerful enabler of risk taking at the frontier of innovation is the possibility of winning financially even if the funded project fails. The much-derided greater fools of the stock market, the "noise traders," are the essential constituency that makes possible the process of trial and error and error and error through which our technologically driven economy evolves. Eliminate equity bubbles from our financial economy? The thought puts me in mind of Sir John Falstaff, a personage devoid of control either of his cash or of himself, when he was first threatened with banishment by Prince Hal in *1 Henry IV*: "Banish plump Jack, and banish all the world."

PART IV

Understanding the game: the role of the state

10 Where is the state?

The history of financial bubbles and crashes – and of the banality yet necessity of the former and the inevitability of the latter – fits nicely with Schumpeter's vision of economic development through waves of creative destruction. Speculation in the financial markets from time to time finances discontinuous innovation that transforms the market economy, redistributing monopoly profits while generating and liquidating transient financial gains. However, for a theorist–practitioner of entrepreneurial finance who has spent well over three decades performing on a stage constructed by government investment in innovation, the game so summarized is incomplete. Where is the state in this story?

From the First Industrial Revolution on, the state has served as an enabler – sometimes as the engine – of economic development, subsidizing if not directing the deployment of transformational technology and, more recently, taking responsibility for funding the advanced science and engineering from which economically significant innovation has come to be derived. Even in liberal nineteenth-century Britain, where the state played no role in planning or funding the build-out of the railways, acts of Parliament were required to reassign property rights from landowners to entrepreneurial "projectors," and the state subsequently acted to promote cartels to limit the destructive competition that followed.[1] Elsewhere – in the United States, across the continent of Europe and throughout Asia – the state has played a central role in sponsoring emergent market economies in an uncertain and competitive world. As Dietrich Rueschemeyer and Peter Evans wrote over twenty-five years ago in their contribution to the foundational collection of essays *Bringing the State Back In*:

[1] F. Dobbin, *Forging Industrial Policy: The United States, Britain and France in the Railway* Age (Cambridge University Press, 1994), pp. 167–171, 200–205.

Effective state intervention is now assumed to be an integral part of successful capitalist development ... Once the assumption of a competitive market
is relaxed ... there are strong theoretical reasons for believing that state
intervention is necessary if capitalist economies are to sustain capital accumulation and reach higher levels of productivity.[2]

Two other responsibilities have intersected the state's role in promoting economic development. As far back as London's banking crisis
of 1825, the central bank, as the agent of the state, has acted to save
the financiers of the market economy from their own folly. From the
Great Depression of the 1930s through current events, and never without controversy, the state has acted more broadly and directly to protect the market economy from the consequences of financial collapse.
Outside of the fantasies of Ayn Rand heroes and their acolytes, it is not
possible to imagine a modern economic world that does not depend
on timely and effective state initiatives. As Dani Rodrik has written,
the "dichotomy between markets and states ... is false and hides more
than it reveals."[3]

   I learned about the intersection of economics and politics at my
father's knee. Eliot Janeway was an acute student of their codepend-
ency. His one book of scholarly stature, *The Struggle for Survival: A
Chronicle of Economic Mobilization in World War II*, is an exhaustive yet enthralling account of FDR's triumph in presiding over the
incoherent and inefficient process through which he "inspired and
provoked" the home front to win the war by "the momentum of production."[4] Thus I was educated from childhood in this dimension
of the Three-Player Game that shapes the world in which we have
worked and spent, saved and invested, learned and played for more
than 200 years.

   Arguments persist over the extent to which markets should determine how resources are allocated and work and capital are rewarded
versus the degree to which the state should intervene to regulate, even

[2] D. Rueschemeyer and P. B. Evans, "The State and Economic Transformation:
    Toward an Analysis of the Conditions Underlying Effective Intervention," in
    P. B. Evans, D. Rueschemeyer and T. Skocpol (eds.), *Bringing the State Back In*
    (Cambridge University Press, 1985), pp. 44–46.
[3] D. Rodrik, *The Globalization Paradox: Why Global Markets, States, and
    Democracy Can't Coexist* (New York: Norton, 2011), p. 9.
[4] E. Janeway, *The Struggle for Survival: A Chronicle of Economic Mobilization in
    World War II* (New Haven, CT: Yale University Press, 1951), p. 18.

direct, the process and to control or cushion its outcomes. By the time I read *The Great Transformation*, Karl Polanyi's summation of this struggle from the time of Adam Smith to the onset of the Second World War, I knew his concept of "the double movement" in my bones:

> The idea of a self-regulating market implied a stark utopia. Such an institution could not exist for any length of time without annihilating the human and natural substance of society: it would have physically destroyed man and transformed his surroundings into a wilderness. Inevitably, society took measures to protect itself, but whatever measures it took impaired the self-regulation of the market, disorganized industrial life, and thus endangered society in yet another way.[5]

To the extent that those who are inescapably dependent on the markets of the economy also have access to the political process, they seek to invent or invoke powers of the state to counter the impact of market forces. Seen in this light, protective tariffs and unemployment benefits are both evidence of the same dimension of the Three-Player Game in process. Throughout the Western world, the progressive extension of the franchise to the propertyless during the nineteenth century shifted this aspect of the game and extended its scope. Those more or less in control of market forces seek to commandeer the state to enforce market discipline as and when they see it to be required. But the state has also been mobilized to play a positive role, undertaking and underwriting investments in furtherance of national development and national security, from Jean-Baptiste Colbert's seventeenth-century France to the strategic role of the US Department of Defense in the construction of the digital economy after the Second World War. Critically, as scientific discovery became the foundation of the Innovation Economy, the central research laboratories of the great corporations were first supplemented and then supplanted by direct state funding of research.

From the massive stimulus of the Second World War, the United States emerged, along with the rest of the world, with a radically enlarged public sector, although in the American case the commitment to national security outweighed that to social security. But contestation over the legitimate scope of the state and the market continued. As

---

[5] K. Polanyi, *The Great Transformation: The Political and Economic Origins of Our Times* (Boston: Beacon, 2001 [1944]), pp. 3–4. Central to Polanyi's argument is the historical role of the state in actively working to free markets from traditional restraints.

Mark Blyth wrote in 2002, extending Polanyi's argument and reflecting on the Reagan–Thatcher counter-revolution of the 1980s:

If ... labor demanded protection ... then was it not reasonable to expect another reaction ... by ... capitalists? The contemporary neoliberal economic order can be seen as merely the latest iteration of Polanyi's double movement. It is an attempt once again to disembed the market from society, to roll back the institutions of social protection and replace them with a more conforming institutional order.[6]

That very success in "liberating" the market economy from the encroachment of the state has potentially dire consequences for the Innovation Economy.

The Hamiltonian tradition

In the history of the Innovation Economy in the United States, Alexander Hamilton stands as the iconic founding father. His *Report on Manufactures*, delivered to Congress in 1791, is the urtext for those seeking to mobilize public support for private enterprise. Hamilton did provide arguments for protective tariffs, export bounties and improvements of the nascent transportation system, but the *Report* itself was not the blueprint of legend for comprehensive state intervention.[7] Hamilton's *Report* was tabled by Congress, and even in diluted form it proved to be no program of action. Although it was adopted in principle by the Whigs under Henry Clay and John Quincy Adams, no major national commitment followed; at the federal level, the one component that came to be embedded in the American political economy was the protective tariff. Only at the level of the individual states, engaged as they were in "rivalistic mercantilism," was the rest of Clay's "American System" widely adopted.[8]

Hamilton's initiative that did prove transformational was directed toward the other player in the Three-Player Game, financial capitalism, whose dynamics he discerned with extraordinary insight. As early as 1779–1781, he had defined the need for a privately owned

---

[6] M. Blyth, *Great Transformations: Economic Ideas and Institutional Change in the Twentieth Century* (Boston: Beacon, 2002), p. 4.

[7] J. R. Nelson Jr., "Alexander Hamilton and American Manufacturing: A Reappraisal," *Journal of American History*, 65(4) (1979), pp. 993–994.

[8] Dobbin, *Forging Industrial Policy*, p. 24.

central bank modeled on the Bank of England and had envisioned the national debt as a "national blessing" because it bonded quite literally the interests of the "monied" class to the survival, indeed the prosperity, of the new republic.[9] At the end of the Revolution, Hamilton won not only the argument within Washington's cabinet for establishing the Bank of the United States. He also won the opportunity to make the "bold gamble" of nationalizing the debts of the newly federated states – although at the cost of moving the capital from New York to a malarial swamp on the banks of the Potomac River.[10]

Hamilton's "financial revolution" was accompanied by the proliferation of state-chartered banks: by 1825, the United States had 330 incorporated banks in addition to the twenty-five branches of the Second Bank of United States, at a time when Britain was limited to the Bank of England plus several hundred banking partnerships, each of which was legally restricted to no more than six partners, all exposed to unlimited liability.[11] Richard Sylla summarizes:

By 1795, the United States had all the institutional components of a modern financial system – strong public finances and debt management, a national dollar monetary unit based on precious metals, a central bank, a banking system, thriving securities markets … When the industrial and transportation revolutions of early U.S. history took place, a modern financial system was there to finance them.[12]

Sylla's enthusiasm may overstate the modernity of the early American financial system, much of whose focus was on the provision of short-term commercial credit and unproductive speculation in land. But, as Naomi Lamoreaux has documented for New England in her study *Insider Lending*, family controlled, state-chartered banks did provide the capital critical to the rapid development of manufacturing in

[9] R. Sylla, "The Political Economy of Early US Financial Development," in S. Haber, D. C. North and B. Weingast (eds.), *Political Institutions and Financial Development* (Palo Alto, CA: Stanford University Press, 2008), pp. 64–66.

[10] *Ibid*. 66. There is an obvious resonance between Hamilton's effective exercise in nation building through financial and fiscal integration and the stalemate crippling the Eurozone since 2009, for, unlike the creators of the euro, Hamilton understood that financial integration could survive only if backed by fiscal integration.

[11] *Ibid*. 79. This was a lingering consequence of legislative response to the South Sea Bubble.

[12] *Ibid*. 61–62.

early nineteenth-century America.[13] More generally, Hamilton's vision encompassed the deliberate state sponsorship of financial capitalism as the critical enabler of both economic growth and political stability. There may be no more explicit, institutionally embodied statement of one thesis of this book in its most positive form. However, Hamilton's program would be crippled at its core in barely a generation when the Jacksonian Revolution threw the Three-Player Game into reverse.

With respect to state promotion of innovation, Hamilton (like Benjamin Franklin) was an advocate of prizes and subsidies, support for which "in the United States has always been sporadic and limited in scope."[14] But from early days Americans were pioneers in exploiting the most obvious opportunity available to technological followers: expropriation of the intellectual property already developed by others. Samuel Slater was the signal vector, emigrating by stealth from Britain in 1790, at a time when the export of machinery was prohibited by law. Slater was master of the most advanced textile manufacturing technique, "Arkwright's Patents." Backed by Moses Brown of Providence, he reproduced from memory a state-of-the-art mill on the Blackstone River in Pawtucket, Rhode Island.[15] Nonetheless, respect for the returns to original invention was evident in the Constitution's remarkable injunction to Congress in Article I, Section 8: "to promote the Progress of Science and useful Arts, by securing for limited Times to Authors and Inventors the exclusive Right to their respective Writings and Discoveries."

In direct and conscious contrast with the prevalent European patent systems, characterized by extremely high fees and subject to pervasive political influence, the American system was open and accessible, dedicated to

providing broad access to a well-specified and enforceable property right to new technology [which] would stimulate technical progress and nearly all of the innovations they made in the design of the patent institutions aimed

[13] N. R. Lamoreaux, *Insider Lending: Banks, Personal Connections, and Economic Development in Industrial New England* (Cambridge University Press, 1994).

[14] B. Z. Khan, "Premium Inventions: Patents and Prizes as Incentive Mechanisms in Britain and the United States, 1750–1930," p. 24. Available at www.international.ucla.edu/economichistory/conferences/khan.pdf.

[15] J. Connell, *Biographical Sketches of Distinguished Mechanics* (Wilmington, DE: Porter and Eckel, 1852), pp. 41–42.

to strengthen and extend inventive activities to a much broader range of the population than would have enjoyed them under traditional intellectual property institutions.[16]

Not only were fees set a level less than 5 percent of those prevailing in Great Britain. The early laws also provided for public dissemination of patented innovations and for the examinations of applications prior to grant, thus reducing uncertainty about the validity of issued patents and increasing their value as financial assets for sale or licensing. "By 1810, despite its lag in industrial development, the United States far surpassed Britain in patenting per capita."[17] Alongside the protective tariff and the subsidies provided by the federal and state government for constructing the transportation infrastructure, patent policy would serve as the third public policy initiative that fueled the technological engine of economic growth in the United States.

In 1989, Arthur Schlesinger Jr. reflected on the Hamiltonian tradition as he considered the role of the state relative to the national economy. Schlesinger's own initial and formidable contribution to scholarship had been *The Age of Jackson*,[18] published forty-four years earlier. In direct challenge to the long-prevailing dogma that Jackson's presidency had represented the entry of the trans-Appalachian frontier into American politics, its thesis was that the politics of Jackson's time had been class-based. Jackson's triumph depended on decisive support from Eastern working men and shopkeepers rebelling against the privileges of legislatively chartered corporations as most visibly and despisedly embodied in the Second Bank of the United States. Now, Schlesinger offered a balanced view of what had been at stake:

The tradition of affirmative government was the tradition of Hamilton … Subsequent statesmen in that tradition, especially John Quincy Adams and Henry Clay, elaborated the Hamiltonian Vision into what Clay called the American System – a great dream of economic development under the leadership of the national state …

The American System, with its program of internal improvements, a protective tariff and Biddle's Bank of the United States was designed to benefit

---

[16] N. R. Lamoreaux and K. L. Sokoloff, Introduction to N. R. Lamoreaux and K. L. Sokoloff (eds.), *Financing Innovation in the United States: 1870 to the Present* (Cambridge, MA: MIT Press, 2007), p. 9.

[17] *Ibid.* 5.

[18] A. M. Schlesinger Jr., *The Age of Jackson* (Boston, MA: Little, Brown, 1945).

the business classes; but this was not the whole truth. The Whig program was also designed to benefit the nation and so accelerate the pace of economic growth. In retrospect, the Hamiltonians had a sounder conception of government and a more constructive policy of economic development than the anti-statist Jacksonians.[19]

The mercantilism represented by the Hamilton–Clay tradition transcends the history of the American political economy in its significance. Prior to the Industrial Revolution, France stood out for state commitment to internal improvements: in 1666, Colbert had convinced Louis XIV to finance the Canal du Midi as one aspect of the generations-long campaign to establish centralized state authority over the still feudal French nation.[20] Since time immemorial, however, the public credit of the state had been predominantly devoted to the financing of war, whether the state was in the hands of a feudal king, an absolute monarch, a republican city-state, or the conflation of royal power circumscribed by parliamentary representatives of the propertied classes and tempered by "the mob" that emerged in Britain from 1688. The game between the financial markets and the state was played out over the terms on which the owners of liquid capital would fund the state's armies relative to the problematic likelihood of their being repaid.

The economic consequences of wars so financed could be substantial – and certainly had been during the Napoleonic Wars – both in the state's exceptional demand for resources and in the inflation regularly generated by military consumption of scarce commodities and disruption of their supply, but these were unintended consequences. The American System, by contrast, was explicitly statist, emulating the French tradition of mobilizing public credit in pursuit of economic development for its own sake, thereby triangulating the relationships between the state, the market economy and financial capitalism for positive gain, not for reciprocal destruction. Although the implementation of the American System was limited at the national level, at the state level it produced the salient success of the Erie Canal, and it attracted capital from abroad to fund an extensive array of other canals and turnpikes and then the railroads. But consistent with state engagements in support of the emerging market economies that

---

[19] A. M. Schlesinger Jr., "The Ages of Jackson," *New York Review of Books*, 36(19) (1989), pp. 49–50.
[20] Dobbin, *Forging Industrial Policy*, p. 101.

followed, it also produced rampant corruption that fed the Jacksonian assault on financial interests.[21]

Jacksonian reversal

Jackson's successful war against the Bank of the United States and the east coast financiers reversed the dynamic of the Three-Player Game, as a most energetic president mobilized the government to limit the reach of financial capitalism. Liberation came at a cost for the market economy. As Sylla notes, "The United States without a central bank ... suffered more financial instability than other leading nations into the twentieth century."[22] Jackson's activism was succeeded by a generation of passivity, as the emerging sectoral conflict paralyzed the political processes. Richard Franklin Benzel has comprehensively argued that

the state that early American nationalists had previously attempted to establish ... had become a mere shell by 1860 – a government with only a token administrative presence in most of the nation and whose sovereignty was interpreted by the central administration as contingent on the consent of the individual states.[23]

The Hamilton–Clay tradition of mobilizing public resources, including the public credit, for national economic development was renewed in the program of the Whigs' institutional successor, the Republican Party of Lincoln. The Republicans added to the traditional protective tariff and broad program of internal improvements the grand project of a Pacific Railroad. But any such initiatives were blocked by the Southern-controlled Senate, since their direct effect would be to strengthen the northeastern industrial economy and to tie the developing agrarian economy of the Midwest more closely to it, at the comparative expense of the Southern plantation economy. Because the initiatives legitimized the central state's intervention into the institutions of the market economy, their potential indirect consequence was even more threatening: federal action directed against slavery when the South lost its grip on national power.

---

[21] *Ibid.* 44–47 and J. Macdonald, *A Free Nation Rich in Debt* (New York: Farrar, Straus and Giroux, 2003), pp. 385–386.

[22] Sylla, "The Political Economy of Early US Financial Development," p. 86.

[23] R. F. Benzel, *Yankee Leviathan: The Origins of Central State Authority in America, 1859–1877* (Cambridge University Press, 1990), p. ix.

The only federal initiative sanctioned by the South was enforcement of the Fugitive Slave Act, especially after the Southern-controlled Supreme Court opened the entire country to property rights in human beings with the Dred Scott decision in 1857.[24] Contrariwise, one result of Southern secession was removal of the roadblocks to state support of economic development, whose need was both legitimized and amplified by the North's mobilization for war. By the summer of 1862, the key components were in place: protective tariffs against foreign manufactures; the Pacific Railway Act, which provided for land grant subsidies on a massive scale; and the Morrill Act to finance agricultural colleges on public lands in the developing West.[25]

The land grants to the railroads subsidized a massive mobilization of private financial capital to construct the foundations of the new economy that emerged in the decades after the Civil War. The availability of such capital at unprecedented scale was itself a consequence of the institutional innovations required to pay for the war in the North.[26] In turn, the history of corruption at the state level was replicated at the national level, most notoriously in the Credit Mobilier scandal surrounding the financing of the Union Pacific. This galvanized antistatist sentiments "by fulfilling the Constitution's prophecy that state power breeds corruption."[27] Of the American System, only protective tariffs remained when state subsidies to the construction of infrastructure were abandoned. However, with their powerful assistance and as a model for future rising economies, the United States moved into a substantial and sustained trade surplus beginning in the mid-1870s.[28] In the future, national development would no longer legitimize direct interventions in the market economy by the American state. Such initiatives would need to be explicitly justified in the name of national security.

Technology's emerging dependence on science

The requirements of war induced the first exercise in mobilizing science for national needs. On March 3, 1863, Lincoln signed the act of

---

[24] *Ibid.* 63–64.   [25] *Ibid.* 69 n. 1, 173–174, 178.
[26] *Ibid.* 238 and Macdonald, *A Free Nation Rich in Debt*, pp. 382, 396–399.
[27] Dobbin, *Forging Industrial Policy*, pp. 55–56.
[28] S. B. Carter, S. G. Gartner, M. R. Haines, A. L. Olmstead, R. Sutch and
    G. Wright (eds.), *Historical Statistics of the United States*, millennial edn.
    (Cambridge University Press, 2006), table Ee362–375.

incorporation of the National Academy of Sciences (NAS), chartered as a private, nonprofit organization to "investigate, examine, experiment, and report upon any subject of science or art" when called upon by any department of the government. During the Civil War, the Navy Department was the most significant client of the NAS, asking for guidance on protecting the bottoms of its new iron-hulled vessels against corrosion and on correcting magnetic deviations of compasses on iron ships.

After the end of the war, when its principal project was to evaluate the longevity of metal headstones for the countless graves of dead soldiers, the NAS faded into irrelevance. Beyond generating reports on such subjects as "Means of Distinguishing Calf's Hair from Woolen Goods" (1875) and "The Restoration of the Declaration of Independence" (1880), its only two lasting contributions were its recommendations that led to the creation of the US Geological Survey in 1878 and the Forestry Service in 1905.[29] Apart from the NAS, direct investment in the scientific and technological sources of economic growth was modest: in the armories that perfected the "American system of manufactures," characterized by interchangeable mechanical parts,[30] and in the experimental stations of the Department of Agriculture, founded through the same impulse that led to passage of the Morrill Act.[31]

It was by indirection that public policy contributed to technology-driven economic growth. Preceding the mercantilist policies that extended the war's massive stimulus to industrial expansion and accompanying them through the remainder of the nineteenth century, a vibrant market for technology developed in the United States. As documented by Naomi Lamoreaux and Ken Sokoloff, this was the offspring of the distinctively accessible American patent system, especially after the process of examination by professionals was introduced by the Patent Act of 1836.[32] By 1870, the emergence of a class

---

[29] The National Academies, "The NAS in the Late Nineteenth Century" (Washington, DC: The National Academies, n.d.). www7.nationalacademies.org/archives/late19thcentury.html.

[30] D. C. Mowery and N. Rosenberg, *Technology and the Pursuit of Economic Growth* (Cambridge University Press, 1989), p. 27.

[31] R. R. Nelson, M. J. Peck and E. D. Kalacheck (eds.), *Technology, Economic Growth and Public Policy* (Washington, DC: The Brookings Institution, 1967).

[32] N. R. Lamoreaux and K. L. Sokoloff, "Inventive Activity and the Market for Technology in the United States, 1840–1920," National Bureau of Economic Research Working Paper 7107 (1999), p. 8.

of professional inventors in association with an active trade in patent rights is evident in the data. This market mechanism for transforming invention into commercializable innovation expanded through the early years of the twentieth century, increasingly intermediated by professional agents operating on an increasingly national scale.[33]

By the First World War, a new institution was emerging to serve as the nexus of technological innovation: the industrial research laboratory. The relevance of science to industry had been discovered by that most entrepreneurial of capitalists, Andrew Carnegie, who reflected on the economic benefits of systematic assays of iron ore by a trained chemist:

What fools we had been! But then there was this consolation: we were not as great fools as our competitors ... Years after we had taken chemistry to guide us [they] said they could not afford to employ a chemist. Had they known the truth then, they would have known they could not afford to be without one.[34]

The more general recognition, a generation later, of science-based research and development as a source of competitive advantage may be read as an indirect impact of the railroads in the context of the American version of *laissez-faire*. As we saw in Chapter 7, the creation of a national market, along with the radical decline in manufacturing costs as companies exploited the "economies of scale and scope" analyzed by Alfred Chandler, engendered the merger movement enabled by the trust bubble. Not only did companies have a need and an opportunity to rationalize "the facilities and skills of the constituent companies by making concentrated investments in manufacturing, marketing and management,"[35]

the mergers and corporate reorganizations of the late nineteenth and early twentieth centuries hastened the growth of industrial research ... In firms such as American Telephone and Telegraph, General Electric, U.S. Steel or Du Pont, the development of a strong central office was closely

---

[33] *Ibid.* 22, 30–33.
[34] Quoted in Mowery and Rosenberg, *Technology and the Pursuit of Economic Growth*, p. 30.
[35] A. D. Chandler, *Scale and Scope: The Dynamics of Industrial Capitalism* (Cambridge, MA: Harvard University Press; Belknap Press, 1999), p. 229.

associated with the establishment or significant expansion of a central research facility.[36]

Thus the great corporations moved into a space that previously had been haphazardly funded, principally by wealthy individuals guided by motives that combined curiosity and philanthropy. Darwin, for example, was the beneficiary of a rentier father whose highly successful angel investments in the first industrial revolution were accompanied by dynastic alliances with the enormously wealthy Wedgwood family. The Cavendish Laboratory at Cambridge University, founded in 1874 under the initial Cavendish professor James Clerk Maxwell, was a gift of William Cavendish, Seventh Duke of Devonshire. A distant echo of such initiatives can be found in the extraordinary story of Alfred Loomis: having sold out of his successful investment banking firm before the Crash of 1929, he created a physics laboratory on his estate in Tuxedo Park, New York, where he personally financed and participated actively in work that contributed to the invention of radar in time for the Second World War.[37] What links these and a host of other instances is the funders' utter lack of interest in economic or financial return.

By the early twentieth century, regional stock exchanges had opened up to funding entrepreneurial companies, especially in the Midwest, but the first generation of high-tech industries mobilizing the sciences of chemistry and electricity were embodied in the large-scale industrial enterprises of the mid-Atlantic region.[38] From the 1920s through the 1970s, central research laboratories were funded by the monopoly profits of the great corporations. Whether established by legislation (AT&T's), based on patent monopolies (RCA's and Xerox's) or generated from a combination of innovative research and commercial dominance (DuPont's and IBM's), the leading research laboratories could afford to invest upstream in the fundamental science from which

[36] Mowery and Rosenberg, *Technology and the Pursuit of Economic Growth*, p. 71.
[37] J. Conant, *Tuxedo Park: A Wall Street Tycoon and the Secret Palace of Science that Changed the Course of World War II* (New York: Simon & Schuster, 2002).
[38] N. R. Lamoreaux, K. L. Sokoloff and D. Sutthiphisal, "Reorganization of Inventive Activity in the United States during the Early Twentieth Century," National Bureau of Economic Research Working Paper 15440 (2009), pp. 24–25.

technological innovations of commercial significance might evolve. Seemingly secure monopolies created environments in which science for its own sake could be indulged and pursued within the for-profit enterprise.[39]

Prior to the Second World War, federal support of research remained trivial in terms of both absolute dollars and scientific impact. Only agriculture was favored for federal research support, thanks to the Morrill Act and the Agriculture Department's Extension Service: in 1940, the $30 million of research funding for agriculture exceeded that for the combined departments that would make up the postwar Department of Defense.[40] Although the original National Institute of Health emerged from the combined Public Health and Marine Hospital Service in 1930, public funding of life sciences research remained marginal.[41]

State support of science

The First World War did leave a legacy that lingered through the inter-war decades. In 1916, as the United States was drawn more deeply into the European conflict, the NAS "could not keep up with the volume of requests for advice regarding military preparedness." In response, Wilson asked the NAS to establish the National Research Council, whose purpose would be:

to bring into cooperation government, educational, industrial, and other research organizations with the object of encouraging the investigation of natural phenomena, and increased use of scientific research in the development of American industries, the employment of scientific methods in

[39] Of course, the role of the great corporations in the American social economy transcended investment in science and engineering. Beyond Social Security and before Medicare, they also became the principal vehicles for delivering the haphazard and incomplete welfare state – specifically, pensions and medical insurance – whose fragile base was thus also vulnerable to the same loss of entrenched competitive power that terminated the scientific mission of the central industrial research labs.

[40] Mowery and Rosenberg, *Technology and Pursuit of Economic Growth*, pp. 92–93.

[41] National Institutes of Health, "Chronology of Events" (Bethesda, MD: National Institutes of Health, n.d.). www.nih.gov/about/almanac/historical/chronology_of_events.htm.

strengthening the national defense, and such other applications of science as will promote the national security and welfare.[42]

Wilson perpetuated the Council by executive order, and its general mission enjoyed the support of the most activist member of the Republican cabinets of the 1920s, Herbert Hoover, whose Commerce Department worked broadly to promote the application of science and technology for the benefit of American business.

As David Hart has documented, Hoover's "associationalism," which looked to voluntary cooperation among industrial competitors and between industry and the academic research community, collapsed under the weight of the Depression.[43] Its progressive faith was challenged from the right and the left. On the right, Frank Jewett, president of the Bell Telephone Laboratories and of the NAS from 1938, argued that "federal meddling with patent laws and research funding would slow the pace of scientific and technological progress."[44] On the left, although one faction of New Dealers argued for job-creating investment in technology-enabled enterprise, exemplified by the Tennessee Valley Authority, others sought to curb the job-destroying impact of productivity-enhancing innovation.[45]

Jewett's fear that government bureaucrats would distort research priorities exemplified a more general rejection of state intervention in the market economy. In *Business Cycles*, published in 1939, Schumpeter stated the case in the most comprehensive terms:

What we know from experience is not the working of capitalism as such, but of a distorted capitalism which is covered with the scars of past injuries inflicted on its organism ... The very fundaments of the industrial organisms of all nations have been politically shaped. Everywhere we find industries which would not exist at all but for protection, subsidies and other political stimuli, and others which are overgrown or otherwise in an unhealthy state because of them ... Such industries and assets are of doubtful value, in any case a source of weakness and often the immediate cause of breakdowns or

[42] The National Academies, "Organization of the National Research Council" (Washington, DC: The National Academies, n.d.). www7.nationalacademies. org/archives/nrcorganization.html.

[43] D. M. Hart, *Forged Consensus: Science, Technology and Economic Policy in the United States, 1921–1953* (Princeton University Press, 1998), pp. 30–61.

[44] Ibid. 18.   [45] Ibid. 66.

depressive symptoms. This type of economic waste and maladjustment may well be more important than any other.[46]

It was strictly to the private sector and increasingly to the large-scale firm that Schumpeter looked for innovation. In the "perennial gale of creative destruction," the restrictive practices and price-setting power of monopolists and oligopolists were "incidents of a long-run process of expansionism which they protect rather than impede."[47] As specific evidence, anticipating Mowery and Rosenberg's research, Schumpeter remarked:

The first thing a modern concern does as soon as it feels that it can afford it is to establish a research department every member of which knows that his bread and butter depends on his success in devising improvements. This practice does not obviously suggest aversion to technological progress.[48]

By the time that Schumpeter wrote these sentences in 1943, the dynamics of the Innovation Economy had been transformed by the advent of the Second World War. The profit-seeking monopolistic enterprise that funded applied research for immediate economic reward, as characterized by Schumpeter, was supplanted by the national security state funding research that extended all the way back upstream to quantum physics in its struggle for survival.

Beginning in 1939, as the threat of war grew imminent, Vannevar Bush came to play a decisive role in the mobilization of science for war. As president of the Carnegie Corporation and chair of the National Advisory Committee for Aeronautics, Bush joined with Harvard president James Conant, MIT president Karl Compton and Frank Jewett, who was no longer resistant to a role for the state in the allocation of resources to research for national security. Jointly they urged creation of a central directing authority in the federal government. Bush was the author of the proposal for the National Defense Research Committee (NDRC), which secured the president's approval in May 1940 as the German armies swept through France. When, a year later, the NDRC was subsumed into the Office of Scientific Research and Development

---

[46] J. A. Schumpeter, *Business Cycles: A Theoretical, Historical and Statistical Analysis of the Capitalist Process*, 2 vols. (London: McGraw-Hill, 1939), vol. 1, p. 13.

[47] J. A. Schumpeter, *Capitalism, Socialism and Democracy*, 4th edn. (London: Allen & Unwin, 2010 [1943]), pp. 87–88.

[48] *Ibid.* 96.

(OSRD), Bush moved from serving as chair of the former to being director of the latter. Under his leadership, OSRD directed the work of some 30,000 scientists and technologists in the development of sonar, radar, the proximity fuse, the Norden bombsight and, until administration of the Manhattan Project was transferred to the Army in 1943, the atomic bomb.[49]

Once again, the direct mobilization of science ended with the termination of hostilities, and OSRD was wound down. This time, however, the commitment of the state was renewed. After five years of Washington infighting, the Korean conflict triggered the reconstruction in nominal peacetime of the national security state. Small as it was militarily in comparison with the Second World War, the Korean War had a massive economic impact. The defense budget, originally set at $10 billion for fiscal year 1951, was increased by emergency appropriations to $42 billion and the following year reached $60 billion. Military R&D tripled to $1.8 billion. By the mid-1950s, the defense budget amounted to some two-thirds of total federal spending and about 9 percent of gross domestic product.[50] This spending was accompanied by the nascent and incomplete welfare state initiated through Social Security and to be augmented by Medicare. The United States had found its own path to big-state capitalism.

Well before the mid-1970s, when I began my education in the disciplines that underlay computing, "most of the basic electronic development that made digital technology feasible was in place."[51] By the mid-1950s, the Department of Defense had already funded some twenty research projects to construct digital computers,[52] even before the Soviet launch of Sputnik catalyzed creation of the Defense Advanced Research Projects Agency (DARPA). From microelectronics and semiconductor devices through computer hardware and software and on to the internet, development of all of the components of digital

---

[49] G. P. Zachary, *The Endless Frontier: Vannevar Bush, Engineer of the American Century* (New York: The Free Press, 1997), pp. 171–203.

[50] Hart, *Forged Consensus*, pp. 195, 203.

[51] H. Kressel, *Competing for the Future: How Digital Innovations are Changing the World* (Cambridge University Press, 2007), p, 56.

[52] K. R. Fabrizio and D. C. Mowery, "The Federal Role in Financing Major Innovations: Information Technology During the Postwar Period," in N. R. Lamoreaux and K. L. Sokoloff (eds.), *Financing Innovation in the United States, 1870 to the Present* (Cambridge, MA: MIT Press, 2007), table 7.2 (p. 296).

information and communications technology reflected state policies for both R&D and procurement that

encouraged the entry of new firms and interfirm technology diffusion. In addition, federal procurement supported the rapid attainment by supplier firms of relatively large production runs, enabling faster rates of improvement in product quality and cost than otherwise would have been realized. Finally, Federal support of innovation in IT contributed to the creation of a large-scale R&D infrastructure in federal laboratories and, especially, in U.S. universities.[53]

The deployment of the SAGE air defense computer network served both to accelerate the development of relevant technologies by its prime contractor, IBM, and as a "software university" for hundreds of programmers, "laying the foundations for the software industry's development within the United States." As the dominant source of demand for computers, the Defense Department was able to establish standards such as the COBOL programming language, in which business applications would be written for a long generation. Even as commercial demand for semiconductor devices and computers began to outstrip military demand, the Defense Department extended its innovative investment in IT to communications, including the foundation of the internet through DARPA. With its principal design objective specified as survival in the event of nuclear war, the packet-switched network initially deployed as ARPAnet linked more than 100 nodes at universities and other major research sites by 1975. In keeping with its commitment to open standards in IT, the Defense Department sponsored the TCP/IP suite of protocols for digital communications. These won out over a variety of proprietary alternatives and contributed decisively to the open architecture of the internet as it evolved into a universal medium for digital communications and transactions.[54]

During prior technological revolutions that have defined the succession of new economies since roughly 1750, large-scale government support of the deployment of more or less proven technologies had been significant, even at times decisive, most notably in the United States, where state credit was used to fund canal building and where the gift of public lands subsidized railroad construction. But the post-Second World War engagement of the US Department of Defense to finance

---

[53] *Ibid.* 286–287.   [54] *Ibid.* 301–302, 305–306.

both fundamental research at the frontier of scientific experimentation and the technological development necessary to produce reliable devices and systems was entirely unprecedented. Much of the funding was directed to the major industrial research labs of the great corporations – AT&T, IBM, RCA – whose monopoly rents had funded scientific advance and innovative engineering from the late nineteenth century to the Second World War. But much was distributed more broadly as well, especially to universities. Moreover, the major corporations were required to share the results of research not only with each other but with new entrants. When their monopoly profits came under pressure beginning in the 1970s and all the industrial sponsors pressured their central labs for product-oriented, applied R&D, the new academic networks of research and innovation were in place.[55]

By the mid-1960s, the commercial applications of IT had begun to exceed the government's share. When, in the early 1960s, IBM made its enormous commitment to construct System 360, the first comprehensive line of computers that would open wide the commercial market, the company's CEO, Tom Watson Jr., had to fight free from the operational and cultural constraints imposed by its military projects, especially SAGE.[56] On the other hand, IBM's education in the new science and technology of silicon semiconductors was accelerated through collaboration with Texas Instruments, one of the emerging innovators that had been sponsored by the military in the previous decade.[57] By the end of the 1970s, the "milspec" (military specification) market for semiconductors and computers had become a marginally relevant niche, where requirements were dictated by absolute performance regardless of cost and by the ability to function in extreme environments. When the Defense Department announced its Very High Speed Integrated Circuit program in 1980, I recall learning that Intel chose not to participate lest its star designers be distracted from the

[55] For an authoritative summary of the rise and fall of the industrial research laboratory as the locus for technological innovation, see Kressel, *Competing for the Future*, chapter 3. For an updated overview of the impact of military investment, see D. C. Mowery, "Military R&D and Innovation," in B. H. Hall and N. Rosenberg (eds.), *Handbook of the Economics of Innovation*, 2 vols. (Amsterdam: North-Holland, 2010), vol. 2, pp. 1219–1256.

[56] S. W. Usselman, "Learning the Hard Way: IBM and the Sources of Innovation in Early Computing," in Lamoreaux and Sokoloff (eds.), *Financing Innovation*, p. 337.

[57] *Ibid.* 341–342.

exploding demand for commercial microprocessors as the personal computer revolution gathered momentum.

Collectively, the American approach stood in sharp contrast to the European model of tight security and concentration on "national champions." Decoupled from any direct concern with economic return, the Defense Department could fund numerous alternative research agendas, underwriting the "wasteful" search for solutions that inevitably accompanies any effort to push back the frontiers of knowledge. Moreover, the defense establishment insisted on an intellectual property rights regime that was scandalously – and productively – loose relative to what has evolved over the three decades since then. Legitimized by considerations of national security, postwar US policy fostered a complex of commercial industries whose products and services would, some forty years on, combine to create another new economy. In doing so, the federal government also enabled the generation of a host of investment opportunities that would first feed a new class of professional venture capitalists whose work product – the firms they founded – would, in time and in turn, fuel the speculative greed of the great dotcom/telecom bubble of 1999–2000. In the meantime, the American model was emulated globally: as Josh Lerner summarizes, "virtually every hub of cutting-edge entrepreneurial activity in the world today had its origins in proactive government intervention."[58]

After Vannevar Bush's proposal to institutionalize state funding of science became public policy due to the contingency of the Cold War, the economists Kenneth Arrow and Richard Nelson separately provided a theoretical rationale for state investment in research and development. Both emphasized that the social return to discovery and invention exceeds its private return, as the cost of sharing information is minimal. Arrow emphasized how private firms are inhibited by the inevitable uncertainty that besets such investment, especially when potential returns depend on long-term, indivisible efforts to generate new knowledge, which, in turn, can only be partially appropriated and monetized by individual firms.[59] Nelson identified the long lag

---

[58] J. Lerner, *Boulevard of Broken Dreams: Why Public Efforts to Boost Entrepreneurship and Venture Capital Have Failed – and What to Do about it* (Princeton University Press, 2009), p. 42.

[59] K. J. Arrow, "Economic Welfare and the Allocation of Resources for R&D," in K. J. Arrow (ed.), *Essays in the Theory of Risk-Bearing* (New York: American Elsevier, 1971 [1962]), pp. 144–163.

between initiation of research and commercially relevant application and focused on the conditions of emergent industries, where business success usually turned on investment in fundamentally new technologies whose economic value was difficult for the pioneering firms to estimate, let alone capture.[60]

Yet arguments for state intervention to address such market failures have proved only marginally compelling, and not just in the American context. Rather, it has been mission-oriented state investments that have, time after time and across national boundaries, proved effective in driving the individual sectors of the Innovation Economy. David Mowery summarizes the historical record:

Although the market failure rationale retains great rhetorical influence in justifying public investments in R&D programs, casual empiricism suggests that its influence over such public investments is modest at best ...

Also noteworthy ... is the relatively small share of central-government R&D spending accounted for by the "Bush–Arrow" form of R&D spending, nonmission-oriented R&D ... Rather than "scientists" choosing the field in which large investments of public R&D funds were made, allocation decisions were based on assessments by policymakers of the research needs of specific agency missions in fields ranging from national defense to agriculture.[61]

Writ large, the strategic state interventions that have shaped the market economy over generations have depended on grander themes – national development, national security, social justice, liberation from disease – that transcend the calculus of welfare economics and the logic of market failure.

---

[60] R. R. Nelson, "The Simple Economics of Basic Scientific Research," *Journal of Political Economy*, 67 (1959), pp. 297–306.

[61] D. C. Mowery, "Military R&D and Innovation," pp. 1222–1223.

11 "The failure of market failure"

On either side of the World Financial Crisis of 2008, two of Britain's leading economic commentators each published an article titled "The Failure of Market Failure." The economist John Kay went first, arguing in August 2007 that invocation of market failure to legitimize state intervention "concedes too much to market fundamentalists."[1] By accepting the notion that markets can be complete and efficient – that it is imaginable that markets succeed in delivering a social optimum on their own – center-left politicians implicitly accept the methodological individualism and narrow definition of rationality of neoclassical economics. In so doing, they ignore the fact that interventions at systemic scale, such as Britain's National Health Service, could only be established and maintained by collective action in response to motives (such as compassion and solidarity) not reducible to individual, material incentives.

Some fifteen months later, as the financial crisis paralyzed the market economy, the journalist Will Hutton and his collaborator Philippe Schneider published an article under the same title and began with a similar critique:

The free-market fundamentalists have been so successful in creating an intellectual hegemony that they have managed to steer debate about the market's weak properties as a system into a debate about the scope of particular market failures. The presumption has been that the market paradigm works, even if they admit deviations from the general rule.[2]

Even while assaulting the pretensions of the market's advocates, Kay and Hutton and Schneider separately celebrate what Kay terms the

---

[1] J. Kay, "The Failure of Market Failure," *Prospect* (137), August 1, 2007.
[2] W. Hutton and P. Schneider, "The Failure of Market Failure: Towards a 21st Century Keynesianism," National Endowment for Science, Technology and the Arts, Provocation 08 (November 2008), p. 5. Curiously, Hutton and his collaborator make no reference among their fifty-six footnotes to Kay's preceding article.

"genius" of market economies: "their ability to innovate and adapt in an environment of uncertainty and change."[3] In their turn, Hutton and Schneider assert that despite their "significant shortcomings," markets "remain incredibly effective as 'open access' systems in creating conditions for innovation." They recognize that "market selection provides a way of evaluating and choosing between competing entrepreneurial judgments: successful ones draw resources and expand while ineffective ones free up theirs and are discarded."[4] This is the downstream phase of the Innovation Economy, where exploration of new economic space depends on processes of trial and error. Upstream, however, Kay correctly notes that "markets don't do the basic research, or the training that isn't job-specific, on which the innovative capacity of economic systems depends."[5]

Market failure or failure of markets

These critiques of reliance on the identification of market failure – sound as they are – do not go far enough. I extend them to include the failure of market failure to motivate corrective state action. Hutton and Schneider correctly identify the Crisis of 2008 as "not a market failure but a systemic failure of markets."[6] Yet even such catastrophic events have failed to generate adequate responsive intervention by the state. During the Great Depression, the radically different policy stances of the governments in Britain, the United States and Germany shared one common factor: the refusal to recognize unused human and physical resources at massive scale as, *in and of themselves*, sufficient to justify a correspondingly massive state response. Only mobilization for war – first by Germany, then by Britain, and finally by the United States – provided the political underwriting for state action at the scale required. As I write now in 2011, even in the context of a higher level of economic activity and employment, it is striking how the arguments that rationalize acceptance of the systemic failure of markets echo those of the 1930s.

From the Wall Street Crash of 1929 through the global financial crisis of 1931 to the collapse of the international economic system into

---

[3] Kay, "The Failure of Market Failure," p. 15.
[4] Hutton and Schneider, "The Failure of Market Failure," p. 18.
[5] Kay, "The Failure of Market Failure," p. 18.
[6] Hutton and Schneider, "The Failure of Market Failure," p. 18.

autarchic chaos in 1933, the onset of the Great Depression demonstrated the fragility of the Three-Player Game when all players simultaneously seek to protect themselves by unilateral pursuit of Cash
and Control. In each of the leading industrial nations – Britain, the
United States and Germany – governments were challenged to respond
to mass unemployment of their constituents. The British experience
is peculiarly instructive due to the clarity of the policy debate surrounding the government's consideration of an unprecedented initiative, debt-financed public works to address mass unemployment, not
least because that debate was largely orchestrated by John Maynard
Keynes. In very different ways, the American and German experiences
confirm that, on its own, market failure had limited power to legitimize state intervention to allocate resources even when they would
otherwise have been unemployed.

Examination of this most extreme of historical examples has obvious bearing on evaluation of the joint and several responses of governments to the world financial crisis of 2007–2009 and the consequent
Great Recession. For my own purposes, it can also inform consideration of the role of the state in the longer-term economics of innovation: the haphazard, stepwise invention, deployment and exploitation
of technologies that have successively transformed economic possibili-
ties over the past 250 years.

In 1931, Andrew Mellon famously confronted the third Republican
US president whom he had served as Treasury Secretary over ten years.
Enormously wealthy as a result of his capitalist ventures, Mellon urged
Hoover to stand aside while "the market" performed its necessary,
cleansing function:

Liquidate labor, liquidate stocks, liquidate the farmers, liquidate real estate ...
It will purge the rottenness out of the system. High cost of living and high
living will come down. People will work harder, live a more moral life ...
Enterprising people will pick up the wrecks from less competent people.[7]

---

[7] H. Hoover, *The Memoirs of Herbert Hoover: The Great Depression, 1929–
1941* (New York: Macmillan, 1952), p. 30. In an unpublished paper, Brad
DeLong has shown that the "liquidationist" theory of depression policy, which
emphasized the necessity of freeing resources from uneconomic investments,
had its own coherent rationale and some degree of historical evidence in
its favor, most recently in the swift economic contraction and recovery of
1921. J. B. DeLong, "'Liquidation' Cycles and the Great Depression" (1991).
Available at http://econ161.berkeley.edu/pdf_files/Liquidation_Cycles.pdf.

To his credit, Hoover's response was to move "the greatest Secretary of the Treasury since Alexander Hamilton" from his position of authority in Washington to London as Ambassador to the Court of St. James's. Behind the anecdote lies the conflict that ever drives the formulation of economic policy in a capitalist democracy, a conflict made brutally explicit in Mellon's *laissez-faire* prescription.

The game played between the state and the market economy takes place on a field on which two systems for organizing power to allocate resources and to distribute the costs and benefits of their production and consumption coexist and coevolve. A rough historical rhythm is discernible as the losers from one dispensation appeal to – or invent – the other in search of redress. So, in eighteenth-century Britain, Adam Smith legitimized the market as the alternative both to the restrictions on "natural liberty" imposed by traditional statutes and institutions and to corrupt and corrupting state power, whose economic extension was evident in the granting of monopolies and the provision of patronage. Two hundred years later, Deng Xiaoping followed in Smith's footsteps, with greater directorial authority. Contrariwise, protectionism predictably persists in emerging industrial economies (the United States in the late nineteenth century) and in declining ones (Britain in the mid-twentieth century), as those unable to compete in open markets exercise their political option. As Dani Rodrik has comprehensively documented, deepening globalization of markets intensifies the conflict to the point of calling into question the simultaneous maintenance of both democracy and the autonomous nation-state.[8]

Each distribution of power invokes its own legitimizing ideology. The free market of Adam Smith and Milton Friedman is subject to challenge by the demands both of national security (especially in the United States) and social security (especially in Europe). Capitalism has thrived in epochs of complementary coexistence between politics and markets: for two short generations during the High Victorian age from roughly 1850 in Britain; for one long generation of "repressed capitalism" after the Second World War across the Western world, including Japan. But the potential for conflict is always present, ready to emerge whenever the markets of the private sector fail to deliver or whenever the capture of the state by one interest generates outcomes deemed

---

[8] D. Rodrik, *The Globalization Paradox: Why Global Markets, States, and Democracy Can't Coexist* (New York: Norton, 2011), pp. 184–206.

intolerably unfair by others. From this perspective, the formulation of economic policy in time of crisis takes place in a space contested by competing ideas as well as competing interests. Conflicting definitions of the legitimate limits of state action generate confusion, first for the participants and then for those who retrospectively evaluate the policy process.[9] True as this was of the formulation of economic policy during the Great Depression, it remains so today in the confused and confusing aftermath of the World Financial Crisis of 2008.

Britain's policy paralysis

In Britain, the attempt to fashion political responses to the economic challenges of 1929–1931 was a study in paralysis. Two competing but not mutually exclusive explanations offer themselves. The first is that the political leaders and their principal advisors were victims of ignorance, along with their constituents. The revolution in economic analysis expressed in Keynes's *General Theory*, published only in 1936, would have clarified the issues and liberated the Labour Government to act. The second explanation is that the paralysis of policy reflected deep conflicts in the structure of power relationships that the government inherited and that it was powerless to change in peacetime: specifically, between the responsibility of the private sector to allocate resources and to distribute income and wealth, and the scope allowed for the state to redress market failure. Both explanations are correct. But from the perspective of 2012, when Keynes's work has been available for more than two generations in various guises, it is the latter explanation that must carry the most weight.

The politicians of 1931 were crippled not only by their own ignorance but by the unenlightened self-interest of others: the bankers, investors and businesspeople who controlled access to the cash needed to fund both the state and the investments of the market economy. Determined to restrict the scope of state action in peacetime, they entrenched the economic and financial losses of market failure. The rare exceptions, David Lloyd George and Keynes, stand out as imaginative opportunists, refusing to be constrained by consistency, and

---

[9] M. Blyth, *Great Transformations: Economic Ideas and Institutional Change in the Twentieth Century* (Boston: Beacon, 2002), p. 11.

responsive to the radical transformation of the world around them. In the *General Theory*, Keynes wrote of the "long-term investor":

It is ... he who most promotes the public interest, who will in practice come in for most criticism ... For it is in the essence of his behaviour that he should be eccentric, unconventional and rash in the eyes of average opinion. If he is successful, that will only confirm the general belief in his rashness; and if in the short run he is unsuccessful, he will not receive much mercy. Worldly wisdom teaches that it is better for reputation to fail conventionally than to succeed unconventionally.[10]

In addition to writing a summary prospectus for the aspiring venture capitalist – this passage has hung on the wall of my office since I entered Wall Street – Keynes might also have been writing of his own standing in the world of 1929–1931.

Prior to 1929, and outside of wartime, the deployment of state authority (or quasi-state authority in the case of nominally private central banks, such as the Bank of England) had been limited to last-resort lending to the money market and through it to the banking system, since of all industrializing nations Britain's economic development was least underwritten by state initiatives. The modest beginnings of a social safety net were just discernible in the form of contributory state pensions and unemployment insurance, but intervention to offset contraction of the market economy was unknown to theory or to practice. As Keynes struggled to escape from a mode of thinking that implicitly assumed that all resources are always fully employed, he proposed an abstraction of the state's activities in terms of a generalized investment function: debt-financed expenditure that would fill the gap in aggregate demand when private-sector investment fails. In the *General Theory*, he dramatized the point with characteristic panache:

If the Treasury were to fill old bottles with bank-notes, bury them at suitable depths in disused coalmines which are then filled up to the surface with town rubbish, and leave it to private enterprise on well-tried principles of *laissez-faire* to dig the notes up again ... there need be no more unemployment and, with the help of the repercussions, the real income of the community, and its capital wealth also, would probably become a good deal greater

---

[10] J. M. Keynes, *The General Theory of Employment, Interest and Money*, in E. Johnson and D. Moggridge (eds.), *The Collected Writings of John Maynard Keynes*, vol. 7 (Cambridge University Press and Macmillan for the Royal Economic Society, 1976 [1936]), pp. 158–159.

than it actually is. It would, indeed, be more sensible to build houses and the like; but if there are political and practical difficulties in the way of this, the above would be better than nothing.[11]

What Keynes understood even before he could formulate a comprehensive theoretical explanation was that unemployed resources, human and capital, possess negative productivity. Skills atrophy and become obsolete; machines rust and likewise become obsolete. Putting them to work on whatever projects, even of zero economic return, will augment the flow of income and expenditure that, by definition, have been inadequate. And, incidentally, whatever goods and services those newly reemployed choose to spend their incomes on can be expected to be as economically "efficient" as what those still employed are spending money on. The positive effect will be all the greater if the new income and expenditure are funded by borrowing: as Richard Kahn demonstrated at the time, loan-financed expenditures would finance themselves out of savings from the increased stream of income.[12]

Keynes's attempt to fashion an autonomous macroeconomic role for the state failed to drive economic policy in the Britain of the 1930s. In response to his advocacy of Lloyd George's program, however, the policy debate at the time explicitly addressed the role of the state relative to systemic failure in the markets of the private sector: its potential to deliver corrective action; the barriers such intervention would face; the unintended but countervailing consequences of such initiatives; and, indeed, the legitimacy of undertaking such an effort in the first place. How deep this debate goes – to the foundations of democratic

---

[11] *Ibid.* 129.

[12] R. F. Kahn, "The Relation of Home Investment to Unemployment," *Economic Journal*, 41(163) (1931), pp. 173–198. Estimating the size of the multiplier has become a contentious subject in the academic literature. It is nonetheless clear that its magnitude is context-dependent. It is also clear that it will be at a maximum when economic resources are grossly underemployed and when monetary policy is accommodating, as was the case in Britain between the Wall Street crash in 1929 and the international crisis of the summer of 1931. For a recent, broadly confirmatory exercise in estimating fiscal multipliers generated from the models employed by the leading central banks, see G. Coenen, C. J. Erceg, C. Freedman, D. Furceri, M. Kumhof, R. Lalonde, D. Laxton, J. Lindé, A. Mourougane, D. Muir, S. Mursula, C. de Resende, J. Roberts, W. Roeger, S. Snudden, M. Trabandt and J. in't Veld, "Effects of Fiscal Stimulus in Structural Models," *American Economic Journal: Macroeconomics*, 4(1) (2012), pp. 22–68.

capitalism – is demonstrated by the extraordinary resonance that arguments three generations old have in today's debate over the proper role of the state in response to this generation's crisis. Even more, the terms on which Keynes's critics won the debate illuminates analysis of the state's role more generally. For those who exercised control over state expenditures required that they be evaluated and justified on a case-by-case basis – subject to strict scrutiny as to financial return, economic efficiency and administrative discipline. Only the clear danger of war for national survival would legitimize the state's mobilization of economic resources with the incidental effect of eliminating unemployment.

The circumstances that greeted the British Labour Government that took office in June 1929 were daunting at best. Throughout its life to August 1931, it was a minority government. Although backed by the largest of the three parliamentary parties, it was dependent for survival on at least the abstention of Liberal members of Parliament. Four years before, in 1925, Winston Churchill – thoroughly miscast in the role of Chancellor of the Exchequer – had put Britain back on the gold standard at the now overvalued prewar parity. Although this was generally held to have completed the return to normality, it generated persistent pressure on monetary policy to defend sterling, at the expense of domestic economic conditions. By the time the Labour Government took office, reported unemployment had averaged 10 percent or more for the past seven years, concentrated in the staple export trades, all of which were affected by the overvalued currency: coal, textiles, iron and steel, and shipbuilding. When the government resigned twenty-six months later, reported unemployment had reached 25 percent. Cutting unemployment benefits as the keystone of a program of fiscal austerity, which "responsible" political and financial option required as part of a quixotic attempt to keep the country on the gold standard, had become the issue over which the cabinet divided and fell. It was replaced by a nominally National Government, which was, in fact, dominated by the Conservatives.

During their time in office, members of the Labour cabinet enjoyed an opportunity, never before presented to political leaders of any state, to consider a deliberate and direct assault on mass unemployment. On taking office, the government had been confronted with a radical program of state intervention delivered by Lloyd George, who had launched the proposals in a dramatic attempt to regain the pivotal position he had occupied before, during and immediately following the First World War.

Lloyd George was the most dynamic British politician of his age. Like Lyndon Johnson in the United States two generations later, he was an outsider who fought his way to the citadel of power by skill and cunning. Emerging from rural poverty in Wales, he moved the Liberal Party toward radical initiatives in the years before 1914, most dramatically through the "People's Budget," which he introduced as Chancellor of the Exchequer in 1909. The budget imposed taxes on land plus increased and more progressive income taxes to fund old-age pensions. For the first time since the seventeenth century, the House of Lords exercised its veto to challenge the House of Commons' power of the purse. Two general elections followed to confirm, albeit shakily, the Liberal Government's legitimacy. With the king's pledge to ennoble as many new peers as needed to pass the budget, the supremacy of the House of Commons was confirmed and subsequently enshrined in the Parliament Act of 1911.

In contrast with Johnson, Lloyd George reached his political apotheosis as a war leader. As chancellor in a Liberal cabinet deeply committed to nineteenth-century principles of limited government and individual freedom, Lloyd George seized on the need to mobilize the nation for total war. In 1916, a parliamentary coup made him prime minister with Conservative support and irrevocably divided the Liberals, who never again formed a government. Victory on the battlefield in 1918 was followed immediately by a general election in which the Coalition triumphed. However, when the Conservatives realized they no longer needed Lloyd George, the Coalition Government dissolved, and the Conservatives took power on their own in 1922. The divided Liberals gave way to Labour (now no longer merely an interest group within the Liberal coalition) as the principal opposition.

Like Johnson's, Lloyd George's character was as controversial as his policies. Years afterward, Keynes remembered Lloyd George as he had appeared as a member of the Big Four at the Versailles Peace Conference of 1919:

How can I convey to the reader, who does not know him, any just impression of this extraordinary figure of our time, this siren, this goat-footed bard, this half-human visitor to our age from the hag-ridden magic and enchanted woods of Celtic antiquity? One catches in his company that flavour of final purposelessness, inner irresponsibility, existence outside of or away from our Saxon good and evil, mixed with cunning, remorselessness, love of power, that lend fascination, enthrallment, and terror to the fair-seeming magicians of North European folklore ...

Lloyd George is rooted in nothing; he is void and without content; he lives and feeds on his immediate surroundings; he is an instrument and a player at the same time which plays on the company and is played on by them too; he is a prism, as I have heard him described, which collects light and distorts it and is most brilliant if the light comes from many quarters, a vampire and medium in one.[13]

His character was also subject to question in more mundane terms. Truly a political entrepreneur, he created the Lloyd George Fund as his war chest for fighting electoral battles. It was funded with contributions on an explicitly reciprocal basis, with a set price for each level of "honour," from humble membership in the Order of the British Empire to peerages up to and including earldoms and marquisates.

Although Lloyd George was exiled from power after 1922, he remained a unique source of political energy. Much of the drama of interwar British politics was driven by the shared determination of "responsible" political leaders across the spectrum of ideology and interest to keep him in exile: the very creation of the National Government in 1931 with its pro forma Labour leadership, Conservative base and irreconcilable anti-Lloyd George Liberal support, stands witness. In 1929, he made his last throw of the dice by offering a radical response to Britain's economic slump.

Lloyd George's assertion in the 1929 election campaign that "We can conquer unemployment" represented the first deliberate effort to design a countercyclical macroeconomic policy of fiscal stimulus, not only in Britain but anywhere in the world. The significance of this initiative is heightened by the support it received from Keynes, who had first gained public standing in 1920 through his exposition in book form of *The Economic Consequences of the Peace*[14] and, most particularly, his denunciation of Lloyd George for his role in constructing "the bad peace." When challenged for this turnabout, Keynes's

---

[13] J. M. Keynes, *Essays in Biography*, in E. Johnson and D. Moggridge (eds.), *The Collected Writings of John Maynard Keynes*, vol. 10 (Cambridge University Press and Macmillan for the Royal Economic Society, 1972 [1933]), pp. 23–24.

[14] J. M. Keynes, *The Economic Consequences of the Peace* (New York: Harcourt, Brace and Howe, 1920).

characteristic retort was: "The difference between me and some other people is that I oppose Mr. Lloyd George when he is wrong and support him when he is right."[15] His pamphlet, "Can Lloyd George Do It?" provided an aggressively affirmative response to the question its title asked.[16]

The central thrust of Lloyd George's pledge to conquer unemployment was a two-year, £200 million debt-financed program of public works. National income was then on the order of £4 billion. A direct stimulus equal to 5 percent would have been significant, although its economic weight would have been diluted by being spread over several years. Hobbled also by his deserved reputation for opportunistic recklessness, Lloyd George's initiative ran headlong into obstacles deployed from within the Treasury, then and still the core of Britain's permanent government, and from both major political parties. In the debate that ensued over the next two years, three parameters of policy were invoked again and again:

(1) Economically, any works funded by the state must be "useful" and "remunerative."
(2) Administratively, centrally subsidized or funded projects must not circumvent the machinery of local government.
(3) Financially, state aid could only be funded out of current revenue.[17]

At the time and since, the financial criterion was the principal focus of theoretical debate. The original round of that argument, conducted in the context of 1929–1931, was the catalyst that triggered the process through which Keynes thought his way to the theoretical rationale for a stimulative fiscal policy and, indeed, to macroeconomic theory in its broadest sense. But the other parameters of policy have proved to be

---

[15] R. Harrod, *The Life of John Maynard Keynes* (New York: Harcourt Brace, 1951), p. 396.

[16] J. M. Keynes and H. Henderson, "Can Lloyd George Do It?" in E. Johnson and D. Moggridge (eds.), *The Collected Writings of John Maynard Keynes*, vol. 9 (Cambridge University Press and Macmillan for the Royal Economic Society, 1972 [1929]), pp. 86–125.

[17] The evolution of public works policy is exhaustively documented in W. H. Janeway, "The Economic Policy of the Second Labour Government: 1929–1931," unpublished Ph.D. thesis, University of Cambridge (1971), pp. 26–69.

at least as significant in constraining state economic initiatives. Most critically, debate over the specification of what can constitute an economically legitimate object of state expenditure has persisted to this day, defining and limiting the role of the state in the market economy in good times as in bad – whether state expenditures are proposed in response to the market economy's failure to generate adequate aggregate demand in the short term or in order to increase the market economy's growth potential in the longer run.

As promulgated at the time, the financial parameter expressed two overlapping conceptual confusions. The first lay in the difficulty of comprehending the existence of persistent unemployment through a mode of analysis that assumed full employment. If all resources are fully employed, according to the hypothesis, then borrowing and spending money can only result in inflation. In fact, in Britain and around the world mass unemployment prevailed and prices of all goods and services were falling, with disastrous consequences for all who had to service fixed amounts of debt from declining revenues and income. The second confusion was generated by the economic logic that defines the volume of employment as inversely related to the level of real wages. The existence of unemployment was considered evidence that real wages were too high. Any attempt to reduce unemployment could only operate by reducing real wages through inflation: that is, by driving prices up relative to nominal wages. Either way, debt-financed spending by the state could be condemned as an inflationary threat both to Britain's already challenged competitive position in the international marketplace and also to the domestic standard of living.

The most extreme form of the financial parameter came to be known as the Treasury dogma. Winston Churchill, in his last budget speech as Chancellor of the Exchequer before the general election of June 1929, set it forth in absolute terms:

It is the orthodox Treasury dogma, steadfastly held, that whatever might be the political or social advantages, very little additional employment and no permanent additional employment, can, in fact and a general rule be created by State borrowing and State expenditure.[18]

---

[18] Quoted in Keynes and Henderson, "Can Lloyd George Do It?" p. 115.

The Treasury's formal response to Lloyd George and Keynes, in April 1929, was more nuanced:

The large loans involved, if they are not to involve inflation, must draw on existing capital resources. These resources are on the whole utilized at present in varying degrees of active employment; and the great bulk is utilized for home industrial and commercial purposes. The extent to which any additional employment could be given by altering the direction of employment is therefore strictly limited.[19]

It was to this statement that Keynes was explicitly responding when, in the preface to the *General Theory*, he emphasized the core lesson of the book: to explain how "changing views about the future are capable of influencing the quantity of employment and not merely its direction."[20]

At the time, Keynes attacked the Treasury dogma head on, invoking common sense rather than high theory:

There is nothing in the argument which limits its applicability to State-promoted undertakings ... It must apply equally to any new business enterprise entailing capital expenditure. If it were announced that some of our leading captains of industry had decided to launch out boldly, and were about to sink capital in new industrial plant to the tune, between them, of £100 millions, we should all expect to see a great improvement in employment. And we should be right. But, if the argument we are dealing with were sound, we should be wrong. We should have to conclude that these enterprising business men were merely diverting capital from other uses, and that no real gain to employment could result.[21]

Missing from Keynes's argument, however, was that business investment, as opposed to state investment, definitionally satisfies the first two parameters of policy: it is economically efficient and administratively legitimate.

The challenge Keynes failed to overcome in 1929 – and that has been evident in every debate over stimulative fiscal policy in peacetime from the Great Depression to the Great Recession – was to justify debt-financed expenditures abstracted and decoupled from the specific

---

[19] "We Can Conquer Unemployment," Memoranda by Ministers on Certain Proposals Relating to Unemployment,' Cmd. 3331 (London: HMSO, 1929), p. 53.

[20] Keynes, *General Theory*, p. xxii.

[21] Keynes, "Can Lloyd George Do It?" pp. 115–116.

projects and programs through which cash is actually dispensed. Nonetheless, under pressure from Keynes, the senior officials of the Treasury – the "Treasury knights" – begged off from the extreme version of the dogma. In his draft notes for the evidence he gave to the Macmillan Committee on Finance and Industry, Sir Richard Hopkins referred to the statement in the April 1929 white paper as "perhaps rather telescopic." In his direct confrontation with Keynes before the committee, Hopkins was "prepared to give [Keynes] that argument" – that in theory loan-financed public works would "pay for themselves." And Chancellor of the Exchequer Philip Snowden himself, in his parliamentary statement in response to a renewed Liberal plan for "national development," directly contradicted his predecessor, Churchill:

It has sometimes been crudely said that a view obtains in the Treasury that any money borrowed by the State automatically cancels another loan of equal amount to enterprise ... This is a misrepresentation. But it is necessary also to say that in the economics of Government borrowing there are regions which are disputed and only partially explored.[22]

Yet even as Keynes won the public debate over the Treasury dogma, an alternative barrier to action took the first rank. The fear that radical economic policy would undermine confidence in sterling and threaten Britain's ability to remain on the gold standard had been explicit in official statements from the beginning of the debate. Now this concern was complemented by the line opened up by Hubert Henderson, who warned of the potential domestic economic consequences of any substantial program of public works.

Henderson was strategically placed as secretary to the government's Economic Advisory Council (EAC), a newly formed body whose existence reflected at least some sense that economic advice was needed. Henderson was a protégé of Keynes and had coauthored "Can Lloyd George Do It?" with him. But, as early as May 1930, his position had shifted. He wrote privately to Keynes, repudiating the view that Britain's unemployment problem was "a short-period, transitional problem":

If you launch a ... £200 million two year's programme ... there are solid grounds at once for believing that that means that taxation is likely to be

---

[22] CP 329(30), para. 63, quoted in Janeway, "The Economic Policy of the Second Labour Government", pp. 176–177.

increased ever higher, year by year … I should say that the alarm might quite easily serve to counter-act finally the employment benefits of the pro-gramme, and you would then be in a vicious circle of requiring a still bigger programme, still more unremunerative in character, with an increasing hole in the Budget, and increasing apprehension, until you were faced with either abandoning the whole policy or facing a real panic-flight from the pound.[23]

Henderson here invoked "Ricardian equivalence," the idea that state borrowing is economically the equivalent of state taxation since the lenders and everyone else in the private sector "know" that the bor-rowings will have to be paid back out of future tax revenues. Of course, Ricardian equivalence exhibits exactly the same fallacy as the Treasury dogma, the assumption that all resources are already fully employed. If they are not, increased employment and income generated by govern-ment stimulus will increase the tax base from which to service the gov-ernment's debt with no necessary increase in tax rates. Keynes could only assert that the increase of business profits would, "after the first blush, have more effect on them than anything else." Henderson won the debate due to his mobilization of the confidence argument to aug-ment the economic parameter, as his subsequent contributions to the policy discussion would show.

Henderson repeated his position publicly to the EAC's Committee of Economists in October 1930, and he drafted the section of its report dealing with public works, despite the fact that Keynes had been the driving figure in the creation of the committee in the first place and that Kahn was its co-secretary. Explicitly rejecting the Treasury dogma and sketchily referring to the multiplier, the report justified only works that satisfied the economic parameter by being "useful and product-ive," that could be "put into production and carried out with speed" and that would "not … create later a difficult 'demobilisation' prob-lem." "Finally," the report concluded,

The scope and scale of the programme as a whole must be such as to com-mend itself as reasonable and sensible to public opinion … While … we do not believe that employment created by public works need involve a diminu-tion of resources devoted to private investment, it might easily do so, if it took a form which aroused apprehension as to the stability of the public credit.[24]

---

[23] H. Henderson to J. M. Keynes, May 30, 1930, Keynes Papers EA/1, quoted in Janeway, "The Economic Policy of the Second Labour Government," p. 280.

[24] CP 363(30), para. 68, quoted *ibid*. 281.

No doubt, the controversial personalities of the political sponsors of such radical programs – Lloyd George, Keynes himself and Sir Oswald Mosley, who had served as an activist member of the Labour cabinet before resigning to found the British Union of Fascists – contributed to the apprehension that Henderson invoked. But what emerges as of lasting importance from this episode is the requirement that the components of state programs of expenditure be evaluated by the same criteria – "useful and productive" – that financial capitalists would apply to the investment projects of the market economy.

Implicit in this argument from confidence that trumped Keynes's economic logic is the same presumption that animates the oxymoronic notion of expansionary fiscal austerity today. State initiatives to stimulate aggregate demand are deemed inherently wasteful and, therefore, destructive of private-sector confidence. Conversely, a reduction of aggregate demand resulting from the imposition of fiscal discipline on the state will be more than offset by the blossoming of private-sector investment, animated by what Paul Krugman has memorably personified as "the confidence fairy." Henderson's arguments of eighty years ago could have been written yesterday.[25]

Thus, British economic policy at the time of the global financial crisis of 1931 shows the Three-Player Game as an exercise in stalemate. Despite mass unemployment, the crisis in the market economy was insufficient to liberate the Labour Government either from the inherited ideas that constrained its policy choices or from the threat of punishment at the hands of the financial markets if it should try to expand its options. In September 1931, the National Government, which succeeded Labour, had the political legitimacy to execute one of the great exercises in pragmatic opportunism: it abandoned the gold standard. Britain was thus freed from the market forces that drove deflation for eighteen more months in the United States and Germany and fully five more years in France. Currency depreciation of some 30 percent gave Britain access to

---

[25] See, for example, R. Barro, "The Coming Crises of Governments," *Financial Times*, August 3, 2011, or the numerous self-justifying speeches of Britain's Chancellor of the Exchequer available at www.hm-treasury.gov.uk/newsroom_and_speeches.htm. For a thorough and balanced critique of "expansionary fiscal contractions," see International Monetary Fund, "Will it Hurt? Macroeconomic Effects of Fiscal Consolidation," in *World Economic Outlook* (Washington, DC: International Monetary Fund, 2010). Available at www.imf.org/external/pubs/ft/weo/2010/02/pdf/c3.pdf.

the positive cash flow that confers autonomy of action at the national level as at the level of the individual bank or venture capitalist.

Yet the constraining power of ideas persisted: fear of loss of confidence still limited action by a government exempt from external financial and domestic political challenge. As the opponents of government stimulus in 1929–1931 abandoned their argument from first principles, they succeeded in keeping the Labour Government and the National Government from the path of experimentation that Franklin Delano Roosevelt pursued in the United States, however haphazardly and inadequately. And unemployment in Britain, while roughly halving from the 1932 peak, did not fall below 10 percent, even as the depreciated pound and the cheap money consequent on relief from adherence to gold combined to generate a slow recovery. Only mobilization for war at the end of the decade would finally drive the British economy to full employment.

The New Deal

In contrast with Britain, both the United States and Germany witnessed activist programs of public works financed by central government deficits. The economic devastation in these countries was manifestly worse than in Britain, as the economic contraction was accelerated and amplified by domestic banking crises that liquidated savings as well as jobs. And, in each case, the failure of an incumbent conservative government to respond effectively to the Depression created the political opening for radical initiatives. Yet the history of civilian public works in the two hugely different regimes – the New Deal and the Third Reich – serves perversely to confirm the lessons to be drawn from the British experience of political paralysis.

The centerpiece of FDR's initial program of recovery and reform was the National Industrial Recovery Act, passed into law on June 16, 1933. Title II of the act created the Public Works Administration (PWA), endowed with an enormous appropriation of $3.3 billion, more than $50 billion in current dollars, 165 percent of then total federal revenues and almost 6 percent of 1933 gross domestic product (GDP).[26] The PWA drew on the distant history of US state and federal

---

[26] J. S. Smith, *Building New Deal Liberalism: The Political Economy of Public Works, 1933–1956* (Cambridge University Press, 2006), p. 2.

governments' funding of internal improvements: turnpikes, canals and railroads. More recently and relevantly, countercyclical public works had been advocated as an instrument of public policy to offset periodic waves of unemployment by the economists William Foster and Waddill Catchings in their 1928 book *The Road to Plenty*[27] and embraced reluctantly and to a limited and indirect extent by Hoover through the Reconstruction Finance Corporation.[28] Characteristic of the first New Deal's incoherent experimentation, however, the PWA had been preceded by the Economy Act of 1933, which was intended to fulfill FDR's campaign pledge to balance the budget and mandated a $500 million reduction in federal spending, then running at only $3.6 billion.

The conflict between the orthodoxy of public finance and the demands of the economic emergency were duplicated in the operations of the PWA. Harold Ickes, administrator of the PWA as well as Secretary of the Interior, was a cantankerous, utterly honest progressive who served FDR loyally for the full thirteen years of his tenure. He was "determined that no money under his jurisdiction should be wasted or corruptly spent."[29] Under Hoover's Reconstruction Finance Corporation, projects had been required to be self-liquidating: that is, revenues from tolls and fees were to offset the capital costs of construction. This limited both the volume of projects funded and any impact on unemployment or aggregate demand.

Although Ickes and the PWA relaxed the Hoover-era requirement that projects be self-liquidating, the change was made only on paper. The PWA proclaimed that projects would be chosen based on their social and economic "desirability", their fit with pre-existing plans, their engineering and technical "soundness", the financial stability of the applicant, and the "legal enforceability" of any securities bought by the federal government in order to fund the project. In fact however, only the last three factors – engineering, legal and financial soundness – were formally measured and reviewed by the PWA.[30]

Criticism of Ickes's disciplined approach was widespread from the beginning, as exemplified by *Business Week*'s editorial comment: "Mr.

---

[27] W. Foster and W. Catchings, *The Road to Plenty* (Boston: Houghton Mifflin, 1928).

[28] Smith, *Building New Deal Liberalism*, pp. 27, 136.

[29] A. J. Badger, *The New Deal: The Depression Years, 1933–1940* (New York: Hill & Wang, 1989), p. 83.

[30] Smith, *Building New Deal Liberalism*, p. 86.

Ickes is running a fire department on the principles of a good, sound bond house."[31] After the fact, John Kenneth Galbraith estimated in the official review conducted in 1940 that "total off-site and on-site employment" generated by the PWA and related federal construction projects averaged slightly less than 1.2 million during the years 1934–1938, at the start of which period unemployment was over 10 million. Many of the jobs ascribed to the PWA were indirect, the result of derived demand for construction materials; the count was not based on the mathematics of the multiplier.

FDR had no patience with such calculations, and he was not alone: frustration with the PWA's limited direct impact on unemployment led to the June 1935 creation by executive order of the Works Progress Administration (WPA) as the vehicle for providing direct "work relief." Although the WPA made a widespread contribution to the creation of public works of value, it was under continuous assault for funding uneconomic waste ("boondoggles") and for political patronage. Nonetheless, it managed to create some 1.6 million jobs on average, again as estimated by Galbraith.[32]

The New Deal's accounting maintained the fiction of a balanced normal budget, from which such emergency programs as the PWA and the WPA were excluded. In fact, the aggregate federal deficit reached $3.2 billion in 1936, as the growth in GDP averaged some 10 percent per year from the Depression low of $56.4 billion, and unemployment declined from the peak count approaching 15 million at the time of FDR's inauguration to below 5 million in the summer of 1937 – still (as in Britain) about 10 percent of those working or looking for work.[33]

The administration then snatched defeat from the jaws of incipient victory by means of an aggressive shift back to fiscal orthodoxy. Spending cuts and tax increases – notably including the $1.4 billion, first-year impact of Social Security taxes with no offsetting benefits paid out – killed recovery and generated a recession that drove unemployment back above 11 million in 1938.[34] Only then did the

---

[31] Quoted *ibid.* 99.   [32] *Ibid.* 101.

[33] See www.nber.org/databases/macrohistory/rectdata/08/m08084a.dat.

[34] Among my father's first career-making insights as an apprentice economic analyst was his anticipation of the "Roosevelt recession." See M. C. Janeway, *The Fall of the House of Roosevelt: Brokers of Ideas and Power from FDR to LBJ* (New York: Columbia University Press, 2004), p. 93.

"proto-Keynesians" of the second New Deal, led by Federal Reserve chair Marriner Eccles, convince FDR to commit explicitly to fiscal stimulus, embodied in a $3.75 billion spending package.[35] Two years later, when the war in Europe exploded from its "phony" stage into Hitler's blitzkrieg in France, the United States followed Britain into mobilization for total war, even though rearmament by stealth remained a political necessity in the United States through the 1940 presidential election.[36]

The Third Reich

In Germany's case, it was at the start of his regime that Hitler needed to exercise stealth while investment in armaments drove economic recovery. Still subject to the restrictions on ground, naval and air forces imposed by the Versailles Treaty, the Third Reich adopted the civilian "work creation" programs it inherited from the last administrations of the Weimar Republic and aggressively propagandized their importance.[37] But, as the leading scholar of the Third Reich's economic history, Adam Tooze, writes: "the 'Keynesian' issues of work creation and unemployment were never as prominent in the agenda of Hitler's Government as commonly supposed."[38]

The monies appropriated confirm the relative magnitudes of investment in war-fighting capability versus civilian public works. The two "Reinhardt Programs" of work creation approved in 1933 amounted to some 1.5 billion Reichsmarks.[39] Even augmented by the much-heralded autobahn construction program, which was explicitly legitimized by its importance to national defense, the economic weight was marginal compared with the secret four-year, 35 billion Reichsmarks rearmament program to which Hitler committed in June 1933 at the same time as he eliminated formal international constraints by declaring a moratorium on foreign debts. "In every respect except propaganda," writes Tooze, "the civilian work creation measures of 1933 were

[35] Badger, *The New Deal*, pp. 111–113.
[36] See R. J. Gordon and R. Krenn, "The End of the Great Depression, 1939–1941: Policy Contributions and Fiscal Multipliers," National Bureau of Economic Research Working Paper 16380 (2010).
[37] R. Evans, *The Third Reich in Power* (New York: Penguin, 2005), p. 329.
[38] A. Tooze, *The Wages of Destruction: The Making and Breaking of the Nazi Economy* (London: Allen Lane, 2006), p. 38.
[39] *Ibid*. 42–48.

dwarfed by the decisions taken in relation to rearmament and foreign debt. The military spending package vastly exceeded anything ever contemplated for work creation." Despite continuing promotion of the "Battle for Work," Tooze reports, "not a single Reichsmark was allocated to national work creation in 1934 or at any point thereafter."[40]

Creatively financed by off-budget credits laundered through a state-sponsored financing vehicle in which such major industrial companies as Krupp and Siemens participated, rearmament was the engine of German recovery. From 1 percent of national income in 1933, such expenditures reached 10 percent in 1935 and more than 20 percent in 1938, as national income itself doubled from the 43 billion Reichsmark level of 1933.[41] In no way subject to the tests applied to proposed civilian public works in Britain or the United States – or, indeed, in Germany itself – Hitler's Four Year Plan generated uncoordinated chaos as the armed forces competed for labor and materials: the first imposition of price controls and rationing on consumer foodstuffs came as early as 1937, and "by 1939, shortages of raw materials were leading to grotesque consequences for the everyday life of ordinary Germans."[42] More relevant to the regime's priorities, aircraft production actually declined between 1937 and 1938.[43] But in response to headlong spending on armaments, and amplified by the manipulation of statistics, the reported number of people unemployed declined from the Depression peak of 6 million in the winter of 1932–1933 to fewer than 1 million in 1937.[44]

Parallel stories

Considering the radically different paths of policy in Britain, the United States and Germany, one observes that Britain preempted its industrial rivals by leaving the gold standard early, and then, with appalling consequences, Germany trumped both Britain and the United States by seizing mobilization for war as its economic motive force. Less than ten years after the fall of the Labour Government and Britain's departure from the gold standard, the potential for loan-financed government spending to stimulate final demand and eliminate unemployment

---

[40] *Ibid.* 55, 59.   [41] *Ibid.* 53, 62–63.
[42] Evans, *The Third Reich in Power*, pp. 363–364.
[43] *Ibid.* 362.   [44] *Ibid.* 333.

was conclusively demonstrated country by country through the economic impact of rearmament. From 1937 to 1942, British "Public Authorities' Current Expenditures on Goods and Services" rose from £536 million, or 10.5 percent of gross national product, to £4,581 million, or 47.3 percent of GNP.[45] Over the same period, unemployment fell from 10.8 percent to 0.6 percent.[46]

Unsurprisingly, the story in the United States runs in parallel. In 1929, total expenditures by all levels of American government had amounted to a mere 9 percent of GDP; of this, only 1.7 percent was federal spending. The increase in the public-sector share to 15.4 percent in 1933 was entirely a function of the collapse in GDP by no less than 46 percent in then current prices, from $103.6 billion to $56.4 billion. The trivial increase in federal expenditures, from $1.7 billion to $2.3 billion, was more than offset by a decline in state and local spending. While total government savings did decline from $2.6 billion to a deficit of $0.5 billion – of which two-thirds was at the federal level – the $3.1 billion contribution to final demand amounted to only one-fifth of the catastrophic decline in private-sector gross fixed investment, which fell by no less than 90 percent, from $16.5 billion to $1.7 billion, and was the primary engine of economic contraction.[47]

During the summer of 1964, I served as a research assistant to Lester Chandler of Princeton, a doyen of old-school money-and-banking finance. Chandler was on the way to publishing *American Monetary Policy, 1929–1941*,[48] a useful, if underappreciated, corrective to Milton Friedman and Anna Jacobson Schwartz's much better known *Monetary History of the United States*,[49] which attributed the Depression's dynamics to monetary policy alone. At the time, the concept of the full-employment budget deficit was being promulgated by the Council

[45] B. R. Mitchell, *British Historical Statistics* (Cambridge University Press, 1988), p. 834.

[46] "Labour Force 8: Adjusted Estimate of Overall Percentages Unemployed 1855–1965 and Percentages of Insured Unemployment 1913–1980," *ibid.* 124.

[47] Bureau of Economic Analysis, US Department of Commerce, National Economic Accounts, tables 1.1.5, 1.1.10, 3.1 and 3.2. Available at www.bea.gov/national/nipaweb.

[48] L. V. Chandler, *American Monetary Policy, 1929–1941* (New York: Harper & Row, 1971). The published work does not refer to the back-of-the-envelope exercise Chandler conducted with me.

[49] M. Friedman and A. J. Schwartz, *A Monetary History of the United States, 1867–1960* (Princeton University Press, 1963).

of Economic Advisors as a useful rationale for the Kennedy–Johnson tax cuts of that year. Professor Chandler guided me through a back-of-the-envelope calculation to estimate the magnitude of the federal deficit in 1933 that would have been roughly consistent with a return to full employment. As I recall, the number we came up with was on the order of three times the size of total federal expenditures in 1932.

The peacetime scale of the public sector in both countries was simply incommensurate with the magnitude of the collapse in private-sector economic activity. In the United States as in the United Kingdom, mobilization for war demonstrated the economic potential of government stimulus. As total government spending rose from $13.8 billion in 1938, or 16 percent of GDP (of which federal spending was less than half), to no less than $62.7 billion in 1943, or 48 percent of a GDP that in aggregate had itself doubled, unemployment fell from 20 percent in June 1938 to 0.2 percent in June 1942.[50] In July 1940, Keynes took rueful note in an article published in the *New Republic:* "It is, it seems, politically impossible for a capitalist democracy to organize expenditure on the scale necessary to make the grand experiment which would prove my case – except in war conditions."[51]

From the perspective of today's Great Recession, the authors of the most comprehensive analysis of the economic effect of transnational fiscal and monetary policies during the Great Depression broadly concur:

Fiscal policy made little difference during the 1930s because it was not deployed on the requisite scale, not because it was ineffective ... The real Keynesian stimulus, when it came, would be associated with military expenditure during World War II, producing very rapid growth in countries like the United States. In our view, peacetime stimulus packages, which could have halted the rise in unemployment that ultimately led to the election of Adolf Hitler ... would have been preferable to the stimulus of war.[52]

[50] See www.nber.org/databases/macrohistory/data/08/m08292a.db.

[51] J. M. Keynes, "The United States and the Keynes Plan," *New Republic* (July 29, 1940), in E. Johnson and D. Moggridge (eds.), *The Collected Writings of John Maynard Keynes*, vol. 22 (Cambridge University Press and Macmillan for the Royal Economic Society, 1978), p. 149.

[52] M. Almunia, A. S. Bénétrix, B. Eichengreen, K. S. O'Rourke and G. Rua, "From Great Depression to Great Credit Crisis: Similarities, Differences and Lessons," National Bureau of Economic Research Working Paper 15524 (2009), p. 25.

This is precisely why scrutiny of the peacetime stimulus programs of the 1930s is so relevant. For if the state is blocked when it asserts the authority to allocate resources in pursuit of full employment when they are manifestly not scarce, how will it legitimize such interventions in the market economy under normal conditions? Echoing Keynes, Badger asks the right questions with specific reference to the United States in the 1930s but with broader reach across time and space:

Could policy-makers in the 1930s have devised ways of spending enough money to secure full economic recovery? Did the expertise and mechanisms exist for a larger public works programme than that operated by the PWA? How big did the deficit need to be to secure full employment? Would such a deficit have been politically feasible and economically successful in the face of intransigent business opposition? Do Keynesian economic policies work only in time of war?[53]

[53] Badger, *The New Deal*, p. 117.

12   Tolerating waste

Efficiency is *the* virtue of economics. By definition, in efficient markets resources are optimally allocated to satisfy expressed individual preferences; free competition and the price mechanism ensure the absence of waste in a persistent general equilibrium. But any such notional economy is frozen outside of time, either locked into a once-and-for-all Arrow–Debreu general equilibrium, where all the infinity of possible transactions have been already enacted, or alternatively replicating itself endlessly in an imaginary steady state. In either case, innovation is banned by hypothesis. Forty years ago, I left academic economics because I was unable to internalize and propagate the notion of an efficient general equilibrium as a plausible representation of economic reality.

Of course, economic inefficiency is not itself virtuous. And, of course, economists have long been aware of market failures. The literature on external economies and diseconomies and on imperfect competition induced by increasing returns to scale has evolved for generations. More recently, Nobel Prizes have been awarded to the theorists who have analyzed the consequences of asymmetrical information between market participants and those who have evaluated psychological biases previously excluded from the discipline's domain. The recognition of strategic behavior by market players operating under conditions of incomplete information has become widespread, nowhere more so than in financial economics, where there is a great blossoming of work on markets populated by heterogeneous agents whose expectations are ever imperfect and whose ability to stand against the market is limited in time and extent. Yet the cultural center of gravity in consideration of markets in financial assets and in real goods and services remains drawn to the promise of waste-free, efficient outcomes.

The necessity of waste

In this context, taking economic waste seriously is both needed and challenging. This I have come to do both as a theorist and as a practitioner, concerned with the historical reality of two very different types of economic waste. First, in my doctoral study of the formulation of economic policy in the Great Depression, the presenting issue was what – if anything – to do about the pervasive waste to which Keynes addressed himself: the underemployment of resources due to an inadequate level of aggregate demand in a stubbornly persistent short run. Then, as a reflective practitioner of venture capital over four decades, I came to appreciate the necessity of waste on the long-run, supply side of the market economy: in the uncertain processes of scientific discovery, which have been the primary source of technological innovation over the past 150 years, and in the speculative exploitation of such innovation for commercially rewarding uses. I refer to the productive waste required for creative destruction in the Innovation Economy as Schumpeterian, in conscious disregard of Schumpeter's indictment of all political intervention in the market economy.

Here is the irony. The same appeal to economic efficiency serves both to rationalize the toleration of Keynesian waste and to limit the toleration of Schumpeterian waste, and the double-edged impact is compounded by the interaction between the two effects. When Keynesian waste is at a minimum – that is, in a high-growth, fully employed economy – the consequences of Schumpeterian waste are likely to be more creative and less destructive. More innovations will be profitably exploited, and the people and capital stranded in legacy occupations will be more rapidly redeployed. And very much vice versa.

To explore this interaction, a good place to start is with the essay "Endogenous Growth and Cycles," published by Joseph Stiglitz in 1993. It begins with a critique of Schumpeter's "Austrian" view of the beneficial consequences of economic contractions:

Schumpeter emphasized the long-run efficiency enhancing aspects of economic downturns. We argue here that by ignoring the deleterious effects on R&D he underestimated the negative effects of recessions, and that on balance macro-economic policies that stabilized the economy are more likely to be conducive to long run growth.[1]

---

[1] J. Stiglitz, "Endogenous Growth and Cycles," in Y. Shionnoya and M. Perlman (eds.), *Innovation in Technology, Industries and Institutions: Studies in Schumpeterian Perspectives* (Ann Arbor, MI: University of Michigan Press, 1994), p. 5. Although Schumpeter did, indeed, share the Austrian view of the cleansing properties of periodic recessions, writing in 1939 he conceded that

Stiglitz recognizes that because financial markets are necessarily incomplete, firms "cannot fully divest themselves of all the risks which they face."[2] So, in times of economic contraction, the riskiest expenditures are the most likely to be cut. Moreover, productivity gains from learning by doing will likely be less than in periods of high growth.[3] Taking account of the positive feedback processes that reciprocally relate current output and income to past R&D spending, and current R&D spending to future output and income, Stiglitz is able to construct a simple model to illustrate how

there are real costs to economic fluctuations which extend well beyond the temporary loss in output and the economic waste resulting from unused resources: the future productivity of the economy is adversely affected. These long run losses are likely to be far more significant than any temporary gains from any induced cost-cutting.[4]

More recently, a team of economists led by Giovanni Dosi set out to extend Stiglitz's creative attempt "to explore the feedbacks between the factors influencing aggregate demand and those driving technological change."[5] I find this work of striking interest for three reasons. First, Dosi and his colleagues incorporate the critical features of

once recession had spiraled into self-reinforcing depression: "There seems in fact to be an element of truth in the popular opinion that there must be help from outside of the business organism, from government action or some favorable chance event for instance, if there is to be recovery at all or, at any rate, recovery without a preceding period of complete disorganization and of indefinite length." J. A. Schumpeter, *Business Cycles: A Theoretical, Historical and Statistical Analysis of the Capitalist Process*, 2 vols. (London: McGraw-Hill, 1939), vol. 1, p. 154.

[2] Stiglitz, "Endogenous Growth and Cycles," p. 10.

[3] In imperfect support of Schumpeter's position, it should be noted that Alexander Field has mobilized evidence to suggest that the greatest measured increase in US total factor productivity occurred during the Great Depression, when industrial laggards took advantage of the proven benefits of electrification and when public investment in road building enabled major improvements in transportation and distribution. However, Field's data do not capture the consequences for future growth in productivity of a forced reduction in discretionary corporate spending on R&D. A. J. Field, *A Great Leap Forward: 1930s Depression and US Economic Growth* (New Haven, CT: Yale University Press, 2011), pp. 19–41.

[4] Stiglitz, "Endogenous Growth and Cycles," p. 44.

[5] G. Dosi, G. Fagiolo and A. Roventini, "Schumpeter Meeting Keynes: A Policy-Friendly Model of Endogenous Growth and Business Cycles," *Journal of Economic Dynamics and Growth*, 34 (2010), pp. 1748–1767.

Stiglitz's simple model, notably imperfect capital markets. They also honor George Akerlof's "dream" of escaping the Rational Expectations Hypothesis by developing a "behavioral macroeconomics ... in the original spirit of Keynes' *General Theory*," one that emphasizes "the role of psychological and sociological factors, such as cognitive bias, reciprocity, fairness, herding and social status."[6] Finally, in order to explore the resulting systemic modes of behavior, they construct the sort of agent-based simulation that I found so compelling almost forty years ago.

Dosi's work in progress, disciplined by the comparison of model output with empirical data, confirms the intuition of

a strong complementarity between Schumpeterian policies addressing innovative activities and Keynesian demand-management policies. Both types of policies seem to be necessary to put the economy into a long-run sustained growth path. Schumpeterian policies *potentially* foster economic growth, but they do not appear to be able alone to yield sustained long-run growth ... By the same token, demand shocks (in the simplest case, induced by government fiscal policies) bear persistent effects upon *output levels, rates of growth* and *rates of innovation*. Keynesian policies not only have a strong impact on output volatility and unemployment, but seem to be a necessary condition for long-run economic growth.[7]

In an exercise that demonstrates the inverse of Hyman Minsky's identification of the strategic role of the state in "stabilizing an unstable economy," when the government sector is shut down, "the economy experiences wider fluctuations and higher unemployment rates in the short run." Critically:

output growth in the long-run [is] not far from nil. Countercyclical Keynesian policies ... act indeed as a parachute during recessions, sustaining consumption and, indirectly, investment on the demand side. However, they also bear *long-term effects* on the supply side: in particular on the rates of growth of productivity and output ... A vicious feedback loop goes from low output to low investment in R&D, low rates of innovation.[8]

---

[6] G. A. Akerlof, "Behavioral Macroeconomics and Macroeconomic Behavior," *American Economic Review*, 92(3) (2002), p. 411.

[7] Dosi, Fagiolo and Roventini, "Schumpeter Meeting Keynes," p. 1750; emphasis in original.

[8] *Ibid.* 1763; emphasis in original.

Thus, participation in – let alone leadership of – the Innovation Economy turns on the existence of a politically legitimate state with the resources and the understanding required to sustain the market economy over time. This is where possession of Cash and Control, those twin sources of autonomy in an uncertain world, come into their own at the level of the nation-state. Cash and Control are the assets that permit independent policy formation, even as they invite the charge of mercantilism from market fundamentalists. Perversely, they are what today empower Germany to force fiscal austerity and Keynesian waste on its dependents across Euroland. Equally, they are what empower China to pursue its broad commitment to Schumpeterian waste, from building multiple high-speed train lines to aggressively investing in the science and engineering of solar energy.

Asymmetry of power is built into the global financial economy. The various ways in which that power is applied are functions of the balance of differing domestic political interests, the evolution of distinctive political cultures and the expression of perceived national purpose: economic development, financial control, military security or social justice. Those nations enjoying Fred Adler's "positive cash flow from operations" – translated to this domain as a surplus in the current account of the international balance of payments – enjoy, for their own and their neighbors' good or ill, freedom to choose.

The Great Depression and the Great Recession

During the 1930s, the requirement that projects of civilian public works be useful and productive on their own terms limited the ability of the state to offset the failure of private investment. The prospect of wasteful boondoggles financed with borrowed money drove the "argument from confidence" that carried the day against Keynes's proposal for debt-financed fiscal stimulus and the New Deal's halting experiments along similar lines. For, indeed, an extended and diverse history of incompetent and mendacious disposition of state-controlled resources was available for all to observe. It was not for nothing that the pre-Victorian British political establishment had been known as "Old Corruption." In the United States of 1933, the theft of the Navy's petroleum reserves at Teapot Dome a decade earlier was living memory. But, in consequence, only when Britain and the United States were compelled to respond to Hitler's mobilization for war was unemployment finally conquered, by the ultimate engine of economic waste.

The world financial crisis of 2007–2009 and the Great Recession that followed came in a world institutionally transformed from that of the 1930s. In 1936, Keynes had expressed his frustration over the inability of peacetime Britain to generate an adequate response to the Great Depression in his "Concluding Notes on the Social Philosophy Toward Which the General Theory Might Lead":

> I conceive, therefore, that a somewhat comprehensive socialization of investment will prove the only means of securing an approximation to full employment; though this need not exclude all manner of compromises and devices by which public authority will co-operate with private initiative.[9]

The term "socialization" sounds revolutionary. And, in historical fact, something not unlike what Keynes suggested has occurred: a revolution in the scale of the state relative to the private sector and, in particular, of government expenditures relative to private investment. I find it astonishing that the voluminous literature written to compare and contrast the Great Depression of the 1930s and the Great Recession that began in 2008 has paid so little attention to this most obviously significant fact.

In today's Britain, general government expenditures exceed private-sector fixed capital formation, and they have done so for years.[10] In the United States, combined federal, state and local government expenditures exceed gross private domestic fixed investment.[11] Thus, the public sector is of a scale to cushion abrupt reductions in the most volatile element of private sector spending. In both cases, this is without taking into account the macroeconomic role of social welfare transfer payments, which serve as automatic stabilizers when private sector income and employment contract. Reflecting the impact of the Great Recession, combined US government spending rose from 31 percent of gross domestic product (GDP) in 2006, with the federal

---

[9] J. M. Keynes, *The General Theory of Employment, Interest and Money*, in E. Johnson and D. Moggridge (eds.), *The Collected Writings of John Maynard Keynes*, vol. 7 (Cambridge University Press and Macmillan for the Royal Economic Society, 1976 [1936]), p. 378.

[10] *United Kingdom National Accounts* (The Blue Book) (2008), table C1.

[11] United States Bureau of Economic Analysis, National Economic Accounts, table 1.1.5. Available at www.bea.gov/national/nipaweb.

share at two-thirds, to more than 35 percent in 2009, with virtually all of the increase at the federal level (in this comparison, transfer payments are taken into account, as they should be because this source of private-sector income is stable regardless of macroeconomic conditions).[12] And the public sector of the United States is smaller as a component of the national economy than that of any other developed or substantial emerging economy in the world.

Even as the increased scale and scope of the public sector has transformed and stabilized the institutional architecture of the market economy, its legitimacy has been challenged. The return of market fundamentalism gained momentum during the Reagan–Thatcher era of the 1980s and peaked as the World Financial Crisis of 2007–2009 began. In its origins, it was in good part a negative reaction to over-reaching by political leaders, especially in Washington. There, Lyndon Johnson's Great Society asserted the authority of the state across a broad frontier: to take up the abandoned struggle for civil rights; to establish Medicare as the first extension of the American welfare state since social security; and to initiate a limited and compromised War on Poverty. Both LBJ's historic achievements and evident failures at home came to be read through the lens of the Vietnam catastrophe, as his liberal coalition dissolved.

The lesson from the failure of policy was critically reinforced by innovation in economic theory. Here the cause and context lay in the stagflation that followed the first global oil shock of 1973, when the previously observed trade-off between inflation and unemployment – the Phillips Curve – appeared to collapse. As inflation and unemployment rose in parallel, what had been a standard guide to policy, indicating whether stimulus or restraint was in order, failed.[13]

The apparent breakdown of the Phillips Curve created a historic opening for Robert Lucas of the University of Chicago. From the late 1960s, Lucas and his colleagues had been working to complete the neoclassical program by showing that rational agents operating in the markets of the economy would render any policy initiatives ineffective by shifting their behavior in response to the state's interventions. The expectations of those rational agents would dominate the purposes of the policy makers.

[12] *Ibid.*, tables 3.1, 3.2 and 3.3.
[13] As recounted in Chapter 2, this was the shock to macroeconomic theory and econometric practice that drove me to discover computers.

The assertion that expectations matter was, of course, as central to the economics of Keynes as it is to the economics of Lucas. For Keynes, expectations are necessarily precarious, to use his term, and behavior consequently unstable. For Lucas, expectations are defined to be rational in terms of the stationary neoclassical model of the world, which all actors are assumed to share and which is asserted to be true. When participants in efficient markets are defined to exhibit rational expectations, only unanticipated shocks can have even a transient effect on economic outcomes.

The theoretical appeal of the Lucas Critique reflected its insistence that macroeconomics be derived consistently from microfoundations. Rational expectations themselves are internally consistent by definition, at the expense of decoupling those who are asserted to hold them from the manifestly inconsistent and uncertain world in which human beings live. From the underlying microfoundations of rational representative agents maximizing their various utility and production functions as they consume and produce, Lucas and his colleagues constructed an alternative macroeconomics whose prime virtue was precisely its consistency with those rational expectations.[14]

The macroeconomics constructed on Lucas's microfoundations allowed little scope for a financial system capable of generating endogenous shocks as bubbles formed, blossomed and burst. And its logic purported to demonstrate that no macroeconomic intervention by the state could have any sustained effect on the real variables of the market economy. Any intervention by the state could be expected only to introduce inefficient distortions to the equilibrium allocation of resources.

Hence arose the fatal undermining of the neoclassical synthesis of the "bastard Keynesians." To Keynes's followers in Cambridge, England, Paul Samuelson and his colleagues in Cambridge, Massachusetts, had skimmed the surface of Keynes's economics to invoke discretionary macroeconomic policy as capable of assuring that all resources could always be counted on to be fully employed. Now, the apparent failure

[14] See R. E. Lucas Jr, "Nobel Lecture: Monetary Neutrality," *Journal of Political Economy*, 104(4) (1996), pp. 661–682. For accessible and insightful reviews of the rise of the Rational Expectations Hypothesis as the capstone of the Efficient Market Hypothesis, see J. Cassidy, *How Markets Fail: The Logic of Economic Calamities* (New York: Farrar, Straus and Giroux, 2009), pp. 97–107 and P. Mehrling, *The New Lombard Street: How the Fed Became the Dealer of Last Resort* (Princeton University Press, 2010), pp. 88–89.

in practice of Keynesian macroeconomic policy in the face of stagflation rendered Keynesian macroeconomic theory vulnerable to the
charge of internal inconsistency.

Broad acceptance of the Rational Expectations revolution was reinforced by two other exercises in overreaching by those in charge of the
state during the 1970s. In the United States, Richard Nixon imposed
peacetime wage and price controls, an unprecedented exercise in
opportunism that contributed to his landslide reelection in 1972. In
the United Kingdom, later in the decade, the Labour Government then
in power attempted to fend off inflation through an "incomes policy"
that depended on voluntary restraint on the part of its allied labor
unions. Both initiatives failed, and in failing they legitimized the libertarian program to role back the state, popularized most effectively by
Milton Friedman and implemented to varying extents in Britain and
America by the Thatcher and Reagan administrations.

There is a historical irony here whose significance extends beyond
the realm of academic economic theory. At the time of the first oil
shock, very few analysts and commentators – one of them was Richard
Cooper of Harvard[15] – correctly read the quadrupling of oil prices by
the OPEC governments' cartel as a massive excise tax imposed on
energy consumers in the advanced countries, industrial and residential
alike. Radically augmenting already apparent cost–push wage inflation, it drove up the cost of doing business and, as producers sought
to maintain profit margins, it also drove up prices and the cost of
living. But it *was* a tax: cash was drained from energy-deficit economies, where the propensity to consume was high, and flowed to the
underdeveloped producing states, so global aggregate demand was
depressed. No wonder unemployment and inflation were observed to
rise in tandem.

Reducing the impact of this tax depended on increasing the elastic-
ity of demand with respect to the price of energy – that is, increasing the efficiency of energy production and consumption. And that,
in turn, depended on investment in new products and new processes,
investment that was not forthcoming as the economy slumped while
interest rates rose in line with inflation. Even with banks incentivized

[15] See R. Cooper, "Oil and the International Monetary System," in Patrick
Boarman and David Tuerck (eds.), *World Monetary Disorder* (New York:
Praeger, 1976).

to work out how to recycle petrodollars back into the financial systems of the developed world, and with the assistance of state initiatives such as minimum fuel standards for autos, this was the work of years. So the intellectual revolution that expelled the state from the market economy was legitimized by a willed misreading of the economic consequences of state action by OPEC.

A long, honorable and increasingly influential range of critiques is trained on the Rational Expectations Hypothesis. Most productive in my view has been the gradual integration of game theory with approaches to understanding human behavior from the other social sciences. This allows rigorous modeling of strategic behavior on the part of agents who understand that the outcome of their own behavior depends on the behavior of others. From within the discipline, Hashem Pesaran defined "The Limits to Rational Expectations" as long ago as 1987:

It may be possible to defend the representation of exogenous uncertainty by means of stable probability functions ... where individuals through their own actions cannot influence the data generating process. Unfortunately, the same cannot be said when the source of uncertainty is behavioral.[16]

Nonetheless, the neoclassical counterrevolution has dominated academic economics. From it, two distinct strands of policy-oriented macroeconomics emerged.

The New Classicals and the New Keynesians

The New Classical freshwater economists, principally located in the American Midwest, with the Universities of Chicago and Minnesota as home bases, rationalized a return to *laissez-faire*. Their Real Business Cycle Theory held that the friction-free, self-adjusting market system can be disturbed only by shocks from the outside – exogenous shocks such as natural disasters or techno-scientific discoveries or the characteristically misguided interventions of the state. In a kind of Minsky process at the level of theory, the so-called Great Moderation in macroeconomic volatility that prevailed during the 1980s and 1990s – itself the result of repeated interventions by the institutions of big-state

---

[16] H. Pesaran, *The Limits to Rational Expectations* (Oxford: Basil Blackwell, 2007), p. 15. See also Akerlof, "Behavioral Macroeconomics."

capitalism and the counterpart in the real economy of the super-bubble in the financial system – encouraged emergence of a macroeconomics that excluded the state save as a source of exogenous disruption.[17]

The New Keynesians, or saltwater economists, typically to be found on the east and west coasts of the United States, with roots in Cambridge, Massachusetts and Berkeley, California, preserved an intellectual basis for state intervention in response to manifest macroeconomic shortfalls from optimal performance. Acting as pragmatists, they incorporated frictions of various sorts, notably sticky prices and wages, into their models. In consequence, their models are able to demonstrate the inconsistent collective outcomes – the coordination failures characterized by unemployed resources – that are endemic to macroeconomic life.[18]

Both New Classicals and New Keynesians, however, allowed money into their models only to a limited extent. The money supply was considered fixed, provided by the central bank from outside the system, rather than endogenously generated by the financial system. Consequently, their models made only marginal provision for the way increased liquidity preference in the face of heightened uncertainty decouples demand and supply or even for the effect on the real economy of the relative availability and cost of credit. And thus they generally failed to anticipate the real economic consequences of the financial Crisis of 2008: as late as the fourth quarter of that year they were predicting real economic growth in 2009.

The immediate effects of the crisis have been, first, to discredit Real Business Cycle Theory and, second, to induce elaboration of the New Keynesian models by adding specifically financial frictions as further sources of disequilibrium. The first, I would assert, represents an unequivocal increase in the net sum of human knowledge. The second invites comparison with the ever more complex addition of epicycles to the pre-Copernican, Ptolemaic model of the solar system in the effort to keep the earth at the center of the universe.

---

[17] I owe this insight to Ira Katznelson of Columbia University.
[18] For a positive view of "modern macro," presented just as the Crisis of 2008 was gathering force, see M. Woodford, "Convergence in Macroeconomics: Elements of the New Synthesis," prepared for the annual meeting of the American Economics Association, January 4, 2008. Available at www. columbia.edu/~mw2230/Convergence_AEJ.pdf. For a negative view, see P. Krugman, "How Did Economists Get it so Wrong?" *New York Times Magazine* (September 2, 2009).

Especially where and when finance theorists and economists operate in close proximity to each other, as at Princeton, a more profound effort has become discernible.[19] This entails reconstruction of the core of macroeconomics by drawing on innovative approaches to understanding behavior in the peripheral financial markets. Ricardo Caballero observes:

> In the context of the current economic and financial crisis, the periphery gave us frameworks to understand phenomena such as speculative bubbles, leverage cycles, fire sales, flight to quality, margin- and collateral-constrained spirals, liquidity runs, and so on – phenomena that played a central role in bringing the world economy to the brink of a great depression. This literature also provided the basis for the policy framework that was used to contain the crisis.[20]

The challenge remains: to construct integrated models of a financial economy whose participants both are aware of the limits and fragility of their own knowledge and condition their behavior on that of others similarly aware. Whether it will prove possible to generate general equilibrium from such realistic microfoundations remains an open question. Perhaps frustration in that pursuit will encourage alternative efforts to explore the space of potential macroeconomic outcomes through models that explicitly represent those heterogeneous agents, as I once dreamed would be constructive when I discovered computers close to forty years ago.

Stimulus and austerity after 2008

The universal turn toward fiscal stimulus by the major governments in the winter of 2008–2009 was informed by history – the culturally embedded experience of the 1930s as evaluated by such scholars as Ben Bernanke, Barry Eichengreen and Peter Temin – and rationalized by reference to New Keynesian macroeconomic models. And, once again, big-state capitalism proved capable of putting a floor under the economic consequences of a financial crisis. In the institutional

---

[19] An example of such research is M. K. Brunnermeier and Y. Sannikov, "A Macroeconomic Model with a Financial Sector." Available at http://scholar.princeton.edu/markus/files/macro_finance.pdf.

[20] R. J. Caballero, "Macroeconomics after the Crisis, Time to Deal with the Pretense-of-Knowledge Syndrome," *Journal of Economic Perspectives*, 24(4) (2010), p. 88.

context of the early twenty-first century, the measure of that success was that unemployment rose to only about 8 percent to 10 percent in the developed nations, versus the 25 percent to 30 percent experienced during the Depression. It should not be surprising that the regulatory response has been muted to somewhat the same degree. One might say that with 25 percent unemployment you get Glass–Steagall; with 10 percent unemployment you only get Graham–Dodd.

Across the world, central banks reduced their policy rates (the short-term interest rates that they directly control) to the "lower bound" – that is, approximately zero. And the leading central banks – the Federal Reserve, the Bank of England, the European Central Bank, the Bank of Japan – augmented conventional monetary ease with "quantitative easing," the direct purchase of (generally) government debt of relatively long maturity. This phenomenon signaled, to use Paul Krugman's prescient phrase, "the return of Depression economics."[21] For the enormous increase in risk aversion and liquidity preference proved resistant to efforts to induce a generalized shift out of the liquidity trap and back into consumption and investment. To summon a traditional notion curiously absent from policy discussions, the central bankers of the world committed themselves to pushing on the strings at their disposal.

Initially, the activist response to the global financial crisis was itself global. In particular, the emerging nations of East and South Asia, led by China, demonstrated the will and the ability to defend themselves by pursuing nakedly mercantilist trade and currency policies: the invocation of Cash and Control at the national level. They had experienced in the late 1990s the threatened or actual imposition from abroad of exactly the sort of deflationary discipline that the gold standard had existed to enforce – but was this time asserted in the name of the Washington Consensus. Now those countries' accumulated reserves bought them time, and now they knew what to do with it: they deployed programs of fiscal stimulus and credit expansion on a scale unprecedented in peacetime. Unencumbered by fear that the capital markets would exercise an effective veto over political initiative, China most particularly has demonstrated the relevance of Keynes's economics to today's crisis:

[21] P. Krugman, *The Return of Depression Economics* (New York: W.W. Norton & Company, 2009).

According to Fitch Ratings, fiscal stimulus packages as a percentage of gross domestic product amounted to 6.9 percent for Vietnam, 7.7 percent for Thailand, 8 percent for Singapore, 13.5 percent for China, and a whopping 14.6 percent for Japan. Taiwan, with a relatively modest stimulus of 3.8 percent, gave $100 spending vouchers to each of its 23 million inhabitants, including convicts. The Singaporean government subsidised businesses that retained staff. In China, the mother of all stimulus packages funnelled $585bn of spending into the economy, and even more through directing state-controlled banks to increase credit.

Unlike in the west, there is little debate in Asia about how well the stimulus worked. It has been spectacular.[22]

Indeed, Lucas himself reluctantly allowed, during the winter of 2008–2009, that "everyone is a Keynesian in a foxhole."[23] The existence proof represented by mobilization for the Second World War suggests that Lucas's metaphor is more apt than he intended.

Yet, in the West, scarcely had the world been saved from the threat of a second Great Depression than the threat of a sovereign debt crisis emerged to compromise the stumbling return to economic growth. First in Berlin and then in London, politicians called for fiscal consolidation and then, more explicitly, for fiscal austerity, preempting capital markets that remained content to fund unprecedented state borrowings at minimal rates of interest. However, except on the fundamentalist fringes of the debate, the assault on stimulative public policy did not express a retreat to a confused model of the world in which, by definition, all resources must always be fully employed.[24] Rather, it was Hubert Henderson's argument from confidence that was deployed: On the one hand, fiscal deficits on the scale necessary would invite the vigilantes of the bond and foreign exchange markets – James Carville's bullies – to punish spendthrift states. On the other, the imposition of fiscal discipline in the public sector would, against relevant experience, stimulate confidence in the private sector to the extent needed to generate recovery.

---

[22] D. Pilling, "Asia's Keynesians Take Pride in Prudence," *Financial Times* (July 21, 2010).

[23] Quoted in J. Fox, "Bob Lucas on the Comeback of Keynesianism," *Time* blog (October 28, 2008). http://business.time.com/2008/10/28/bob-lucas-on-the-comeback-of-Keynesianism.

[24] Attempts to summon the hard-core Treasury dogma back into battle in 2008, notably by Eugene Fama and John Cochrane of the University of Chicago, played no substantive role in the policy debate.

Whether deployed by German disciplinarians distributed between Berlin and Frankfurt, by Oxonian blue bloods in the Palace of Westminster, or by America's home-grown Tea Party activists, this radical repudiation of the pragmatic policies that saved both financial capitalism and the market economy is best understood as a ploy in the ongoing contest over the legitimate scope of the state relative to the market economy. Of course, such argumentation is the substance of politics. And, of course, capture of the state by private interests and privileged expropriation of economic rents – as in contemporary Greece – are suitable targets. But in the United States and other apparently mature political economies, justifying austerity today in anticipation of excessive Social Security payouts a generation hence serves only to underline the political content of the ploy. After all, only twelve years ago the looming fiscal crisis with which the American government was threatening its own and the world's financial markets was the potential repayment of the entire national debt and, thus, the elimination of the risk-free asset that has been the foundation of the financial system for more than half a century. It took inspired fiscal irresponsibility, delivered through two wars of choice *un*financed by massive tax reductions, to produce the threat of uncontrolled deficits spiraling toward default. It would, alternatively, take only a modest amount of the sort of collaboration evident as recently as the Reagan and Clinton presidencies to bring back fiscal balance in the longer term.

In the context of the Three-Player Game, the consequences of explicitly invoking the financial markets as the judges and disciplinarians of state behavior can be anticipated, and they are dangerous. The most general lesson to be learned from observing the centuries of financial history summarized by Carmen Reinhart and Kenneth Rogoff is that, given the opportunity, financial markets will go to extremes.[25] Some twenty years ago, my wife's doctor responded to her inquiry as to whether our cat could accompany her during an extended hospital stay by asking, "Can you guarantee his behavior?" "Yes," she responded, "it will be bad."

Thus, an economic orthodoxy that has manifestly failed and that is itself in process of reconstruction from the inside out has been invoked

---

[25] C. M. Reinhart and K. S. Rogoff, *This Time is Different: Eight Centuries of Financial Folly* (Princeton University Press, 2009).

to rationalize the tolerance of Keynesian waste, albeit on a materially smaller scale than the last time around. Policies that force economic contraction through fiscal cutbacks in defense of national solvency are likely to be self-defeating. Evidence that fiscal austerity will generate expansion is limited to those few instances when a relatively small and open economy enjoyed the offsetting benefits of major reductions in both long-term interest rates and its effective exchange rate, usually while its principal trading partners were enjoying economic booms.[26] Canada in the early 1990s is a prime example. The United States in the early 2010s cannot be. In Europe, the vicious cycle of fiscal austerity inducing economic contraction, resulting in lower tax revenues, larger deficits and the "logical" requirement of further cuts was already evident in Britain and Spain by the end of 2011.[27]

Britain in 1931 offers some modest support for the proposition that there are conditions under which fiscal discipline can be more than offset by cheap money and a cheap currency; Britain in 2011 demonstrates that such conditions do not apply today. But Britain in 1815 offers signal support for the proposition that even an astonishingly high level of public debt is most productively addressed by the acceleration of economic growth through leadership in the Innovation Economy. Britain exited the Napoleonic Wars with a national debt no less than 250 percent of its estimated national income. Far from suffering default, Britain saw its gilts (government bonds) come to represent the highest-quality risk-free asset in the world as British leadership of the First Industrial Revolution generated economic growth at unprecedented rates. Decade after decade, as the economy expanded, the public debt fell on a relative basis, though it declined in absolute terms only after 1860. By 1890, it was less than 50 percent of

[26] See the analysis by a chastened International Monetary Fund, "Will it Hurt? Macroeconomic Effects of Fiscal Consolidation," in *World Economic Outlook* (Washington, DC: International Monetary Fund, 2010). Available at www. imf.org/external/pubs/ft/weo/2010/02/pdf/c3.pdf. Also D. Baker, *The Myth of Expansionary Fiscal Austerity* (Washington, DC: Center for Economic and Policy Research, 2010).

[27] For a thoughtful, concise summary of the lessons to be drawn from post-2007 experience for economic policy, see D. Romer, "What Have We Learned about Fiscal Policy from the Crisis?" paper presented to the International Monetary Fund Conference on Macro and Growth Policies in the Wake of the Crisis, March 2011. Available at www.imf.org/external/np/seminars/eng/2011/res/pdf/ DR3presentation.pdf.

gross national product.[28] Sixty years later, the United States emerged from the Second World War as the unquestioned leader both in current production of goods and services and in technological innovation, and with public debt equal to almost 120 percent of GDP. In this instance, the pace of economic growth was markedly more rapid. By 1965, only twenty years later, even though it had grown by 20 percent in absolute terms, the US national debt had likewise fallen to less than 50 percent of GDP.[29]

The United Kingdom in the nineteenth century and the United States in the mid-twentieth century were unequivocal leaders of the Innovation Economy. That each grew itself out from under a debt burden at a level now conventionally deemed crippling is the measure of that fact. The adoption of fiscal austerity at a time of extraordinary deleveraging and liquidity preference across the private sectors of the Western world will not only raise the odds that Japan's lost decade will be the model for other developed economies. For the United States in particular, it is also bound to accelerate surrender of leadership in the Innovation Economy. At the level of the microeconomics of innovation, fiscal austerity will doubtless reduce the "unproductive" funding of upstream scientific discovery and technological experimentation on which depend both the development of innovative economic infrastructure and the novel candidates competing to populate new economic space. And at the level of the macroeconomy, the prospect of extended stagnation offers an environment in which the needed speculative investment in infrastructure and in its exploitation will be muted at best.

---

[28] Public Finance 7, "Nominal Amount of the Unredeemed Capital of the Public Debt of the United Kingdom at the End of Each Financial Year, 1691–1980" and National Accounts 2, "Gross National or Domestic Product by Sector of Origin, Great Britain, 1801–1924, and United Kingdom, 1920–80," in B. R. Mitchell, *British Historical Statistics* (Cambridge University Press, 1988), pp. 601–602 and 822, respectively.

[29] United States Treasury, "Historical Debt Outstanding." Available at www.treasurydirect.gov/govt/reports/pd/histdebt/histdebt_histo3.htm. And Bureau of Economic Analysis, National Economic Accounts, table 1.1.5.

Coda

The Innovation Economy evolves through interactions between scientific discovery and technological invention, between basic and applied research, between the pursuit of fundamental understanding and considerations of practical use.[1] Hence emerge the transformational innovations – general-purpose technologies like the steam engine, electricity and digital electronics – whose deployment and exploitation create the successive waves of new economies.[2]

All of the stages of development are dependent to some degree on speculative forays into the unknown. None lends itself to optimal management in accord with a strict accounting of expected returns relative to costs incurred, whether conducted by a central planner or an established, profit-making enterprise. When scientific advance was funded by the profits of the great corporations through the first half of the twentieth century, the costs of the central research labs could no more be rationalized by the calculus of prospective financial returns than could the costs of the National Science Foundation (NSF) or the Defense Advanced Research Projects Agency (DARPA) or the National Institutes of Health (NIH) – which is why they were all required to shift resources toward explicitly applied research and development when profits came under pressure.

Thus, the prime and critical constituent elements of the Innovation Economy are sources of funding decoupled from concern for economic return. This is clearly so with respect to the unfettered pursuit of scientific curiosity, but support for such research may be fully available from the state only during transient moments of national self-confidence when economic competition seems least threatening.

[1] See D. Stokes, *Pasteur's Quadrant: Basic Science and Technological Innovation* (Washington, DC: The Brookings Institution, 1997), pp. 73, 79–80.
[2] See T. Bresnehan, "General Purpose Technologies," in B. H. Hall and N. Rosenberg (eds.), *Handbook of the Economics of Innovation*, 2 vols. (Amsterdam: North-Holland, 2010), vol. 2, pp. 761–791.

Perversely, investment in scientific research is likely to be challenged as the nation's competitive position weakens.

So the Haldane principle, invoked in Britain to defend the autonomy of scientific research from political pressures, dates back to the First World War, when the sun still did not set on the British Empire. It was radically revised by the Rothschild Report in post-Empire 1971 to draw a bright line between pure and applied research and to subject the latter to the test of a customer–contractor relationship.[3]

In the United States, Vannevar Bush's vision of public investment in science transcended near-term considerations of return, economic or political. Two generations later, the NIH and NSF are collaborating under the tortuous acronym STAR METRICS – "Science and Technology for America's Reinvestment: Measuring the Effects of Research on Innovation, Competitiveness and Science" – in response to "increasing pressure to document the results of … research investments in a scientific manner and to quantify how much of the work is linked to innovation."[4] The attempt to manage scientific research in narrow pursuit of "value for money" can be expected to reduce its potential for creative exploration of the unknown.

As I learned from my engagement with computing, the state has directly and indirectly accelerated construction of technology platforms to support the speculative exploits of entrepreneurs and the capitalists who finance them. Financial bubbles, in which returns are decoupled from the economic fundamentals, are the complementary engine of Schumpeterian waste. There are some examples of efficient deployment of new technological infrastructure: the construction of the French railroad system under state direction was a model of engineering efficiency and proceeded *pari passu* with the railroad systems in Britain and the United States, but without their duplicative waste. But, regardless of how potentially revolutionary networks have been planned, their financing has exploited the essential and inevitable

---

[3] Rothschild Report, *The Organisation and Management of Government Research and Development*, Cmnd. 4814 (London: HMSO), in Parliamentary Papers (House of Commons and Command), Session 2, November 1971–October 1972, vol. 35, pp. 747–775. Unsurprisingly, the Secretary of State for Education and Science who commissioned the report and drove the shift in policy toward marketlike discipline was Margaret Thatcher.

[4] J. Lane and S. Bertuzzi, "Measuring the Results of Science Investments," *Science*, 331 (2011), p. 678.

herding behavior of investors. And, for the final phase of the Innovation Economy, there is no substitute for the speculative wastefulness of financial markets and the proliferation of hosts of hopeful commercial monsters funded thereby to explore the new economic space.

When the great technology corporations were still funding basic research in their central labs, their monopoly positions in the markets they served inhibited their ability to exploit the technologies derived therefrom. Three times I directly observed signal examples of such failure. During the 1980s, I witnessed repeated instances of "fumbling the future" at Xerox when none of the innovations delivered by PARC could measure up to the profits of the entrenched, patent-protected copier business.[5] Like all investors in the birth of client–server computing, I was an indirect beneficiary of AT&T's failure to capitalize on the extraordinary information technologies created within its Unix Systems Laboratory. And at BEA, I was both the direct beneficiary of AT&T's invention of Tuxedo and, in equal measure, of IBM's inability to sacrifice the profits from its proprietary products to compete directly in the new world of open and distributed computing. Joseph Schumpeter expressed the view that large firms have an inherent advantage in innovation relative to smaller enterprises.[6] But, as Josh Lerner summarizes the experience of the biotech and internet revolutions: "The enabling technologies were developed with government funds at academic institutions and research laboratories. It was the small entrants ... who first seized upon the commercial opportunities."[7]

In defiance of Schumpeter's expectation, economic innovation has not been effectively bureaucratized by the great corporations. Rather, it tends to be delivered by new companies. But funding those new companies depends on access to financiers who have access to financial markets prone to speculative excess. This is the lesson both of my professional life as a practitioner and of my research into the sources of venture capital returns. And it is a lesson drawn not only from the most recent iteration of the Innovation Economy or from the

---

[5] D. K. Smith and R. C. Alexander, *Fumbling the Future: How Xerox Invented, then Ignored, the First Personal Computer* (San Jose, CA: Excel, 1999).

[6] J. A. Schumpeter, *Capitalism, Socialism and Democracy*, 4th edn. (London: Allen & Unwin, 2010 [1943]), pp. 132–134.

[7] J. Lerner, *Boulevard of Broken Dreams: Why Public Efforts to Boost Entrepreneurship and Venture Capital Have Failed – and What to Do about it* (Princeton University Press, 2009), p. 46.

long-term development of the British and American economies. Even
in the bank-based industrial economies of Germany and Japan, the
stock exchange played a critical role in funding aggressive investment
in frontier technologies during their initial high-growth decades of
the late nineteenth and early twentieth centuries.[8] The vast expansion
of the German and Japanese banking systems took place to finance
post-Second World War recovery, precisely when innovation was a dis-
traction from the defined task of literally reconstructing the physical
assets of the economy.

The most recent new economy – the digital economy in whose development I have passed my professional career – was built through the
combined forces of state funding of research and speculative financing of the companies created to transform the fruits of research into
commercial goods and services. But the discrediting of LBJ's Great
Society in the context of Vietnam, followed by the stagflation of the
1970s, opened the door to the return of market fundamentalism as a
constraint on state initiatives.

Meanwhile, as a body of scholarship has documented, a "hidden
developmental state" has stealthily survived. Fred Block describes it:

The hidden quality of the U.S. developmental state is largely a result of
the dominance of market fundamentalist ideas over the last thirty years.
Developmental policies have lived in the shadows because acknowledging
the state's central role in promoting technological change is inconsistent
with the market fundamentalist claim that private sector firms should simply be left alone to respond autonomously and spontaneously to the signals
of the marketplace.[9]

The lack of political legitimacy means that continuity of funding is
uncertain and efforts are uncoordinated. Its crippling effects are most
clearly and critically evident in the nexus of discussion that reaches
from the science of climate change to the invention and deployment of
green-tech and low-carbon technologies.

---

[8] See R. Tilly, "Public Policy, Capital Markets and the Supply of Industrial
Finance in Nineteenth-Century Germany," in R. Sylla, R. Tilly and G. Torella,
The State, the Financial System and Economic Modernization (Cambridge
University Press, 1999), pp. 134–157 and T. Hishi and K. Kashyap, *Corporate
Finance and Governance in Japan: The Road to the Future* (Cambridge, MA:
MIT Press, 2001), pp. 3–27.

[9] F. Block, "Swimming Against the Current: The Rise of a Hidden Developmental
State in the United States," *Politics and Society*, 36(2) (2008), p. 170.

More than thirty years ago, the first oil shock seemed to offer an opportunity to mobilize resources under the banner of energy independence. When President-Elect Carter proposed the creation of a Department of Energy toward the end of 1976, I was one of those who urged James Schlesinger, when he was offered the role of founding secretary, to accept the challenge of forging energy policy into "the economic equivalent of war." But the initiative failed as soon as oil prices retreated at the end of the decade, and it was comprehensively rolled back by the Reagan administration.

A generation on, President Obama's attempt to catalyze broad state investment in the science and engineering required to enable the low-carbon new economy has been deferred and marginalized. Obama's invocation of a Sputnik moment met with much more than the imposed criterion of economic efficiency in the context of fiscal austerity. This time the ideological rejection goes far deeper. At the end of December 2010, a leading climate scientist visited Cambridge University and recounted his meeting with key members of the Republican majority in the House of Representatives shortly after their victory in November 2010: not only did talk of climate change express a "socialist conspiracy" whose purpose is "to justify state control of our lives," but no action would be appropriate because "global warming would be God's will."

Yet the next new economy can already be defined in broad strokes. Like the digital one we are currently still learning how to exploit and enjoy, that low-carbon economy can be built only on a base of substantial state investment and agreed rules of engagement across both public and private sectors. To advance the frontier of needed innovation, much science remains to be done. A host of technologies – batteries and solar cells and fuel cells, among them – require extended investment to improve both absolute performance and the ratio of performance to cost. And the protocols for bringing alternative, renewable energy sources online and into the intelligent grid that is yet to be designed, let alone deployed, will need to be standardized, as were the networking and internetworking protocols of the digital economy.[10]

However, no significant private-sector investment in the new infrastructure, let alone the speculative funding necessary to finance

---

[10] For one of many frustrated calls to action, see Bill Gates's guest editorial in *Science:* "The Energy Research Imperative," *Science*, 334 (2011), p. 877.

deployment at scale, can be expected while the return on that investment remains exposed to the volatile markets of conventional energy sources. Only collective state action – the prospect for which is not at all visible – can protect the new alternative energy technologies and accelerate the step-function increases in thermal efficiency necessary to compete with conventional sources without state subsidy. In parallel, advances in materials and in information technologies to reduce the carbon content of consumer goods and services are similarly required and at risk.

At present, there is little reason to believe that the next new economy will be made in America. On the contrary, the spectacle of the United States bringing China to the World Trade Organization for allegedly subsidizing clean-tech innovation is as telling as it is humiliating. No doubt, had there been such a body fifty years ago, European governments would have been entitled to attack the US government's commitment to underwriting the technologies that made the digital revolution.

By 2010, China's investment in clean-energy technologies was estimated to have reached $54.4 billion, more than 50 percent above the US level in an economy less than half the size.[11] Commitment to what ought to be a core initiative in the United States is significant only symbolically: the first-year funding for the Advanced Research Projects Agency–Energy (ARPA–E) was the $400 million included in the American Recovery and Reinvestment Act of 2009; that amount was reduced to $180 million in the budget appropriation for fiscal year 2011.[12] But, even as it seems inevitable that the federal science budget will be constrained, China's leadership is pushing national spending on research to and beyond 2 percent of GDP, about the level achieved in the post-Second World War United States.[13]

The next leader of the Innovation Economy can learn from the post-Second World War example of the United States. It is a given

---

[11] Pew Charitable Trusts, "Who's Winning the Clean Energy Race: Growth, Competition and Opportunity in the World's Largest Economies," in *G20 Clean Energy Factbook* (Washington, DC: Pew Charitable Trusts, 2011), fig. 9 (p. 11).

[12] An overview of the United States Department of Energy, ARPA–E is available at arpa-e.energy.gov/About/FAQs/ARPAEOverview.aspx.

[13] R. Stone, "China Bets Big on Small Grants, Large Facilities," *Science*, 331 (2011), p. 1251.

that the leader must begin with the bulwarks of autonomy: Cash and Control. Only a state so positioned can resist the persistent demands that public funds be deployed only on projects that are demonstrably "useful and productive" – that meet the test of static efficiency. For the Innovation Economy depends on an entrepreneurial state that can play two roles as needed: to invest in speculative science and technology before commercially motivated firms and their investors can envision either an economic or financial return; and to ensure that the burden of Keynesian waste on economic growth is minimized.[14]

The first challenge as the public's cash is put to work is to keep the "corruption tax" sufficiently small so as not to discredit the whole exercise, while disbursing funds freely enough to have substantive impact. Straightforward bribery is not the only form of corruption. Political earmarking of research funds is a soft version. Both were managed well enough when national security provided the rationale for US leadership in information technology, and they have also been well managed for two generations by the NIH. Despite congressional efforts to the contrary, the integrity of the scientific enterprise in the United States remains generally intact, as it does in Europe and Japan.

The second challenge – arguably more difficult – is to relinquish control in two dimensions. First, the funding of scientific discovery will be compromised by the strict separation of basic and applied science advocated by Lord Rothschild forty years ago in Britain. As Donald Stokes points out, such separation

confronts us with a notable puzzle … The annals of research so often record scientific advances simultaneously driven by the quest for understanding and considerations of use that one is increasingly led to ask how it came to be so widely believed that these goals are inevitably in tension and that the categories of basic and applied science are radically separate.[15]

The state also needs to relinquish control when science-based innovation enables commercial exploitation. It must resist the temptation to pick winners, to designate national champions such as, in the world of computing, Britain's ICL, France's Bull and Germany's

---

[14] For a useful attempt to "unpack the role of the state in fostering radical growth-enhancing innovations," see M. Mazzacuto, *The Entrepreneurial State* (London: Demos, 2011), p. 21 and *passim*.

[15] Stokes, *Pasteur's Quadrant*, p. 24.

Siemens: failures all.[16] Along this dimension, the successive East Asian "miracle" economies, from Japan to China by way of the "Tigers," generated growth initially through protection and subsidy and then, once a sufficient degree of competitive maturity has been established, backed off and opened up.[17] More particularly, by endowing multiple players in the Three-Player Game with access to the scientific and technological sources of innovation, the state can sponsor the open-ended process of trial and error that alone has the potential to explore new economic space.

It is worth emphasizing once again the role of the US defense agencies a generation ago as imaginative and generous customers for innovative digital technologies. By setting specifications open for any supplier to meet, the Defense Department sponsored competition at the frontier that its funding of research continued to advance. By contrast, today's program of loan guarantees by the Department of Energy is fundamentally misconceived: targeting such high-risk candidates as Solyndra and Tesla with capital subsidies is the opposite of the successful programs that induced the digital electronic revolution.

In this context, it should be recalled that the regime of intellectual property rights under which the scientific and technological platform of the digital economy was constructed in the United States was radically at odds with present standards: software was not patentable, and business processes were not even subject to copyright, let alone patent; cross-licensing of patents was widespread and in some instances mandatory; and the requirements of national security forced the active creation of second sources. Recognition that technology spillovers are key to the generation of economic growth goes as far back as Keynes's mentor, Alfred Marshall, and resides at the core of New Growth Theory.[18]

Appropriation of some portion of the return to innovation is essential to stimulate and finance new firms; in certain sectors, such as

---

[16] For a summary of "a flagrant example of government incompetence in promoting innovative activities" – the French government's support of established electronics and computer firms – see Lerner, *Boulevard of Broken Dreams*, pp. 74–75.

[17] D. Rodrik, *The Globalization Paradox: Why Global Markets, States, and Democracy Can't Coexist* (New York: Norton, 2011), pp. 142–156.

[18] For an intellectual history of growth theory, see D. Warsh, *Knowledge and the Wealth of Nations: A Story of Economic Discovery* (New York: W. W. Norton and Company, 2006).

medical devices, a restrictive patent regime may be required to allow new products from new companies to be born, let alone survive. But, as Adam Jaffe and Josh Lerner have documented, reform of patent law in the 1980s spawned a monster, creating a deadweight burden by way of a vast extension of what is patentable and an equally vast expansion of related and consequent litigation.[19] A retreat to defensive citadels of discovery and invention may well be accelerated as the nations playing catch-up in the Innovation Economy, led by China, have transformed what in previous epochs was the uncoordinated appropriation of intellectual property by diverse entrepreneurs – recall Samuel Slater and Arkwright's Patents – into organized state policy.

While we necessarily await some external impulse from outside the market economies of the developed world, the prospect looms of an extended epoch of debt repayment and hoarding of cash reserves across the spectrum: from consumers, through enterprises small and large, to the banking system. This is the "New Normal" aptly styled by Mohamed El-Erian of the global investment management firm PIMCO.[20] In the language of corporate finance that I learned forty years ago, this is the environment of the "earn-out": far to be preferred to the alternative of liquidation that threatens the financially overextended, but hardly one to be welcomed with exuberant enthusiasm. The political economies of the Western, industrial world have all reached positions of stasis: the recovery of the market economy remains incomplete, the overhang of financial excess persists, and the space for political initiatives to address each is constrained.

Closest to my intellectual and professional home, in the developed economies of the world the forward movement of the Innovation Economy is stalled. Having managed to convince themselves they are out of Cash, their leaders have jointly and severally lost Control over their technological and economic future. In a frustrating and needless echo of Britain eighty years ago, when the scale of small-state

---

[19] See A. B. Jaffe and J. Lerner, *Innovation and its Discontents: How Our Broken Patent System is Endangering Innovation and Progress, and What to Do about it* (Princeton University Press, 2004). Whether the most recent reform of patent law – the America Invents Act of 2011 – will materially reduce the cost remains to be seen.

[20] See M. El-Erian, "Navigating the New Normal in Industrial Countries: Per Jacobsson Foundation Lecture," October 10, 2010. www.imf.org/external/np/speeches/2010/101010.htm.

capitalism institutionally constrained the scope for activist response, paralysis is the political consequence of the first crisis of big-state capitalism.

In the meantime, there remains ample scope for filling in the many open spaces still available for discovery and exploitation in the internet-enabled, digital new economy. We remain in the early stages of understanding and exploiting the unique characteristics of a medium that reciprocally integrates communicating and transacting, a medium that simultaneously captures the traces generated by all who use it – data that can be intelligently transformed into commercially valuable information (incidentally requiring innovations in the management of privacy and security).

Especially intriguing to me is the notion of the web as an environment in which the practices of work are transparently embedded, even as those for whom Facebook and Twitter are home live in a social environment that integrates the real and the virtual. In this environment, the enterprise software applications that we spent a full generation and perhaps $1 trillion building and deploying are static repositories of reference data, drawn on as necessary to inform the real-time, mobile context in which actual work gets done. As the technical infrastructure is abstracted and virtualized into "the cloud" – beyond the concern of developers, let alone users of innovative applications – this is an economic landscape whose investment opportunities will not be exhausted for decades.

Even while we are forced to wait in frustration for the next new economy, there is work for the practitioner in completing the rollout of this one, even if that work will become increasingly routine and exposed to competition in kind. There is also much work for the theorist. I did not expect to live to see the economics I had absorbed at Cambridge more than forty years ago – the economics of Keynes; of uncertainty at the level of the individual investor, consumer, firm and government; and of consequent instability at the level of the integrated financial economy – again become so relevant and so broadly recognized as such within the discipline. Over three decades, I learned as a practitioner the role that prudent provision of Cash and Control plays in providing an effective hedge against that which cannot be anticipated. In less than three years, the world learned again how the forced pursuit of Cash and Control by all parties in times of crisis paralyzes financial capitalists and forces contraction to the point of liquidation on the market economy. In such conditions only the state can command access to the cash needed to ensure the continuity of financial and economic institutions. Incorporating these realities of financial and economic life into models that can be challenged by data is the most demanding and immediate theoretical challenge.

The intellectual entrepreneurs who have accepted the challenge to reconstruct financial economics are largely motivated by recognition that the markets of the financial economy are not the mechanical, self-regulating systems of neoclassical theory. And so the state may be let back in at the macroeconomic level, as required to stabilize the inherently unstable economy. But the reconstruction of financial economics will remain incomplete so long as its scope excludes a positive role for the state in the Three-Player Game of innovation. The intellectual framework that relates how Schumpeterian waste can be productively sponsored by the state is as urgently required as theories that subvert the toleration of Keynesian waste.

Bibliography

Aghion, P. and Howitt, P., *The Economics of Growth* (Cambridge, MA: MIT Press, 2009).

Akerlof, G. A., "Behavioral Macroeconomics and Macroeconomic Behavior," *American Economic Review*, 92(3) (2002), pp. 411–433.

Allen, F., Babus, A. and Carletti, E., "Financial Crises: Theory and Evidence," *Annual Review of Financial Economics*, 1 (2009), pp. 97–116.

Allen, F. and Gale, D., *Understanding Financial Crises* (Oxford University Press, 2007).

Almunia, M., Bénétrix, A. S., Eichengreen, B., O'Rourke, K. S. and Rua, G., "From Great Depression to Great Credit Crisis: Similarities, Differences and Lessons," National Bureau of Economic Research Working Paper 15524 (2009).

Angeletos, G.-M., Lorenzoni, G. and Pavan, A., "Beauty Contests and Irrational Exuberances: A Neoclassical Approach," National Bureau of Economic Research Working Paper 15883 (2010).

Arrow, K. J., "Economic Welfare and the Allocation of Resources for R&D," in K. J. Arrow (ed.), *Essays in the Theory of Risk-Bearing* (New York: American Elsevier, 1971 [1962]), pp. 144–163.

Arrow, K. J. and Debreu, G., "Existence of an Equilibrium for a Competitive Economy," *Econometrica*, 22 (1954), pp. 265–290.

Badger, A. J., *The New Deal: The Depression Years, 1933–1940* (New York: Hill & Wang, 1989).

Bagehot, W., *Lombard Street: A Description of the Money Market* (New York: Charles Scribner's Sons, 1999 [1873]).

Baker, D., *The Myth of Expansionary Fiscal Austerity* (Washington, DC: Center for Economic and Policy Research, 2010).

Bannerjee, A. and Duflo, E., "Growth Theory Through the Lens of Development Economics," in P. Aghion and S. N. Durlauf (eds.), *Handbook of Economic Growth* (Amsterdam: Elsevier North-Holland, 2005).

Barro, R., "The Coming Crises of Governments," *Financial Times*, August 3, 2011.

Baumol, W. J., *Welfare Economics and the Theory of the State*, 2nd edn. (Cambridge, MA: Harvard University Press, 1969).

BBC News, "The 19th Century iPhone," May 17, 2010. http://news.bbc.co.uk/1/hi/technology/8668311.stm.

Benzel, R. F., *Yankee Leviathan: The Origins of Central State Authority in America, 1859–1877* (Cambridge University Press, 1990).

Berle, A. and Means, G., *The Modern Corporation and Private Property* (New York: Macmillan, 1932).

Black, F. and Scholes, M., "The Pricing of Options and Corporate Liabilities," *Journal of Political Economy*, 81(3) (1973), pp. 637–654.

Blanchard, O. and Watson, M., "Bubbles, Rational Expectations and Financial Markets," National Bureau of Economic Research Working Paper 945 (1982).

Block, F., "Swimming Against the Current: The Rise of a Hidden Developmental State in the United States," *Politics and Society*, 36(2) (2008), pp. 169–206.

Blyth, M., *Great Transformations: Economic Ideas and Institutional Change in the Twentieth Century* (Boston: Beacon, 2002).

Bond, P., Edmans, A. and Goldstein, I., "The Real Effects of Financial Markets," National Bureau of Economic Research Working Paper 17719 (2012).

Braudel, F., *Afterthoughts on Material Civilization and Capitalism* (Baltimore, MD: Johns Hopkins University Press, 1977).

   The Wheels of Commerce, trans. Sian Reynolds, vol. 2 of *Civilization and Capitalism, 15th–18th Century*, 3 vols. (New York: Harper & Row, 1982).

Bresnehan, T., "General Purpose Technologies," in B. H. Hall and N. Rosenberg (eds.), *Handbook of the Economics of Innovation*, 2 vols. (Amsterdam: North-Holland, 2010), vol. 2, pp. 761–791.

Brooks, J., *The Go-Go Years: When Prices Went Topless* (New York: Ballantine, 1974).

Brown, J. R., Fazzari, S. M. and Petersen, B. C., "Financing Innovation and Growth: Cash Flow, External Equity, and the 1990s R&D Boom," *Journal of Finance*, 64(1) (2009), pp. 151–185.

Brunnermeier, M. K. and Sannikov, Y., "A Macroeconomic Model with a Financial Sector." Available at http://scholar.princeton.edu/markus/files/macro_finance.pdf.

Bush, V., *Science, the Endless Frontier: A Report to the President on a Program for Postwar Scientific Research* (Washington, DC: US Office of Scientific Research and Development, 1960 [1945]).

Caballero, R. J., "Macroeconomics after the Crisis: Time to Deal with the Pretense-of-Knowledge Syndrome," *Journal of Economic Perspectives*, 24(4) (2010), pp. 85–102.

Cambridge Associates LLC and National Venture Capital Association, "Difficult Q3 2011 Did Not Slow Improvements in Long Term Venture

Performance," press release, January 24, 2012. Available at www.nvca. org/index.php?option=com_content&view=article&id=78&Itemi d=102.

Carret, P. L., *The Art of Speculation* (Columbia, MD: Marketplace Books, 2007 [1927]).

Carroll, P., *Big Blues: The Unmaking of IBM* (New York: Crown, 1993).

Carter, S. B., Gartner, S. G., Haines, M. R., Olmstead, A. L., Sutch, R. and Wright, G. (eds.), *Historical Statistics of the United States*, millennial edn. (Cambridge University Press, 2006).

Cassidy, J., *How Markets Fail: The Logic of Economic Calamities* (New York: Farrar, Straus and Giroux, 2009).

Chancellor, E., *Devil Take the Hindmost: A History of Financial Speculation* (New York: Penguin, 1999).

(ed.), *Capital Account: A Money Manager's Reports from a Turbulent Decade, 1993–2002* (New York: Thomson Texere, 2004).

Chandler, A. D., *Scale and Scope: The Dynamics of Industrial Capitalism* (Cambridge, MA: Harvard University Press; Belknap Press, 1999).

The Visible Hand: The Managerial Revolution in American Business (Cambridge, MA: Harvard University Press; Belknap Press, 1977).

Chandler, L. V., *American Monetary Policy, 1929–1941* (New York, Harper & Row, 1971).

Chernow, R., *The House of Morgan: An American Banking Dynasty and the Rise of Modern Finance* (New York: Atlantic Monthly Press, 1990).

Christiansen, C., *The Innovator's Dilemma: When New Technologies Cause Great Companies to Fail* (Cambridge, MA: Harvard University Press, 1997).

Coenen, G., Erceg, C. J., Freedman, C., Furceri, D., Kumhof, M., Lalonde, R., Laxton, D., Lindé, J., Mourougane, A., Muir, D., Mursula, S., de Resende, C., Roberts, J., Roeger, W., Snudden, S., Trabandt, M. and in't Veld, J., "Effects of Fiscal Stimulus in Structural Models," *American Economic Journal: Macroeconomics*, 4(1) (2012), pp. 22–68.

Conant, J., *Tuxedo Park: A Wall Street Tycoon and the Secret Palace of Science that Changed the Course of the Second World War* (New York: Simon & Schuster, 2002).

Connell, J., *Biographical Sketches of Distinguished Mechanics* (Wilmington, DE: Porter and Eckel, 1852).

Cooper, R., "Oil and the International Monetary System," in Patrick Boarman and David Tuerck (eds.), *World Monetary Disorder* (New York: Praeger, 1976).

Davidson, P., *John Maynard Keynes* (New York: Palgrave Macmillan, 2007).

Defense Advanced Research Projects Agency, "Our Work." www.darpa.mil/our_work.

Defoe, D., *The Anatomy of Exchange Alley; Or, a System of Stock-Jobbing* (Stamford, CT: Gale ECCO, 2010 [1719]).

DeLong, J. B., "Profits of Doom," *Wired*, 11(4) (April 2003).

DeLong, J. B., Shleifer, A., Summers, L. and Waldmann, R., "Noise Trader Risk in Financial Markets," *Journal of Political Economy*, 98(4) (1990), pp. 703–738.

Dobbin, F., *Forging Industrial Policy: The United States, Britain and France in the Railway Age* (Cambridge University Press, 1994).

Dosi, G., *Further Essays on Economic Organization, Industrial Dynamics and Development* (Cheltenham: Edward Elgar, forthcoming).

Dosi, G., Fagiolo, G. and A. Roventini, "Schumpeter Meeting Keynes: A Policy-Friendly Model of Endogenous Growth and Business Cycles," *Journal of Economic Dynamics and Growth*, 34 (2010), pp. 1748–1767.

Dosi, G. and Nelson, R. R., "Technical Change and Industrial Dynamics as Evolutionary Processes," in B. H. Hall and N. Rosenberg (eds.), *Handbook of the Economics of Innovation*, 2 vols. (Amsterdam: North-Holland, 2010), vol. 1, pp. 51–127.

Dreyfus, H. and Dreyfus, S. E., *Mind over Machine* (New York: The Free Press, 1986).

Eatwell, J., "Useful Bubbles," in J. Eatwell and M. Milgate (eds.), *The Fall and Rise of Keynesian Economics* (Oxford University Press, 2011).

Eichengreen, B., *Golden Fetters: The Gold Standard and the Great Depression, 1919–1939* (Oxford University Press, 1992).

El-Erian, M., "Navigating the New Normal in Industrial Countries: Per Jacobsson Foundation Lecture," October 10, 2010. www.imf.org/external/np/speeches/2010/101010.htm.

Epstein, J. M., *Generative Social Science: Studies in Agent-Based Computational Modeling* (Princeton University Press, 2006).

Evans, R., *The Third Reich in Power* (New York: Penguin, 2005).

Fabrizio, K. R. and Mowery, D. C., "The Federal Role in Financing Major Innovations: Information Technology During the Postwar Period," in N. R. Lamoreaux and K. L. Sokoloff (eds.), *Financing Innovation in the United States, 1870 to the Present* (Cambridge, MA: MIT Press, 2007), pp. 283–316.

Farmer, J. D. and Foley, D., "The Economy Needs Agent-Based Modeling," *Nature*, 460 (2009), 685–686.

Federal Reserve, Flow of Funds Accounts, L. 129, 1965–2009. www.federalreserve.gov/releases/z1/Current/data.htm.

Field, A. J., *A Great Leap Forward: 1930s Depression and US Economic Growth* (New Haven, CT: Yale University Press, 2011).

Fildes, D. C., "City and Suburban," *The Spectator*, October 3, 1998.

Fogel, R., *Railroads and American Economic Growth: Essays in Econometric History* (Baltimore, MD: Johns Hopkins Press, 1964).

Foster, W. and Catchings, W., *The Road to Plenty* (Boston: Houghton Mifflin Company, 1928).

Fox, J. "Bob Lucas on the Comeback of Keynesianism," *Time* blog, October 28, 2008. http://business.time.com/2008/10/28/bob-lucas-on-the-comeback-of-Keynesianism.

Frehen, R. G. P., Goetzmann, W. N. and Rouwenhorst, K.G., "New Evidence on the First Financial Bubble," Yale International Center of Finance Working Paper 09–04 (2009).

Friedman, M. and Schwartz, A. J., *A Monetary History of the United States, 1867–1960* (Princeton University Press, 1963).

Frydman, R. and Goldberg, M., *Beyond Mechanical Markets: Asset Price Swings, Risk, and the Role of the State* (Princeton University Press, 2011).

"The Imperfect Knowledge Imperative in Modern Macroeconomics and Finance Theory," in R. Frydman and E. Phelps (eds.), *Micro-Macro: Back to the Foundations* (Princeton University Press, forthcoming).

Gaddis, J. L., *The Landscape of History: How Historians Map the Past* (New York: Oxford University Press, 2004).

Galbraith, J. K., *The Great Crash, 1929* (New York: Houghton Mifflin, 1988 [1954]).

Garber, P. M., "Famous First Bubbles," *Journal of Economic Perspectives*, 4 (1990), pp. 35–54.

Gates, B., "The Energy Research Imperative," *Science*, 334 (2011), p. 877.

Geanakoplos, J., "The Leverage Cycle," in D. Acemoglu, K. Rogoff and M. Woodward (eds.), *NBER Macroeconomic Annual 2009*, vol. 24 (University of Chicago Press, 2010), pp. 1–65.

Gompers, P. A. and Lerner, J., *The Venture Capital Cycle*, 2nd edn. (Cambridge, MA: MIT Press, 2004).

Gompers, P. A., Lerner, J., Scharfstein, D. and Kovner, A., "Performance Persistence in Entrepreneurship and Venture Capital," *Journal of Financial Economics*, 96(1) (2010), pp. 18–32.

Gordon, R. J. and Krenn, R., "The End of the Great Depression, 1939–1941: Policy Contributions and Fiscal Multipliers," National Bureau of Economic Research Working Paper 16380 (2010).

Grossman, S. J. and Stiglitz, J., "On the Impossibility of Informationally Efficient Markets," *American Economic Review*, 70(3) (1980), pp. 393–408.

Haacke, C., *Frenzy: Bubbles, Busts and How to Come Out Ahead* (New York: Palgrave Macmillan, 2004).

Haldane, A., "Patience and Finance," paper presented to Oxford China Business Forum, Beijing, September 9, 2010, p. 15. www.bis.org/review/r100909e.pdf.

Harris, R., "The Bubble Act: Its Passage and its Effects on Business Organization," *Journal of Economic History*, 54(3) (1994), pp. 610–627.

Harrod, R., *The Life of John Maynard Keynes* (New York: Harcourt Brace, 1951).

Hart, D. M., *Forged Consensus: Science, Technology and Economic Policy in the United States, 1921–1953* (Princeton University Press, 1998).

Hausman, W. J., *The Historical Antecedents of Restructuring: Mergers and Concentration in the US Electric Utility Industry, 1879–1935*, report prepared for the American Power Association (1937).

Hishi, T. and Kashyap, K., *Corporate Finance and Governance in Japan: The Road to the Future* (Cambridge, MA: MIT Press, 2001).

Hobbes, T., *Leviathan*, ed. R. Tuck (Cambridge University Press, 1993 [1664]).

Hoover, H., *The Memoirs of Herbert Hoover: The Great Depression, 1929–1941* (New York: Macmillan, 1952).

Hughes, T. P., *Networks of Power: Electrification in Western Society, 1880–1930* (Baltimore, MD: Johns Hopkins University Press, 1993).

Hume, D., *An Enquiry Concerning Human Understanding* (Oxford University Press, 2007 [1777]).

Hutton, W. and Schneider, P., "The Failure of Market Failure: Towards a 21st Century Keynesianism," National Endowment for Science, Technology and the Arts, Provocation 08 (November 2008).

International Monetary Fund, "Will it Hurt? Macroeconomic Effects of Fiscal Consolidation," in *World Economic Outlook* (Washington, DC: International Monetary Fund, 2010). Available at www.imf.org/external/pubs/ft/weo/2010/02/pdf/c3.pdf.

Investment Company Institute, *2010 Investment Company Fact Book* (Washington, DC: Investment Company Institute, 2010).

IPO Task Force, "Rebuilding the IPO On-Ramp: Putting Emerging Companies and the Job Market Back on the Road to Growth," presented to the US Department of the Treasury, October 20, 2011.

Jaffe, A. B. and Lerner, J., *Innovation and its Discontents: How Our Broken Patent System is Endangering Innovation and Progress, and What to Do about it* (Princeton University Press, 2004).

James, H., *The End of Globalization: Lessons from the Great Depression* (Cambridge, MA: Harvard University Press, 2001).

Janeway, E., *The Struggle for Survival: A Chronicle of Economic Mobilization in World War II* (New Haven, CT: Yale University Press, 1951).

Janeway, M. C., *The Fall of the House of Roosevelt: Brokers of Ideas and Power from FDR to LBJ* (New York: Columbia University Press, 2004).

Janeway, W. H., "Doing Capitalism: Notes on the Practice of Venture Capital (Revised and Extended)," in W. Drechsler, R. Kattel and E. S. Reinert (eds.), *Techno-Economic Paradigms: Essays in Honour of Carlota Perez* (London: Anthem Press, 2009), pp. 171–188.

"The Economic Policy of the Second Labour Government: 1929–1931," unpublished Ph.D. thesis, University of Cambridge (1971).

Jensen, M. C. and Meckling, W. H., "Theory of the Firm: Managerial Behavior, Agency Costs and Ownership Structure," *Journal of Financial Economics*, 3(4) (1976), pp. 305–360.

Johnson, E. and Moggridge, D. (eds.), *The Collected Writings of John Maynard Keynes*, 30 vols. (Cambridge University Press and Macmillan for the Royal Economic Society, 1971–1989).

Kahn, R. F., "The Relation of Home Investment to Unemployment," *Economic Journal*, 41(163) (1931), pp. 173–198.

Kahneman, D. and Tversky, A., "Prospect Theory: An Analysis of Decision under Risk," *Econometrica*, 47 (1979), pp. 263–291.

Kaplan, S. V. and Schoar, A., "Private Equity Performance: Returns, Persistence and Capital Flows," *Journal of Finance*, 60(4) (2005), pp. 1791–1823.

Kay, J., "The Failure of Market Failure," *Prospect* (137), August 1, 2007.

Keynes, J. M., *The Economic Consequences of the Peace* (New York: Harcourt, Brace and Howe, 1920).

Essays in Biography, in E. Johnson and D. Moggridge (eds.), *The Collected Writings of John Maynard Keynes*, vol. 10 (Cambridge University Press and Macmillan for the Royal Economic Society, 1972 [1933]).

The General Theory of Employment, Interest and Money, in E. Johnson and D. Moggridge (eds.), *The Collected Writings of John Maynard Keynes*, vol. 7 (Cambridge University Press and Macmillan for the Royal Economic Society, 1976 [1936]).

"The General Theory of Employment," *Quarterly Journal of Economics* (February 1937), in E. Johnson and D. Moggridge (eds.), *The Collected Writings of John Maynard Keynes*, vol. 14 (Cambridge University Press and Macmillan for the Royal Economic Society, 1973 [1937]).

"How to Pay for the War: A Radical Plan for the Chancellor of the Exchequer," *Essays in Persuasion*, in E. Johnson and D. Moggridge (eds.), *The Collected Writings of John Maynard Keynes*, vol. 9 (Cambridge

University Press and Macmillan for the Royal Economic Society, 1972 [1940]).

"The United States and the Keynes Plan," *New Republic*, July 29, 1940, in E. Johnson and D. Moggridge (eds.), *The Collected Writings of John Maynard Keynes*, vol. 22 (Cambridge University Press and Macmillan for the Royal Economic Society, 1978).

Keynes, J. M. and Henderson, H., "Can Lloyd George Do It?" in E. Johnson and D. Moggridge (eds.), *The Collected Writings of John Maynard Keynes*, vol. 9 (Cambridge University Press and Macmillan for the Royal Economic Society, 1972 [1929]).

Khan, B. Z., "Premium Inventions: Patents and Prizes as Incentive Mechanisms in Britain and the United States, 1750–1930," p. 24. Available at www.international.ucla.edu/economichistory/conferences/khan.pdf.

Kindleberger, C. P. and Aliber, R. Z., *Manias, Panics and Crashes: A History of Financial Crises*, 6th edn. (New York: Palgrave Macmillan, 2011).

Kregel, J., "Financial Experimentation, Technological Paradigm Revolutions and Financial Crises," in W. Drechsler, R. Kattel and E. S. Reinert, *Techno-Economic Paradigms: Essays in Honour of Carlota Perez* (London: Anthem, 2009), pp. 203–220.

Kressel, H., *Competing for the Future: How Digital Innovations are Changing the World* (Cambridge University Press, 2007).

Kressel, H. and Lento, T. V., *Investing in Dynamic Markets: Venture Capital in the Digital Age* (Cambridge University Press, 2010).

Krugman, P., "The Fall and Rise of Development Economics" (1994). Available at http://web.mit.edu/krugman/www/dishpan.html.

"How Did Economists Get it so Wrong?" *New York Times Magazine* (September 2, 2009).

The Return of Depression Economics (New York: W. W. Norton & Company, 2009).

Kurz, M., "Rational Beliefs and Endogenous Uncertainty," *Economic Theory*, 8(3) (1996), pp. 383–397.

Kynaston, D., *Golden Years: 1890–1914*, vol. 2 of *The City of London*, 4 vols. (London: Pimlico, 1995).

A World of its Own: 1815–1890, vol. 1 of *The City of London*, 4 vols. (London: Pimlico, 1995).

Lamoreaux, N. R., *Insider Lending: Banks, Personal Connections, and Economic Development in Industrial New England* (Cambridge University Press, 1994).

Lamoreaux, N. R. and Sokoloff, K. L., "Inventive Activity and the Market for Technology in the United States, 1840–1920," National Bureau of Economic Research Working Paper 7107 (1999).

Lamoreaux, N. R. and Sokoloff, K. L. (eds.), *Financing Innovation in the United States: 1870 to the Present* (Cambridge, MA: MIT Press, 2007).

Lamoreaux, N. R. and Sokoloff, K. L., "Introduction," in N. R. Lamoreaux and K. L. Sokoloff (eds.), *Financing Innovation in the United States: 1870 to the Present* (Cambridge, MA: MIT Press, 2007).

Lamoreaux, N. R., Sokoloff, K. L. and Sutthiphisal, D., "Reorganization of Inventive Activity in the United States during the Early Twentieth Century," National Bureau of Economic Research Working Paper 15440 (2009).

Lane, J. and Bertuzzi, S., "Measuring the Results of Science Investments," *Science*, 331 (2011), p. 678.

Lawson, T., *Reorienting Economics* (New York: Routledge, 2003).

"The (Confused) State of Equilibrium Analysis in Modern Economics: An Explanation," *Journal of Post Keynesian Economics*, 27(3) (2005), 423–444.

Lerner, J., *Boulevard of Broken Dreams: Why Public Efforts to Boost Entrepreneurship and Venture Capital Have Failed – and What to Do about it* (Princeton University Press, 2009).

Lerner, J. and Tufano, P., "The Consequences of Financial Innovation: A Counterfactual Research Agenda," paper presented to a meeting of the Commission on Finance and Growth, Watson Institute for International Studies, Brown University, December 10, 2010.

List, F., *The National System of Political Economy*, trans. Sampson S. Lloyd (New York: Augustus M. Kelly, 1966 [1841]).

Lucas Jr, R. E., "Nobel Lecture: Monetary Neutrality," *Journal of Political Economy*, 104(4) (1996), pp. 661–682.

Macdonald, J., *A Free Nation Rich in Debt* (New York: Farrar, Straus and Giroux, 2003).

MacKenzie, D., *An Engine Not a Camera: How Financial Models Shape Markets* (Cambridge, MA: MIT Press, 2008).

McKenzie, M. D. and Janeway, W. H., "Venture Capital Fund Performance and the IPO Market," Centre for Financial Analysis and Policy, University of Cambridge Working Paper 30 (2008).

"Venture Capital Funds and the Public Equity Market," *Accounting and Finance*, 51(3) (2011), pp. 764–786.

Mackay, C., *Extraordinary Popular Delusions and the Madness of Crowds* (Petersfield: Harriman House, 2009 [1841]).

Markowitz, H. M., "Portfolio Selection," *Journal of Finance*, 7(1) (1952), pp. 77–91.

Marx, K., *Capital*, vol. 1, trans. S. Moore and E. Aveling (Moscow: Foreign Language Publishing House, 1964 [1887]).

Capital, vol. 3 (Moscow: Foreign Language Publishing House, 1962 [1894]).

Mazzucato, M., *The Entrepreneurial State* (London: Demos, 2011).

Meadows, D. H., Meadows, D. L., Randers J. and Behrens III, W. W., *The Limits to Growth: A Report for the Club of Rome's Project on the Predicament of Mankind* (New York: Universe Books, 1974).

Mehrling, P., *The New Lombard Street: How the Fed Became the Dealer of Last Resort* (Princeton University Press, 2010).

Mendoza, E. G., "Sudden Stops, Financial Crises and Leverage," *American Economic Review*, 100(5) (2010), pp. 1941–1966.

Merton, R. C., "Theory of Rational Option Pricing," *Bell Journal of Economics and Management Science*, 4(1) (1973), pp. 141–183.

Merton, R. K., "The Unanticipated Consequences of Purposive Social Action," *American Sociological Review*, 1(6) (1936), pp. 894–904.

Minsky, H. P., *Can "It" Happen Again?: Essays on Instability and Finance* (New York: M. E. Sharpe, 1982).

Stabilizing an Unstable Economy (New Haven, CT: Yale University Press, 1986).

"The Financial Instability Hypothesis," The Levy Economics Institute of Bard College Working Paper 74 (1992).

Mitchell, B. R., *British Historical Statistics* (Cambridge University Press, 1988).

Moody, J., *The Truth about the Trusts: A Description and Analysis of the American Trust Movement* (New York: Moody Publishing Company, 1904).

Mowery, D. C., "Military R&D and Innovation," in B. H. Hall and N. Rosenberg (eds.), *Handbook of the Economics of Innovation*, 2 vols. (Amsterdam: North-Holland, 2010), vol. 2, pp. 1219–1256.

Mowery, D. C. and Rosenberg, N., *Technology and the Pursuit of Economic Growth* (Cambridge University Press, 1989).

Murphy, A. L., *The Origins of English Financial Markets: Investment and Speculation before the South Sea Bubble*, Cambridge Studies in Economic History, 2nd series (Cambridge University Press, 2009).

Nanda, R. and Rhodes-Kropf, M., "Financing Risk and Innovation," Harvard Business School Working Paper 11–013 (2010).

The National Academies, "The NAS in the Late Nineteenth Century" (Washington, DC: The National Academies, n.d.). www7.nationalacademies.org/archives/late19thcentury.html.

"Organization of the National Research Council" (Washington, DC: The National Academies, n.d.). www7.nationalacademies.org/archives/nrcorganization.html.

National Institutes of Health, "Chronology of Events" (Bethesda, MD: National Institutes of Health, n.d.). www.nih.gov/about/almanac/historical/chronology_of_events.htm.

National Venture Capital Association, *2010 Yearbook* (New York: Thomson Reuters, 2010).

2011 Yearbook (New York: Thomson Reuters, 2011).

Neal, L., "The Financial Crisis of 1825 and the Restructuring of the British Financial System," *Federal Reserve Bank of St. Louis Review* (May/June 1998), pp. 53–76.

Neal, L. and Davis, L. E., "Why Did Finance Capital and the Second Industrial Revolution Arise in the 1890s?" in N. R. Lamoreaux and K. Sokoloff (eds.), *Financing Innovation in the United States: 1870 to the Present* (Cambridge, MA: MIT Press, 2007), pp. 129–162.

Nelson Jr, J. R., "Alexander Hamilton and American Manufacturing: A Reappraisal," *Journal of American History*, 65(4) (1979), pp. 971–995.

Nelson, R. R., "The Simple Economics of Basic Scientific Research," *Journal of Political Economy*, 67 (1959), pp. 297–306.

Nelson, R. R., Peck, M. J. and Kalacheck, E. D. (eds.), *Technology, Economic Growth and Public Policy* (Washington, DC: The Brookings Institution, 1967).

Nelson, R. R. and Winter, S. G., *An Evolutionary Theory of Economic Change* (Cambridge, MA: Belknap, 1982).

Nye, J., *Electrifying America: Social Meanings of a New Technology* (Cambridge, MA: MIT Press, 1992).

Odlyzko, A., "Collective Hallucinations and Inefficient Markets: The British Railway Mania of the 1840s" (2010). Available at www.dtc.umn.edu/~odlyzko/doc/hallucinations.pdf.

"This Time is Different: An Example of a Giant, Wildly Speculative, and Successful Investment Mania" (2010). Available at www.dtc.umn.edu/~odlyzko/doc/mania01.pdf.

Ofek, E. and Richardson, M., "DotCom Mania: The Rise and Fall of Internet Stock Prices," *Journal of Finance*, 58(3) (2003), pp. 1113–1138.

O'Sullivan, M., "Funding New Industries: A Historical Perspective on the Financing Role of the US Stock Market in the Twentieth Century," in N. R. Lamoreaux and K. L. Sokoloff (eds.), *Financing Innovation in the United States: 1870 to the Present* (Cambridge, MA: MIT Press, 2007), pp. 163–215.

Park, A. and Sabourian, H., "Herding and Contrarian Behavior in Financial Markets," *Econometrica*, 79(4) (2011), pp. 973–1026.

Perez, C., *Technological Revolutions and Financial Capital: The Dynamics of Bubbles and Golden Ages* (Cheltenham: Edward Elgar, 2002).

"Finance and Technical Change: A Neo-Schumpeterian Perspective," in H. Hanusch and A. Pyka, *Elgar Companion to Neo-Schumpeterian Economics* (Cheltenham: Edward Elgar, 2007).

Pesaran, H., *The Limits to Rational Expectations* (Oxford: Basil Blackwell, 2007).

"Predictability of Asset Returns and the Efficient Market Hypothesis," in A. Ullah and D. E. Giles (eds.), *Handbook of Empirical Economics and Finance* (Boca Raton, FL: Chapman and Hall/CRC, 2010), pp. 281–312.

Pesaran, H. and Smith, R., "Keynes on Econometrics," in T. Lawson and H. Pesaran (eds.), *Keynes' Economics: Methodological Issues* (London: Croom Helm, 1985).

Pew Charitable Trusts, "Who's Winning the Clean Energy Race: Growth, Competition and Opportunity in the World's Largest Economies," in *G20 Clean Energy Factbook* (Washington, DC: Pew Charitable Trusts, 2011).

Pigou, A. C., *The Economics of Welfare*, 2 vols. (New York: Cosimo Classics, 2010 [1920]).

Pilling, D., "Asia's Keynesians Take Pride in Prudence," *Financial Times* (July 21, 2010).

Pisano, G., *Science Business: Promise, Reality, and the Future of Biotechnology* (Boston: Harvard Business School Press, 2006).

Polanyi, K., *The Great Transformation: The Political and Economic Origins of Our Times* (Boston: Beacon, 2001 [1944]).

Reinhart, C. M. and Rogoff, K. S., *This Time is Different: Eight Centuries of Financial Folly* (Princeton University Press, 2009).

Rodrik, D., *The Globalization Paradox: Why Global Markets, States, and Democracy Can't Coexist* (New York: Norton, 2011).

Romer, D., "What Have We Learned about Fiscal Policy from the Crisis?" paper presented to the International Monetary Fund Conference on Macro and Growth Policies in the Wake of the Crisis, March 2011. Available at www.imf.org/external/np/seminars/eng/2011/res/pdf/DR3 presentation.pdf.

Rothschild Report, *The Organisation and Management of Government Research and Development*, Cmnd. 4814 (London: HMSO), in Parliamentary Papers (House of Commons and Command), Session 2, November 1971–October 1972, vol. 35, pp. 747–775.

Roubini, N. and Mihm, S., *Crisis Economics: A Crash Course in the Future of Finance* (New York: Penguin, 2010).

Rueschemeyer, D. and Evans, P. B., "The State and Economic Transformation: Toward an Analysis of the Conditions Underlying Effective Intervention," in P. B. Evans, D. Rueschemeyer and T. Skocpol (eds.), *Bringing the State Back In* (Cambridge University Press, 1985).

Scheinkman, J. and Xiong, W., "Advisors and Asset Prices: A Model of the Origins of Bubbles," *Journal of Financial Economics*, 89 (2008), pp. 268–287.

"Overconfidence and Speculative Bubbles," *Journal of Political Economy*, 111(6) (2003), pp. 1183–1220.

Schlesinger, A. M., Jr., *The Age of Jackson* (Boston, MA: Little, Brown, 1945).

"The Ages of Jackson," *New York Review of Books*, 36(19) (1989), pp. 49–50.

Schularick, M. and Taylor, A. M., "Credit Booms Gone Bust: Monetary Policy, Leverage Cycles and Financial Crises, 1870–2008," *American Economic Review*, 102(2) (2012), 1029–1061.

Schumpeter, J. A., *Business Cycles: A Theoretical, Historical and Statistical Analysis of the Capitalist Process*, 2 vols. (London: McGraw-Hill, 1939).

Capitalism, Socialism and Democracy, 4th edn. (London: Allen & Unwin, 2010 [1943]).

Shin, H. S., *Risk and Liquidity* (Oxford University Press, 2010).

Shleifer, A. and Vishny, R., "The Limits of Arbitrage," *Journal of Finance*, 52(1) (1997), pp. 32–55.

Simeonov, S., "Metcalfe's Law: More Misunderstood than Wrong?" *HighContrast* (blog) (July 26, 2006). http://blog.simeonov. com/2006/07/26.

Simon, H. A., "Rationality as a Process and Product of Thought," *American Economic Review*, 68(2) (1978), pp. 1–16.

"Rationality in Psychology and Economics, Part 2: The Behavioral Foundations of Economic Theory," *Journal of Business*, 59(4) (1986), pp. 209–224.

"Smith, Adam," *The Money Game* (New York: Random House, 1967).

Smith, A., *The Wealth of Nations* (New York: Random House, 1937 [1776]).

Smith, D. K. and Alexander, R. C., *Fumbling the Future: How Xerox Invented, then Ignored, the First Personal Computer* (San Jose, CA: Excel, 1999).

Smith, J. S., *Building New Deal Liberalism: The Political Economy of Public Works, 1933–1956* (Cambridge University Press, 2006).

Soete, L., Verspagen, B. and ter Weel, B., "Systems of Innovation," in B. H. Hall and N. Rosenberg (eds.), *Handbook of the Economics of Innovation*, 2 vols. (Amsterdam: North-Holland, 2010), vol. 2, pp. 1159–1180.

Soros, G., *The Soros Lectures at the Central European University* (New York: Public Affairs, 2010).

Stiglitz, J., "Endogenous Growth and Cycles," in Y. Shionnoya and M. Perlman (eds.), *Innovation in Technology, Industries and Institutions: Studies in Schumpeterian Perspectives* (Ann Arbor, MI: University of Michigan Press, 1994).

Stokes, D., *Pasteur's Quadrant: Basic Science and Technological Innovation* (Washington, DC: The Brookings Institution, 1997).

Stone, R., "China Bets Big on Small Grants, Large Facilities," *Science*, 331 (2011), p. 1251.

Sylla, R., "The Political Economy of Early US Financial Development," in S. Haber, D. C. North and B. Weingast (eds.), *Political Institutions and Financial Development* (Palo Alto, CA: Stanford University Press, 2008), pp. 60–91.

Sylla, R., Tilly, R. and Torella, G., *The State, the Financial System and Economic Modernization* (Cambridge University Press, 1999).

Tett, G., *Fool's Gold: How the Bold Dream of a Small Tribe at J. P. Morgan was Corrupted by Wall Street Greed and Unleashed a Catastrophe* (New York: Free Press, 2009).

Thomson Reuters and National Venture Capital Association, "Venture Capital Firms Raised $5.6 billion in Fourth Quarter, as Industry Continued to Consolidate in 2011," press release, January 9, 2012, available at www.nvca.org/index.php?option=com_content&view=art icle&id=78&Itemid=102.

Tilly, R., "Public Policy, Capital Markets and the Supply of Industrial Finance in Nineteenth-Century Germany," in R. Sylla, R. Tilly and G. Torella, *The State, the Financial System and Economic Modernization* (Cambridge University Press, 1999).

Tinbergen, J., *An Econometric Approach to Business Cycle Problems* (Paris: Herman & Cie, 1937).

Tirole, J., "Asset Bubbles and Overlapping Generations," *Econometrica*, 53(5) (1985), 1071–1100.

Tobin, J., and Brainard, W. C., "Asset Markets and the Cost of Capital," in R. Nelson and B. Balassa (eds.), *Economic Progress: Private Values and Public Policy, Essays in Honor of William Fellner* (Amsterdam: North-Holland, 1977), pp. 235–262.

Tooze, A., *The Wages of Destruction: The Making and Breaking of the Nazi Economy* (London: Allen Lane, 2006).

United Kingdom National Accounts (The Blue Book) (Basingstoke: Palgrave Macmillan, 2008).

United States Bureau of Economic Analysis, National Economic Accounts. Available at www.bea.gov/national/nipaweb.

Usselman, S. W., "Learning the Hard Way: IBM and the Sources of Innovation in Early Computing," in N. R. Lamoreaux and K. L. Sokoloff (eds.), *Financing Innovation in the United States, 1870 to the Present* (Cambridge, MA: MIT Press, 2007).

Warsh, D., *Knowledge and the Wealth of Nations: A Story of Economic Discovery* (New York: W. W. Norton and Company, 2006).

"We Can Conquer Unemployment," *Memoranda by Ministers on Certain Proposals Relating to Unemployment*, Cmd. 3331 (London: HMSO, 1929).

Woodford, M., "Convergence in Macroeconomics: Elements of the New Synthesis," prepared for the annual meeting of the American Economics Association, January 4, 2008. Available at www.columbia.edu/~mw2230/Convergence_AEJ.pdf.

Zachary, G. P., *The Endless Frontier: Vannevar Bush, Engineer of the American Century* (New York: The Free Press, 1997).

Zweig, J., Introduction to F. Schwed Jr., *Where Are the Customers' Yachts? or A Good Hard Look at Wall Street* (Hoboken, NJ: John Wiley, 2006 [1940]).

Index